**Successful
American
Urban Plans**

Urban America Approaching the Twenty-First Century

Successful American Urban Plans

W.G. Roeseler
Texas A&M University

LexingtonBooks
D.C. Heath and Company
Lexington, Massachusetts
Toronto

Library of Congress Cataloging in Publication Data

Roeseler, W.G.
    Successful American urban plans.

    Includes bibliographical references and index.
    1. City planning—United States—Case studies. I. Title.
HT167.R67   307.7'6'0973   81-47028
ISBN 0-669-04540-3   AACR2

Published simultaneously in Canada

Printed in the United States of America

International Standard Book Number: 0-669-04540-3

Library of Congress Catalog Card Number: 81-47028

To Eva, who is always there

Contents

Contents

List of Figures and Tables

Tables

Preface and Acknowledgments

"Planning is what planners do" has long been the realistic assessment of this avant-garde profession and its relationship to society by one of its deans, Israel Stollman. The ever-changing circumstances that surround us, the constant stream of technological advances in every field affecting the process of urbanization, and the enormous consequences of these changes on human attitudes, consumption patterns, life-styles and characteristics of people from coast to coast and around the world make many people wonder whether a rational, goal-oriented approach to human habitation is still possible, or whether surrender to happenstance, illusion, unbridled greed and moral decay, and the ultimate consequences of chaos are the inevitable consequences of our times.

My personal life experience and my professional work over more than three decades tell me that there is hope—indeed, greater opportunity than ever for a better tomorrow through human will power and the application of the very best that science and technology have to offer within a framework of societal restraint and common objectives. My friend, Frank S. So, deputy director of the American Planning Association, puts it this way: "When planning works, it really works!"

Acknowledgments

I gratefully acknowledge helpful suggestions and information furnished by urban-planning agencies and individual city planners and engineers in response to a survey by Texas A&M University concerning the effectiveness of comprehensive planning in the United States. Also acknowledged is the assistance by officials of the Federal Highway Administration and the Urban Mass Transportation Administration, U.S. Department of Transportation; the highway and transportation departments of the states of California, Kansas, Louisiana, Missouri, Ohio, and Texas; the engineering firms of Wilbur Smith and Associates and Howard, Needles, Tammen and Bergendoff; and the many individuals and colleagues who tested ideas and concepts.

Permission to use photographs and other illustrations was granted by the following companies: Hallmark Corporation of Kansas City, Missouri; J.C. Nichols Company of Kansas City, Missouri; and the Chambers of Commerce of Dallas, Texas, Kansas City, Missouri, Palm Springs, California, Rochester, Minnesota, Tulsa, Oklahoma, and Shreveport, Louisiana. These authorizations are much appreciated. My graduate assistants, Kirt E. Anderson and David Rogers, prepared and adapted the graphics.

My wife, Eva M. Roeseler—having put up with the trials and tribulations of a city planner for more than thirty years—was an invaluable, constructive critic and researcher. I wish to express my gratitude to all these people and organizations for making this book possible.

Introduction

"The reason for your existence," said the late President Harry S Truman on 2 April 1955 in Kansas City to the National Planning Conference of the American Institute of Certified Planners, "is to help create a plan for the future, no matter what the obstacles you have to overcome. They can be overcome when the plan is right, and it don't make much difference what the people say, you have to deal with, of the plan you may offer; if it's right, it will come true!"

I have always believed that, and I thought that it might be of interest to others to travel with me through the land, to go back in time three decades or so, and to tell the story of a part of urban America that perhaps represents most of it and that succeeded in shaping its destiny by the advice of the man from Independence, Missouri.[1]

Urban planning is well established as a function of public administration and private development, having come into its own toward the end of the first quarter of this century. In some form, planning as a process has been around for as long as man has strived to become civilized, and the history of urbanization gives ample evidence of both successes and failures of that function. The derived Latin word *civilization* itself is synonymous with urbanization. In the context here, we are concerned with the contemporary planning experience in America. We are all aware of the overwhelming array of problems and complex issues confronting our society day after day. How do we cope with the political, economic, social, physical, and mental stresses of the times, and are we even trying to approach the issues systematically, with determination and hope of resolution?

Indeed, we are trying, and in many respects we are very successful. Urban planning surely is not a cure-all. However, in the clearly defined area of addressing primarily physical-environmental problems, those presented by nature and those imposed by man, the urban planner will point to opportunity and, given a fair chance, will convert liability into such assets as the public demands and can reconcile with available resources. That area of concern—with its tender relationship to the social, economic, and political spheres—is the subject of this book. It is not a history of urban America of the last thirty or forty years. However, the cases presented here are believed to be representative of the urban-planning movement during that period. The accounts are based on my personal experience in some capacity and are as accurate as my own memory and the recollections of my associates and friends will permit. Those men and women who will appear before you in this context have personally experienced the events reported. What was achieved is a matter of record. It is also a matter of steel, concrete, brick, and mortar—but most of all, of people served by the results of urban planning.

This world is not perfect. To be sure, there are always alternatives to our actions. But the worst of all options is the choice to become frustrated and paralyzed into stagnation in the face of need. The risk of being criticized for having done one thing and not another is the professional hazard of all who dare to take responsibility. Many years ago, in a story about city planning, *Life* magazine made the intriguing observation that a city plan without controversy was probably not worth preparing, for it is incomprehensible that any such effort could satisfy all the conflicting interests of our pluralistic society in any given situation. And, at the conference mentioned earlier, Harry Truman admonished us to beware of the proverbial "Monday morning quarterback who knows what ought to have been done in the football game last Saturday." With an eye on the ever-present political process, Mr. Truman—in his characteristic, dry Missouri humor—continued to remind his audience that the opposition to urban planning typically "gets vociferous about planned economy." He cited the ancient maxim of politics: "If you want to confuse an issue, always talk about what it will do to something that has no relation to it," adding with a broad grin, "and no one knows that better than I do."

In contemporary reference, what is an urban plan and what might be considered a successful plan? By law, and through trial and error over a period of sixty to seventy years, the comprehensive or master city plan is, among other things, a statement of policy by the legislative or governing body of a political entity, frequently acting through an agency that is designated by statute to be the custodian of such a document and is commonly known as a planning commission. Although the plan is a statement of policy, I hasten to add that the policies addressed are those that pertain to provision of facilities and sometimes services of a highly complex character, requiring expression of that policy in technically competent terms. Only appropriately educated and experienced specialists under our system of jurisprudence and government are qualified to compose the plan, and only duly designated, sometimes elected officials are authorized to adopt the plan as a public document on which further action is expected to be taken. In the normal course of public business, such ensuing action will call for the expenditure of public funds and other resources, and frequently for the curtailment of certain property rights.

These measures are taken under the general police power of the state, delegated by law to the state's political subdivisions, and under the power of eminent domain. The police power is said to be inherent in the concept of government of a sovereign state; the power of eminent domain also flows from that concept, and both are limited in scope by the U.S. Constitution and those of the several states. The constitutions stipulate rules of due process of law with respect to protection of life, other general civil liberties, and property of the individual citizen or resident. As we shall see later, in the American judicial tradition, the exercise of these powers must be restricted to situations that make such use of power absolutely necessary, and the means deployed must be humane or without undue oppression.

As to the contents of an urban plan, there is general agreement on the essential, fundamental elements: some understanding of anticipated growth or decline, demographically and economically; adequate information regarding the terrain and all the physiological and other environmental properties of the region; an expression of policies with respect to the numerous aspects of land use, density and intensity, performance, and design; and plans for accessibility and circulation, for educational facilities and recreation, for utilities, and for such other features as may be appropriate under given local conditions. Periodically, attempts are made in various publications to inject a measure of scholastic formalism into the plan-making process. However, such formalism serves only limited purposes. As we look into various plans and their objectives, we shall attempt to develop a better understanding of the topic and allow the readers to formulate their own opinions. Obviously, any formal instrument on which decisions are to be based must be structured, if for no other reason than to document the reasons for the decisions by the public and their representatives. Moreover, implied reasonableness in any public process can often be demonstrated only if it is possible to compare the measure under consideration to the experience of others in a similar position. In other words, it must be compared with what might be called state-of-the-art or normative.

The plan is not a monument. It merely makes a public record of matters that are agreed upon and of the basis for the decisions that are made. In this sense, the plan is simply a landmark in the never-ending planning process. If we could all remember what we did and why we did it, we could do very well without the plan. Imperfect as we are, however, we must write it down. In any case, the law requires that we do so, and for good reasons. Public decisions must be matters of record, and, in planning, there must be a technically defensible justification for the action and a clear case for the cost-effectiveness of public commitments and expenditures. Ignoring that requisite of good public management means a return to pork-barrel public works, patronage, the inevitable corruption that follows, and a general abuse of public power.

The technical justification, the fact base of planning and its roots in the application of scientific principles, will make it more obvious that a public planning document based on nontechnical statements of objectives, no matter how worthy, is not an urban plan. It is like a letter to Santa Claus in which the writer had no idea of the complexity of the wish, let alone the capacity to establish notions of feasibility. A comprehensive plan, competently drawn, establishes feasibility from a physical planning point of view and often also from an economic and fiscal perspective, although the latter is not so critical when first dealing with overall policy. It becomes very significant at the more advanced level of planning, as we move closer to implementation.

Now that we know the general contents of the plan, what makes it a successful one? The answer is simple enough; just as in your own life you consider yourself successful if you achieve what you set out to do, so does the body politic. If plan objectives and resulting programs are achieved, the plan is a successful plan, at least to the point of accomplishing specific proposals. The nature of public and private development is such that plan accomplishments tend to fall within twenty- to twenty-five-year cycles. Within that period, major plan objectives should be attainable.

As in most applied sciences, the literature of urban planning is found primarily in plan documents, as is the theory of and for the planning process. Several years ago, Professor Alan A. Altshuler of the Massachusetts Institute of Technology pointed out correctly that the planner in the planning process must, by necessity, be principally concerned with the definition of public interest, and that, whatever concept emerges, it will change from time to time.[2] The plans themselves, I believe, must directly answer to that issue, and, by and large, they do. Any definition of public interest is not as simple as we would wish, perhaps, or as we are sometimes led to believe in scholarly discourse. In practice, it flows from the analytical treatment of circumstances that prevail with respect to clearly identifiable functions that the planning process must address in ongoing interaction with the decision makers as direct and legal representatives of the public at large. Acceptability of solutions to the general public is further tested by various means of involvement, to the extent that such involvement serves a useful purpose and is manageable—another complex matter. Through the analytical planning process, feasibility is tested as well as public acceptability, and, in this manner, public interest and purpose are defined, thereby establishing the sole justification for the plan. If the public requires a facility or a service, and if it is feasible, by negotiated or given criteria and standards, to provide it, the plan will do so. The crucial matter of the process lies in the eternal wisdom that it is far easier to know what is good to do than to find the proper balance between necessity and acceptability in a democratic society governed by representative officials.

To ascertain the degree of success attained in planning situations, we must become familiar with a given plan, its methodology and techniques, the circumstances that prevailed at the time of plan formulation, and the procedures and ultimate objectives; then we must compare these and other considerations with the actual conditions we may encounter in the field. If what was hoped for years ago is now there, we can assume that success has crowned the deed; if little or nothing has been accomplished, it will not be difficult to detect failure. The demarcation of our venture, then, is that we will look at objectives and achievements, city by city or county by county.

We will certainly not attempt to measure success against superimposed standards, except as these may be widely recognized as representative of this period of American history, which also reflects the general public taste and preferences of our times. Other periods may judge differently, but that is not our concern at the moment, as we live our own lives. In any event, we shall leave abstract notions to other inquiries and shall judge success by the simple yardstick of discernible attainment of the goals the authors of the plans—in the broadest sense of the body politic—expressed in and through their planning efforts.

One other observation should be shared at this juncture. The analytical process and the designs that accompany it, in our frame of reference, must eventually form an integrated, interactive intellectual entity. Although the plan is composed of many elements, it nevertheless has an identity of its own, based on holistic principles and therefore unique; the elements relate to one another, but the sum total gives it life. It is for this reason that we instinctively and easily identify with urban environments that give us a sense of satisfaction because of the apparent harmony of all components. Conversely, we are appalled by dissonance, because centuries of civilization have conditioned us to such response.

The selection of the cases to be reviewed in this book is based on judgment and preference. I will attempt to bring to life personalities and technical particulars that blended under prevailing circumstances into unique human experiences in which men and women of goodwill banded together to act for the general welfare. The results of their efforts, by any reasonable criteria, invariably produced an environment that was superior in their views and in the eyes of their peers to that which would have existed without their courage and dedication. The order of magnitude of this effort is perhaps best illustrated by the fact that the population of the United States has increased by 100 million since the end of World War II, and that most of these people had to be accommodated in urban areas.

The cases presented in this book are arranged by area size and function. The first section deals with the megapolis—the city with more than one million inhabitants. The second section presents major cities below that level, followed by a discussion of representative medium-sized communities under 100,000 population. Finally, the last section addresses the complex problem of the older central areas of the big cities.

Notes
1. Harry S Truman Library, Independence, Missouri. Address before the American Institute of Certified Planners, 1955 (provided by the Missouri chapter of the institute).

2. Alan A. Altshuler, "The City Planning Process," Cornell University, 1965.

Nothing can possibly be conceived in the world which can be called good without qualification, except a good will. Act only on that maxim through which you can at the same time will that it should become a universal law.

—Immanuel Kant, *Metaphysical Foundation of Morals*, 1785

Part I:
The Megapolis
of the Region

Every region in the United States is economically, socially, culturally, and
certainly politically affected by a large urban settlement with a population of
a million or more permanent residents. We call such a settlement a *megapolis*.
It is a convenient and descriptive term borrowed from the Greeks—the
distinguished, ancient city builders and organizers of democracy in our
civilization. Civil rights of the citizens and the guarantee of freedom, combined with clearly conceived duties to society, were the essence of urban life
to the Greeks. Megapolis simply means a very large city—in our reference, a
human settlement with a million or more persons. Incidentally, the term
metropolitan area is used today more for the purpose of describing an urban
entity in its entirety, regardless of size but particularly without regard to
political jurisdiction. A metropolitan area may, for example, consist of a
county and three cities, with a total population of 75,000; or it could refer to
the entire urbanized entity of the San Francisco Bay Area.

Urban planning and development by present-day standards and techniques of physical layout, construction, and financing are deeply rooted in
the megapolis. It was here that the issues of public interest versus private
objectives were first brought into sharp focus on a scale requiring policy
determination and orderly programming of priorities, within the constraints
of available resources, because of sheer magnitude. Where to build, what to
construct, how to perform once operation commenced, who would pay for
what and when, how public interest would be defined, and which agency
would assume regulatory functions locally—and myriads of other technical
problems—had to be resolved when urban growth became an un-
precedented and lasting phenomenon in America. To be sure, there had
been issues of growth and development in the past, but they all would be at-
tended to in good time. The pressure was certainly not of the same
magnitude as that experienced in this century, particularly during the last
thirty years.

In the context of this book, I have avoided the very largest concentrations of people, as they would require penetrating attention of their own,
which would surely overshadow all others. Rather, we want to look at situations that are representative of the urban conditions under which most
Americans live today. Accordingly, I have selected Cincinnati, Ohio,
Kansas City, Missouri and Kansas, and Dallas-Fort Worth, Texas, because
they have become progressive leaders in the management of urban affairs.

1

Cincinnati: Cradle of Urban Theory

The Issue of Police Power

Urban planning, among its other responsibilities, is concerned with the location, general characteristics, and even design of numerous public works and facilities. It also performs managerial and analytical functions with respect to public policy, public services, and the funding of such facilities and functions. These activities are said to be inherent in the concept of government and thus need little justification. Indeed, if they are not performed, we consider the unit of government to be somewhat derelict in its duties.

There is, however, another aspect to urban planning—its responsibilities in regard to environmental policy and regulation. Historically, much of the public concern with environmental issues was private responsibility, closely related to real-property rights. Encroachments and trespasses of one kind or another had to be dealt with on the basis of the law of nuisances or other aspects of the common law. As urbanization became more sophisticated, private contracts in the form of covenants became popular as a means of protecting the urban home owner from the undesirable effects of incompatible activities emanating from neighboring property, particularly from the use of adjacent land.

The complexities brought about by industrialization and by more and more rapid urbanization in America, the revolutionary changes in technology over the last 150 years or so, and the ups and downs of commerce contributed to the public's recognition that the old legal remedies for the protection of private property were no longer very effective and that government, particularly local government, had a responsibility in the broad area of environmental concerns affecting real property. The initial concern was the use of land itself, particularly the establishment of land uses that were not compatible with one another because of the activity on the land, the building setback, height, or bulk, or other reasons. Following the European example—notably that of France or Germany—American cities began to enact regulations of private property, restricting the use of land much as private covenants had done. These regulations became known as zoning laws, and they typically would apply to selected blocks in the city, usually those where property owners had petitioned for their enactment. Frequently, these early zoning regulations, before 1920, were divided into

3

land-use ordinances, height ordinances, setback regulations, and so on. Occasionally, someone would actually attempt to integrate these regulations into a single instrument and would call it comprehensive zoning.[1]

As would be expected, much litigation arose, and the courts attempted to come to grips with this new phenomenon in American jurisprudence. The absence of legal precedent and technical competence on the part of the courts complicated matters further, to a point of utter confusion. So long as private parties agreed contractually to restrict the use of their property for mutual benefit, or so long as the common law of nuisances would operate to stop a clearly detrimental activity, public or private, from affecting other property, equitable adjudication was a matter of routine for the courts, firmly embedded in common-law tradition and contemporary practice.

Suddenly, however, a public body—typically, a municipal corporation without ownership interests—ordained land-use restrictions on private property and actually prohibited certain activities, even before they had been attempted, in anticipation of a potential future problem that might arise from such activities. Not only did such action constitute a fundamental departure from established common-law doctrine, which often has no remedy for a potential trespass, but the entire matter raised a fundamental constitutional issue.

Regulatory measures by a municipal corporation must generally bear a clearly discernible relationship to the police power—one of the basic powers considered to be inherent in the concept of government. The people, having agreed to govern themselves by certain principles laid down in the constitution, further empower their government to make laws and regulations that are necessary to further and protect the public health, safety, morals, and general welfare, so that society may prosper and enjoy the fruits of a common wealth. The U.S. Constitution does that and, at the same time, zealously protects the civil and property rights of the individual. Now, in the face of ever-accelerating urbanization, city governments take it upon themselves, under public pressure, to encroach on the sanctioned rights of property owners by regulating the manner in which they may or may not use their land and buildings.

Property is best understood as a bundle of rights pertaining to a physical object or an intangible issue. In the case of real property, the unrestricted enjoyment of such property is, of course, a fundamental right—unless it is curtailed by contract or covenant. The new zoning concept denies that right. For the courts, in many jurisdictions, the question that had to be settled was whether or not such public action constituted a taking for public purpose under the Fifth and Fourteenth Amendments of the U.S. Constitution and under the constitutions of the states. Indeed, it was not uncommon for lower courts to decree that zoning restrictions were enforceable only under eminent domain and that they required compensation. In other words, if the municipality wanted to restrict the use of private property, it would have to acquire development rights and pay for them. Other jurisdictions held that zoning could be enforced without compensation because of the reciprocal benefits to all property owners flowing from such a regulation. In fact, it was frequently pointed out by courts holding this view that zoning was, indeed, an essential prerequisite to enjoyment of real-property rights in an era of urbanization. Without such constraints, there would be chaos, and zoning was merely an adaptation to real property of restrictions required in the cities today.

Mindful of the evolution of laws such as those regulating the dispensing of alcoholic beverages, with local options, the country divided itself into areas where zoning was simply held unconstitutional, those where the eminent-domain doctrine of compensation prevailed, and those where zoning was viewed as just another necessity of urban life, fully enforceable under the police powers of the state and the state's political subdivisions. There was no generally accepted doctrine, public policy, or standard of guidance, and the U.S. Supreme Court had yet to face the issue. At that juncture, a legal dispute arose in northern Ohio. The village of Euclid, on the outskirts of Cleveland, denied the Ambler Realty Company a permit for the construction of an industrial facility in an area zoned for residential use.[2] The matter was adjudicated in the state courts, and the village lost its case. It decided to appeal to the federal courts, and, eventually, the matter was argued before the U.S. Supreme Court. Ultimately, the Supreme Court ruled in favor of the village of Euclid. It did so by adopting the theories laid before it by Alfred Bettman, a noted constitutional lawyer in Cincinnati, chairman of that city's planning commission, and long-term advocate of city planning and municipal-reform government.

After the attorneys for Euclid had been hopelessly overpowered by the opposition, Alfred Bettman was granted permission by the Supreme Court to enter the case and to file a brief, *amici curiae,* on behalf of the village.[3] This document enunciated the regulatory nature of zoning and effectively dispelled any confiscatory characteristics it had been alleged to possess. Most important, however, Mr. Bettman emphasized the positive effects of planning at the municipal level and the significance of zoning as a means of implementing city plans, viewing city planning as a prerequisite for urban prosperity and as a means of facilitating, if not making possible, a process of urbanization that would allow the public to realize the constitutional promise of the enjoyment of property rights. Moreover, he pointed out that the expertise required to draw up a reasonable plan on which to base zoning regulations was, indeed, available in this country. The year was 1926; this was a remarkably enlightened view for that period. What prompted Alfred Bettman to assume this position, which was to make him the fundamental theorist of urban planning as a municipal function in the United States?

The Bettman-Segoe Theory

Prior to the establishment of a municipal city-planning commission in Cincinnati, Alfred Bettman had organized and was the chairman of a civic group known as the United City Planning Committee, which set out to develop proposals and recommendations for the general improvement of Cincinnati, partly in response to overall-civic reform movements that were attempting to erase the aftershock of lawlessness and bossism that had plagued that city for many years. Realizing that more than goodwill is required to plan a city, the United City Planning Committee, using its own private funds, retained the Technical Advisory Corporation, a New York consulting firm, to assist in the preparation of a city plan. That firm's resident planner was Ladislas Segoe, a Hungarian planning engineer, who assumed his responsibilities there in 1921.

Over the next three decades, Bettman and Segoe developed a close personal relationship, which became a cornerstone of the planning movement in this country. Bettman, twenty years older than Segoe, was, according to Segoe, "a stickler for excellence," whose maxim in public affairs was not to do anything unless there was a compelling reason for it. If he was convinced that something was "the right thing to do," Bettman would go forward and would not be overly concerned with the theoretical or legal aspects of the matter, realizing that the law itself is not static but is capable of adjusting to changing social conditions. This conviction gave Bettman the strength and foresight to encourage Segoe to practice his profession to the best of his ability, not under the stress of doubt because of potential legal issues.

It was in this spirit that Segoe, under the chairmanship of Bettman, set out to develop Cincinnati's first comprehensive plan—the Master Plan of 1925. Segoe introduced with that document a holistic principle that was to give all of his subsequent planning programs distinction and that caused these plans to be the national model to this day.[4] Professor T. Jack Kent, Jr., and others have pointed out that Segoe's principal contribution to urban planning in the United States was his insistence on a comprehensive approach to the management of urban affairs and that his master plan was the tangible symbol of that philosophy.[5] It is equally significant that the extraordinary relationship between Segoe and Alfred Bettman—which Segoe himself described as a father-son relationship—produced the theoretical legal basis for the practical implementation of Segoe's holistic approach to municipal problems, programs, and policies. It was inconceivable to him that the planner, engineer, analyst, or manager could seriously address any one key element of the urban structure without relating it to all others in order to develop a realistic assessment of probable consequences of actions to be taken and of the resources required therefor. Segoe's technical, if not engineering, orientation and his compulsion to find practical solutions within the client's means was complemented by Bettman's speculative mind and his commitment to continued improvement of the social and physical environment of urban America. This relationship is reminiscent of other historical coincidences in our urban history—notably, that of George Kessler and William Rockhill Nelson of Kansas City, which will be discussed in chapter 2.

Without the Bettman-Segoe team, it is doubtful that there would be urban planning as we now know it in this country. The Bettman-Segoe theory was enunciated through actual practice—notably, the 1925 Master Plan of Cincinnati and the Euclid village brief. Essentially, the theory considers the exercise of the broad legislative powers of the municipal corporation—generally referred to as the police power for zoning purposes—to be within the constitutional realm of that power. The essential relationship to public health, safety, convenience, morals, and general welfare, however, must be proved by a competently designed comprehensive plan. Bettman stated that the justification of a plan is "that it does promote the public health and welfare, which means that its justification comes from the fact that those who made the plan made it purposely, and more or less scientifically and organically, for the promotion of those particular public benefits which are recognized as within the police power as the justification of legislative action."[6]

A clear distinction is made between plan and implementing instrument; but the implementing instrument, such as the zoning or subdivision regulation, must be based on the general plan, prescribed and laid out "in accordance with the recognized principles of public health, safety and so on."[7] The key elements of the notion are (1) that there must be a comprehensive plan, as an expression of public policy, to establish the fact that any regulatory steps and others relating to control of private property are within the scope of police power; and (2) that such plan must be designed on the basis of recognized, scientific principles by persons who are competent to apply such principles. Since the theoretical scope of eminent domain is similar to that of mere legislative regulatory power, it became common practice to justify major public works and other capital expenditures on the basis of the comprehensive plan. This concept was to find its way into all federal legislation related to transportation, housing, public works, and other measures. In accepting this fundamental planning theory on the basis of Alfred Bettman's discourse in the Euclid village case, the U.S. Supreme Court established the legal foundation on which the entire modern urban-planning process in this country is based. There is no other theory, nor would there be any need for it.

The Euclid village decision is a logical sequence to the judicial tradition established earlier by the Court regarding eminent domain and police power as a form of intervention in public affairs. As pointed out in several decisions—notably, in *Lawton* v. *Steele*—public intervention is justified only "when absolutely necessary," and the means of such intervention—the exercise of the police power—must not be "unduly oppressive."[8] Both aspects of this philosophy of law, with its roots so clearly in the American version of enlightenment, flow easily and logically from Segoe's holistic technological methodology, by which each and every issue had its carefully designed and purposefully designated place within the spectrum of the urban entity, based on undisputable demonstration of public necessity.

The issues were placed in the perspective of the urban entity and were analyzed in relation to one another. Plan objectives always represented majority consent of public officials, typically through the mechanism of appointed planning commissions, which Bettman had viewed as important catalysts of the public interest—free from the immediate political pressures of legislative bodies but not entirely insensitive to such pressures.

There is no Segoe plan without a clearly motivating focus. Clients came to Segoe not because they wanted a plan but because they had a problem that required attention. The plan became a tool; it did not exist as an object unto itself. It became a vehicle to achieve a clearly perceived community objective. The community, however, had learned to approach its specific problem by looking at the totality of demands and interrelationships that constituted its entirety. In many instances, this holistic approach revealed to those concerned numerous other latent problems and opportunities, concerning not only physical facilities and services but also social and economic issues. It is for this reason that the typical Segoe plan has no difficulty in moving swiftly back and forth from policy to program. In fact, more often than not, it is so intent on problem solving that it brushes aside any clear distinction between goal-setting policy and implementing program.

Subdivisions: The Developer's Responsibility

This attitude was characteristic of Segoe from the very beginning. And because of it, almost accidentally, Segoe was to make one of the most far-reaching contributions of the century to the municipal-management process: the shifting of financial responsibility for new subdivisions from the city to the developer.[9] It is now traditional in the United States to consider the planning commission to be the planning authority. It is the commission's responsibility to assure accurate recording of new urban lots, rights-of-way, and easements, so that future real-estate transactions may be carried out with confidence and with relative ease.[10] It is not unrealistic to say that much urban development and redevelopment is accomplished through the process of subdividing and replatting, and it is largely through this process that the city's two-dimensional form is constantly altered and shaped. Consolidation of subdivision administration in the planning commissions is most directly a result of Herbert Hoover's action as Secretary of Commerce, when, on advice of a blue-ribbon committee of which Bettman was a key member, he issued, first, "A Standard State Zoning Enabling Act" (1926) and then the "Standard City Planning Enabling Act" (1928). Generally, these models were enacted, in due course, by all state legislatures certainly with respect to key provisions, including those pertaining to platting and the designation of the planning commission as the agency responsible for that process at the level of local, general-purpose government.

In his capacity as director of Cincinnati's planning program, which produced the 1925 plan, Ladislas Segoe was the first American planner to persuade his commission and city council that the approval of a plat should be conditioned on the fact that the subdivider would pay for the cost of all street and utility improvements that served the new addition directly, while the city would pay for arterial or trunk lines that served others as well. In the early 1920s, that was a dramatic departure from the practice of having all the costs of a new addition advanced by the city and assessed against the subdivision lots. In very good economic times, that system will work to a point. If sales are slow, however, the city will ultimately end up "holding the bag," as it would have to pay the debt in order to protect its credit rating, although, legally, it could default. Cincinnati escaped that fate, as did other cities that followed its example. It almost cost Segoe his first job; but, in the end, he prevailed.

Planning: A Matter of Coordination

It was important to Bettman that the planning process always relate to an operating unit of government and not "float in space." This was, perhaps, a reflection of his own struggle for recognition in the early days of the municipal-reform movement. He also accepted Segoe's notion that planning must take the entire urbanized area of the subject city into account, not merely the part of the territory that coincidentally happened to be within the legal city limits. Bettman's answer to the problem of inadequate jurisdictions in Cincinnati was an integrated process of capital-improvement programming and corresponding adjustment of taxation by the city of Cincinnati, the Board of Education, and Hamilton County. For years, the Cincinnati Chamber of Commerce listed this arrangement as one of the great locational advantages of the area. Another major step forward was accomplished during the period immediately following World War II, when the City Planning Commission carried out the first major revision of its comprehensive-plan program. However, this time the planning was metropolitan-wide, producing the nation's first Metropolitan Master Plan.[11] As with many of Segoe's programs, it was not without its controversy.

Opponents challenged the legality of spending municipal funds for the planning of areas outside the city limits. The case was lost in the trial court and was not appealed. The court could find no problem in a forward-looking city administration that realized that its issues would not stop at city limits and that it had to cooperate with adjacent communities as a matter of enlightened self-interest.

There is a paradox in Segoe's work: In Cincinnati, where he did his very best design work, only basic elements were implemented. In 1948, Segoe designed a brilliant plan for the Cincinnati riverfront and downtown area. The city followed the riverfront plan in principle, but not in detail—and the details made the difference. In the downtown area, it ignored even the principle.

Segoe's downtown-refurbishing principle was just like the design principle for shopping centers. He often said: "You wrap the shops around the mall, and the parking—and transit facilities—around the shops, mostly horizontally, sometimes vertically." Cincinnati actually has a very compact, symmetrical central business district, which almost invites application of this principle. In urban freeway design, Segoe was much influenced by time-honored railroad design. He called the urban freeways "disorganized railroads," but actually, he appreciated their function very well. It is a little known fact that he single-handedly sketched out the entire Cincinnati freeway system in a few hours; the actual designed locations of the various freeway elements were placed within a few yards of his specified notions, which, of course, reflected years of intimate familiarity with the urban area's topography and man-made infrastructure.

Cincinnati's contribution to planning is manyfold. Although its physical-planning achievements may leave something to be desired, it is to the community's credit that it created an atmosphere within which the genius of Alfred Bettman and Ladislas Segoe could function for the benefit of the nation. In this sense, Cincinnati's urban plans were successful urban plans in America.

Notes

1. E.C. Yokley, *The Law of Zoning* (Charlottesville, Va.: Michie, 1978).

2. Village of Euclid v. Ambler Realty Company, 47 Sup. Ct. Rep. 114 (1926). Brief, *amici curiae*.

3. Alfred Bettman, *City and Regional Planning Papers* (Cambridge, Mass.: Harvard University Press, 1964), p. 157.

4. W.G. Roeseler, "Reflections on Segoe," *Planning,* November 1980.

5. T. Jack Kent, Jr., *The Urban General Plan* (San Francisco, Calif.: Chandler Press, 1965).

6. Alfred Bettman, "The Fact Bases of Zoning" (1925) and "The Master Plan: Is It an Encumbrance?" (1946), in Bettman, *City and Regional Planning Papers.*

7. Bettman, *City and Regional Planning Papers* (Cambridge, Mass: Harvard University Press, 1946).

8. Lawton v. Steele, 152 U.S. 133 (1894).

9. Cincinnati Building Zone Ordinance, 1923.

10. W.G. Roeseler, *General Policies and Principles for Prototype Zoning Ordinances and Related Measures* (Bryan, Texas: EMR Publications, 1976).

11. Metropolitan Master Plan for Cincinnati, Ohio (City Planning Commission, 1948).

Kansas City: The Heart-of-America Metropolis

Prologue: The City Beautiful

In many respects, Kansas City is a remarkable metropolitan area. It staked its initial claim to enter the league of major cities with the securing of the first railroad bridge across the Missouri River in 1869, an event that was to seal the doom of nearby St. Joseph as the center of trade and commerce in western Missouri. Within a few decades, Kansas City rose from oblivion to a major industrial and commercial center of the midwestern United States. Second only to Chicago, it would boast the most extensive rail concentration and transshipment center in America, and, after Detroit, it assembles more motor vehicles than any other city in the United States. Moreover, as evidenced by the prominence of the Kansas City Board of Trade—a leading commodities exchange—Kansas City has maintained a leadership role in agriculture and food processing. There are many other activities, of course, too numerous to elaborate in this context. Suffice it to say that Kansas City enjoys economic stability because of a well-balanced economy. Kansas City's growth pattern has generally paralleled the growth patterns of the nation.

During the second half of the nineteenth century, the Kansas City area grew from its humble beginnings before the Civil War to some 250,000 inhabitants. By the end of World War II, its population had nearly tripled, and, according to the 1980 U.S. Census, it has now passed the 1.5-million mark. Although not as spectacular as the principal growth regions of the United States, the Kansas City area was able to claim its share of the national wealth and, at the same time, was spared many of the severe negative impacts of the economic cycles experienced in most other urban areas.

It has been said that Kansas City is one of America's best-kept secrets. This is an understatement. The city is very beautiful, genuine, and very livable. It has magnificent neighborhoods and commercial centers, fine residential architecture, well-organized industrial districts—unlike the hodgepodge of the typical modern city—and marvelous parkways and boulevards, with hundreds of fountains and countless pieces of Italian sculpture. Where else would you find some 600 square miles of urban area, including 325 square miles in the central city, tied together by 140 miles of mature, landscaped boulevards and some 160 miles of generally well-located and effectively designed urban freeways? I will let readers draw their own conclusions as I report the story of Kansas City's carefully planned accomplishments of the last three to four decades, which, in retrospect, seems incredible.

Nelson and Kessler: Partners in Spirit

To fully appreciate the recent period, we will take a side trip into the past. This prologue is the story of several men, who found themselves in positions of leadership at a critical phase of the city's history. They were all products of nineteenth-century entrepreneurship, and they were overwhelmed by the challenge of an empty continent, the opportunities offered by an emerging technology, and their own ability to function successfully in that environment. They were farsighted and disciplined people, who realized that prosperity, both personal and societal, cannot be sustained without self-imposed constraint.

The leader of this group was William Rockhill Nelson, sole owner and manager of the *Kansas City Star*—a merchant prince in the best tradition. It was his determination to make the "kingdom" he helped "rule" not only a most powerful one but also a center of beauty and culture—perhaps not for the universe but surely for the enormous expanse loosely called the West, somewhere between St. Louis and San Francisco. In the 1860s and 1870s, there was not much competition for such a claim, other than Chicago and perhaps Milwaukee. But they lay far to the north, and, to them, Kansas City was no more than a place north of Texas, where cattle and other animals were brought to market.

The elements of power and skill in dealing with people were essential in the pursuit of the objectives Nelson would set for himself as time went on, to no small measure with the loyal support of his friends in the Commercial Club—an early version of the chamber of commerce. William H. Wilson gives us a splendid report of that period in *The City Beautiful Movement in Kansas City*.[1] In time, such men as August Meyer, Delbert Haff, Thomas Swope, Van Brunt, Armour, Gilham, and Daniel French, in various civic positions, would become part of the power structure guided by William Rockhill Nelson, which would bring about physical improvements and political changes that were fully intended to propel Kansas City into the forefront of urban America. The institution of an independent park board became the vehicle that would carry the governmental aspects of the effort. That entity brought about the adoption of municipal-charter amendments in the 1890s, having established itself in the tumble of politics of that period.

The park board was removed from direct political activity, and it was considered appropriate for businessmen to serve in that capacity for the betterment of the city. The planners of that period, says Wilson, learned quickly that all the planning in the world would accomplish nothing without a solid legal foundation. Diligently, through legal action, the board learned to cope with the complex issues of constitutionality and the use of the power of eminent domain for the acquisition of parks and boulevards. The effective use of power and the diligent application of management skills are the means to a stated end. The planning process is no exception. But power and management operate in a vacuum without technical input and the creative imagination capable of envisioning in physical terms a product that represents the objectives and aspirations of the people concerned.

By coincidence, William Rockhill Nelson made the acquaintance of a talented young German engineer and landscape architect named George Edward Kessler, who practiced in Kansas City and had once been an associate of New York's famed landscape architect, Frederic Law Olmsted. Eventually, Kessler was invited to become the secretary of the park board in Kansas City for the express purpose of designing a plan for the city in much the same manner in which Baron Haussmann had set the standards of city planning for the period that was to become the City Beautiful Movement in the United States.

Nelson and Kessler had much in common: they were hard-nosed, goal-oriented, somewhat egotistical, and, most of all, immensely capable. Nelson's overriding concern for the welfare of the Kansas City business community was matched by Kessler's zest to bring about the best possible urban environment, which would be aesthetically pleasing as well as practical and attainable. Kessler combined with his design genius a pronounced social consciousness typical of his heritage. Both were tenacious, yet persuasive. Neither man was ever known for his diplomatic skills, let alone tact.

Planning, Design, and Construction

By World War I, Kansas City had its third Kessler Plan—not only adopted by park board and city council—but well into implementation. Figure 2-1 shows schematically the evolution of the Kessler plans from the first concept of 1893, through the 1909 issue, to the ultimate plan of 1915. Rockhill Nelson's political instinct, his ability, through the *Kansas City Star,* to shape public opinion and to hold it together through the often stormy ups and downs of Kansas City politics, the leadership of August Meyer and the fine legal expertise of Delbert Haff, and a combination of public finance, careful land-acquisition programs, and considerable private donation of

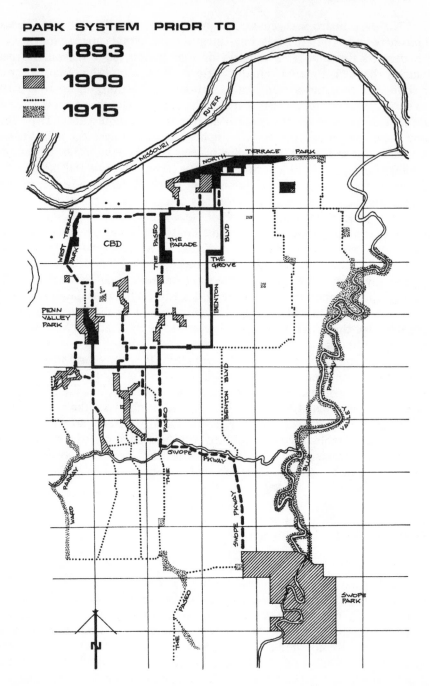

Figure 2-1. Kansas City, Missouri: The Three Stages of Kessler's Plan

cash and land had moved the park and boulevard plan proposed by George Kessler swiftly from the drawing board to reality. With that system, a physical framework was created, which to this day gives Kansas City its distinct character.

Kessler discussed his underlying theories in various reports and communications, particularly in his first major report to the park board in 1893. He correctly critiqued the incompetent layout of the beautiful area by inept surveyors and engineers, who, in the fashion of the times, had superimposed over the charming rolling terrain a rigid gridiron system of streets, which, according to Kessler, had resulted in "an appearance of raggedness that is all but indescribable."[2] Traditionally, streets define the city and give it two-dimensional form. Functionally, streets provide access to the major sections of the city, to private property, and to public places. Moreover, streets provide a variety of significant auxiliary services. They carry surface waters, utilities, and facilities for vehicle storage. To Kessler, streets required classification for major and secondary functions, so that rights-of-way and roadway sections could be designed for efficient discharge of these functions. Like the modern planner, Kessler thought that certain types of major streets would effectively separate land uses that were not compatible.

In establishing his priorities, in his reports to the Park Board, George Kessler advocated the gradual development of a comprehensive boulevard network, which would define land-use areas and connect an ambitious park system. He states that the overriding objective of the boulevards would be twofold: "To provide agreeable driveways, and . . . to make the abutting land . . . especially sought after for residence purposes." Accordingly, he enunciated the following general specifications:

First.   The routes must offer good grades. . . .

Second. They must be located in a naturally sightly locality.

Third.   The lands that abut upon such boulevards must be of a character satisfactory and suitable for good residences.

Fourth. There must be no costly natural or artificial obstacles to remove to permit proper widening of the streets selected.[3]

Kessler had a very good feeling for land form and for maximizing visual effects as well as engineering advantages. His boulevard alignments not only contributed to superb traffic circulation but did much to alleviate surface flooding. Moreover, not only did his planning stimulate the development of major parks for active recreation, but soon the center malls of the boulevards were used as recreational areas by the adjacent residents. A typical boulevard section and a present-day boulevard street scene are shown in figures 2-2 and 2-3.

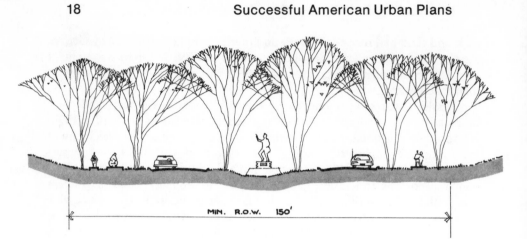

MIN. R.O.W.   150'

Figure 2-2. Typical Cross Section of Boulevard

By Kessler's specifications, location and alignment of the individual boulevards typically fell into natural drainage ways. Kansas City, with its hilly topography, is shaped by a network of streams and rivers, which are all direct or indirect tributaries of the Missouri River, the traditional artery of exploration and commerce of mid-America. What Kessler called a "sightly location" was a relatively high bluff on one side of a streambed, the stream itself, and a slightly rolling approach opposite the bluff. Here, the landscape architect would be stimulated to design the most imaginative and pleasant man-made feature, which would fit perfectly into the natural environment. Therein lies the secret of urban design and the striking difference between inept mechanical application of half-comprehended engineering principles and the work of a true craftsman.

In most situations, the center mall of the boulevard would accommodate the stream, which was often relocated to fit the concept. Grading would be such that surface runoff would also be accommodated in the configuration, so that most flooding, what might now be called 100-year flooding, could be handled without damage to residential areas. On rare occasions, there have been problems, as, for example, in 1978, when a 500-1,000-year-type flood devastated part of the Country Club Plaza.

It is noteworthy that, in locating his parks and boulevards, Kessler kept an eye on removal of slums, a technique deployed in connection with the freeway planning in 1949-1950. However, it is probably reasonable to assume that he was more concerned with the appearance of the city than with social issues—although he was keenly aware of them, not only in Kansas City but also in the other midwestern cities he served. Creating sites for "good residences" paid off handsomely in the long run, particularly from the time that J.C. Nichols, an imaginative Kansas land developer, entered the

Figure 2-3. Typical Boulevard Street Scene

Kansas City scene. Loyally supported throughout his life by banker Crosby Kemper, Sr., J.C. Nichols set out to develop, from the boulevards outward in the southwestern part of Kansas City, what was to become one of America's finest examples of urban design: the Country Club Plaza, the world's first true shopping center away from downtown, and a carefully planned residential area of all types of dwellings, from single family to highrise, extending now over some eighteen square miles and accommodating nearly 300,000 people in Kansas and Missouri. Nichols, who in his later years was to create the well-known Urban Land Institute in Washington, D.C., was a goal-oriented planner-developer who established—on the basis of George Kessler's concepts—a technical base for the development of modern urban areas and the appropriate separation of land uses. The *Community Builders Handbook,* originally written by J.C. Nichols, is still one of the most authoritative works on the subject. Needless to say, Nichols was a great admirer of Kessler's work. Both men were imaginative, creative geniuses, and the work of one inspired the creativity of the other—a classic of urban planning in this century and a classic, too, of a free spirit, a free enterprise, in a free society in constructive action. The work of these men could not be duplicated by a thousand bureaucracies. Figure 2-4, Country Club Plaza, offers a glimpse of that period.

Figure 2-4.   Country Club Plaza

Postscript to Kessler—Harry S Truman

There is an intriguing postscript to that era. In our context, interest is not in
Harry S Truman's presidency, but in his term as presiding judge of Jackson
County, where Kansas City is located. In his capacity as chief administrative officer of one of Missouri's two major urban counties, Mr.
Truman was personally responsible for carrying out an effective planning
program, which he initiated during his first year in office, in 1927. The
results of this effort are documented in a report of the county issued in
1932.[4] Harland Bartholomew, a well-known planning consultant from St.
Louis, and N.T. Veitch, a consulting engineer in Kansas City, were the
technical people responsible for the work. It is also noteworthy that Mr.
Truman's keen political sense made the implementation feasible. Realizing
that politicians often tend to defeat the very purpose of their office by infight-

ing, he borrowed a tactic from William Rockhill Nelson. Since he owned no newspaper, he created and presided over a "nonpolitical" forum, the Greater Kansas City Regional Plan Association, with representation from all the urban counties and cities in both Missouri and Kansas. This was a first, which was to be copied throughout the country under federal guidelines that Truman initiated but that, paradoxically, did not come to fruition until the regime of Richard Nixon.

With that prologue, we go on to present-day Kansas City urban planning, which began with the era of L. Perry Cookingham, dean of the city managers, in the 1940s.

Reform Government and Planning

Management Function

Urban planning is a viable, essential function of urban management. It is not an esoteric exercise. Its sole purpose is to lay before decision makers feasible alternative solutions to perceived issues of public concern. Feasibility in the context of urban planning means (1) that the proposed solution responds effectively to the problem and solves it to the extent that a solution is possible, assuming that the resources, financial and otherwise, could be made available for the undertaking; (2) that the solution will be in the public interest, that is, it will—in the language of Alfred Bettman—be in furtherance of the public health, safety, morals, and general welfare, because, among other reasons, those who designed the solution based their design on recognized scientific principles; and (3) that the public, having been appropriately advised of other options, will support the selected solution. These tests apply whether the plan is initiated by the public, through its mechanisms, or by private interests. As in a court of law, in urban development there is no distinction between a public and private interest insofar as the physical product and the tax liability are concerned. A proposition either is or is not in the public interest. If it is, indeed, in the public interest, it may be implemented; if it is not, it must be rejected. The reason for this premise is that the public cannot very well choose against its own interest in favor of some private gain. Conversely, there is absolutely no objection to private gain in connection with a matter that is otherwise in the public interest, because it is the private gain that would initially motivate someone to take the various risks attendant on such a venture and to carry out a program of development that ultimately enhances the urban environment as a human habitat. There should be no issue here at all, because any reasonable person will readily agree that ventures in urban development are not possible without the numerous actions that produce urban society and its institutions, and it is only fair and equitable that these prior interests be protected as well as the interests of the new venture. Again, our dictum applies to both the public and the private sectors, for in the public sector any reckless use of public powers is as much contrary to public interest as is the exploitation of the commonwealth for direct private gain.

When L. Perry Cookingham accepted the challenge of getting the de facto bankrupt city machinery of Kansas City back on a reasonable track after decades of ruthless bossism under Tom Pendergast he attacked the problem on two fronts: business management and physical-facilities management. The prerequisite of responsible elected officials had been provided by the election of a majority of council members from the non-political Citizens Association. As the "ins" always write history, one must take the array of horror stories about the Pendergast era with the proverbial grain of salt. Nevertheless, it is a matter of record that municipal management in the United States was poor, at least in the major cities, and had yet to achieve the level of professional administration that had been common practice by that time for at least a century and a half in Western Europe and Japan.[5] Mr. Cookingham set out to attempt professionalization of local general-purpose government in Kansas City. This meant dispensing with the traditional American notion that to the victor belongs all spoils, hence that patronage of jobs for loyal party members and hangers-on was no longer to be had, and the power of government was to be used for the benefit of all, just as the law said it would, and not for the principal benefit of the "ins". It meant that bankers would be treated in a businesslike fashion and would have to pay interest on city deposits, which was considered an "unreasonable" policy, even by the supporters of the Citizens Association for a while. It meant that inspections would be based on fact, not on contribution, and that building permits could be had merely by complying with the applicable codes.

Business practice began to govern municipal transactions, which were managed by capable individuals with appropriate professional backgrounds, who were loyal not to the Citizens Association but to the city manager, who now emerged as the new boss. Since his appointment and power base was the city council alone, not a political organization waiting to be fed and clothed, he had few obligations, at least none that would interfere with the conduct of his office directly in a professional, businesslike manner. This included the appointment of department heads and other professionals essential for the conduct of the city's affairs. Modern management practice calls for first-rate staff work, just as in the military, where it had its origin. Staff work is primarily systematic analysis and evaluation of perceived problems and development of solutions on the basis of such scenarios as may be appropriate in order to sort out feasible and infeasible notions until the management is in a solid position to place realistic options for action before the ultimate decision makers. Feasible options are those that may be taken responsibly by elected, reasonably well-informed decision makers and that represent the public interest. They are based on objective fact analysis and on subjective preference, which, to no small measure, flows from experience. That is where the element of *art* enters the scene in management as well as in planning. The process is a human experience, not a machine exercise. Someone accountable makes the final decision, and, in case of failure, it is that person who must answer. It will do little to say, "The computer made me do it," any more than, under other circumstances, "I merely carried out orders."

Cookingham was an artist and a superior craftsman of his trade. He prevailed upon the city council to let him set up staff agencies for physical planning, social planning, and budgetary planning. It was good management practice, and the business community in Kansas City had no problem understanding that. However, there was another motivation. New political movements must show some tangible results of their efforts. Just being good pays few bills and certainly doesn't produce public-works projects with the kinds of contracts that bring money to town and employ people and companies. George Kessler had certainly pointed the way. His planning and programming had converted the country town into a modern city, for the benefit of all. The parallel development to the City Beautiful Movement, which had come out of the depression era in the United States and in Germany, was the highway-development idea, responding to the rapidly increasing motorization of the Western world as a direct result of the technological impact of World War I.

President Roosevelt had suggested an ambitious interregional road system, to be financed by various means, including a tax on unearned-value increment, or an attempt of value recapture by the public on real estate and by other means. Very little was accomplished prior to World War II or, of course, during the war, but it was apparent to all informed people that sooner or later the federal government would get into the highway-construction business with a major injection of federal tax funds. In fact, there was a blueprint for that in the records of the government in the form of a report entitled "Our Cities, Their Role in the National Economy," issued by the National Resources Committee in 1937, ably directed by Ladislas Segoe, executive director of its Urbanism Committee and nationally recognized authority on urban planning.

To be prepared and ready to move when opportunity presents itself is the hallmark of good management, and Cookingham wanted to be ready. He ordered his planners to follow the doctrine laid down by Alfred Bettman and Segoe in connection with the celebrated case, of *Village of Euclid* v. *Ambler Realty Co.*[6]—that all public action in urban development requires the prior existence of a comprehensive plan that clearly enunciates the objectives and policies on which development and public-works construction activity is to be based.[7] This position was aided greatly by the overriding and early-adopted policy of the Missouri State Highway Commission to give top priority to the urban elements of the forthcoming interstate highway system and not to the rural sections—a policy that was to pay handsome dividends for the taxpayers of that state and that enabled the urban planners and engineers to excel in their work.

Urban Highways: A New Concept

City plans of the "city beautiful" era in America showed little, if any, concern for systematic economic or sociological analysis of the urban area they addressed. The focus was primarily on three-dimensional aspects, the building composition of those areas of the city that were then considered to be of civic interest: government buildings, riverfronts, parks, boulevards, and the like. Occasionally, some concern was expressed that the conditions under which recent immigrants or minorities were forced to live in older tenement sections were deplorable and that "something" should be done about it—such as removing the slums to make room for a civic center. "Out of sight, out of mind" was generally considered an adequate "solution" for the social problems of the times.

The common experience of the Great Depression and World War II, the universal recognition of fundamental rights to a life better than bare existence, the emerging concept of social equality or at least equal opportunity, and the decline of bossism in the big cities—all these pressures and others led to the recognition of the public's direct and significant role in the process of formulating goals, plans, and programs for the general betterment of the urban area and its components. The public presents itself to local general-purpose government in several, widely differing forms. First, there is the well-organized, institutionalized public in the political, business, labor, religious, and civic sectors: people of common interest are drawn together by the necessity of having to look out for their specific interests, primarily with respect to any measures that ultimately become legislation designed to further or curtail an interest group.

Second, there is the ad hoc public organization that is created in response to a specific, usually nonrecurring threat to an established system or pattern, such as a contemplated measure that is perceived to be undesirable, as, for example, an unpopular zoning decision relative to a certain neighborhood. Unlike groups in the first category, such organizations will disband when the crisis is resolved. In all these situations, only those members of the body politic will be active who have a discernible, specific interest in the issues at hand. It is interesting that action under either group pattern normally involves only a minority of the public, not in any way the "public at large." In America, more than in most other industrial nations, we suffer particularly from public apathy. For example, barely 54 percent of the eligible electorate bothered to vote in the presidential election of 1980.

Planning Process and Organization

Nevertheless, that public at large, that unorganized public, exists and can become a significant reality in the process of self-government if it is ignored or maligned; it can be a very negative force, indeed, when least expected. No planning process can be effective unless the planners clearly understand the composition and probable short-range and longer-term behavior of that public, its socioeconomic composition, its problems, and its assets. When the Cookingham planners received their orders to initiate an appropriate planning process that would lead to major improvements of the city and metroplitan area of Kansas City, there was no generally accepted methodology for such a task. Some of the pioneers in contemporary urban planning—notably, Ladislas Segoe, Harland Bartholomew, Gordon Whitnall, Russell Blake, John Nolan, and Tracy Augur—had addressed some of the social and economic issues in their comprehensive plans during the approximately twenty years preceding the Kansas City program. However, as a rule, their objectives were to estimate probable changes in city and urban area size, with some vague consideration of population composition—mainly for school population forecasting, not fundamentally, with respect to economic development. Nor did these people have a direct concern with the processes that much later were to be known as "public involvement." Consequently, the older American urban plans of the predepression era contain little more with respect to socioeconomic conditions than a superficial discourse on past population trends and their probable future behavior. Occasionally, the authors would present a description of population composition with respect to age, sex, occupation and employment, and perhaps race. However, these presentations were little more than summaries of the latest available reports from the U.S. Bureau of the Census of the Department of Commerce. From these facts and figures, the planners prognosticated future population for the area as a whole and the probable distribution of that population over the subject areas so that they could make further estimates of the amount of land required over the planning period to accommodate the physical activities generated by the increased population and the facilities and services needed to sustain these activities. The economic studies were simply a means toward a physical planning objective: to identify order of magnitude, scale, and quantities of a wide variety of measures to be accomplished.

The method deployed was by and large the step-down method, by which an urban entity would be related to the next higher unit of civil jurisdiction for which U.S. census material was available. Thus, the subject city would be viewed as an integral part of the county to which it belonged, of the state, possibly of the larger region, in terms of groups of states, and, ultimately, of the United States. Ideally, if past trends indicated that a city behaved proportionately much like the United States—in other words, that its percentage increase in total population for each ten-year period between national censuses would be the same as or close to that experienced by the nation as a whole—the planner would breathe a sigh of relief, for his worries regarding the socioeconomic situation of his client city were over.

If matters remain static and do not change, this methodology is as good as any. Unfortunately—or perhaps fortunately—urban affairs in the United States are not static but are in a constant state of flux. From time to time, we hear a pronouncement that the United States has finally reached its apex. During the 1930s, it was the official position of the U.S. Bureau of the Census, for example, that the United States would reach its ultimate population level of 135,000,000 by 1950. It will therefore be readily apparent that a somewhat more penetrating analysis is required to develop the kind of socioeconomic base from which to draw reliable conclusions—to the extent that such conclusions are at all possible.

L.P. Cookingham's planning team was keenly aware of the issues and realized that it would have to operate to a great extent in uncharted regions, as far as methodology was concerned. The technical planning process is easily understood if it is divided into its functional components: initial survey of the subject area; analysis and forecasting of socioeconomic trends; identification of problems and their respective perception; formulation of common goals and objectives; development or design of feasible options as remedies for problems; priorities; and implementation through capital investment, regulatory measures, and other means. To simplify further, we may distinguish (1) problem identification, (2) problem solution, and (3) implementation.

Management and direction of the Kansas City planning group clearly reflected this functional division. W.G. Bryant, a social scientist, was the initial team leader. He was followed by engineer John M. Picton, who, in turn, was succeeded by landscape architect and planner Philip E. Geissal. The people who followed Geissal after the creative-planning phases in Kansas City, from the late 1950s to the present, were all administrators—appropriately so, for creative people are rarely good at the essential routines that must eventually be established if any discernible results are to be expected from planning as a process.

Ward politics in American cities derived its power from a close-knit relationship of politician and constituency, flowing from the politician's ability to satisfy basic economic needs. It could thrive only where there was significant need. Reform government succeeded on much the same basis, except that the element of basic economic need was replaced by a concept of secondary need that was more closely identified with the life-styles of the middle class. Since, in the United States, there is always an overwhelming majority in the unorganized middle class and traditionally only a small "needy" minority, it takes little statistical know-how to realize that a reform movement based on the organized power of the middle class will win out over ward politics that rely on the needy because of sheer numbers. Such a movement becomes even more certain of control if it takes over the care of the truly needy in a systematic manner. Mr. Cookingham devised the concept of community and neighborhood council organization throughout Kansas City, with permanent representation—through the planning office—of municipal personnel who were capable of providing effective liaison between the public at large—the otherwise unorganized public—and city government. He also organized, as a municipal department under Dr. Hayes Richardson, a first-rate welfare unit, which would attend most effectively over the years to the truly needy.

To achieve these major changes in the municipal infrastructure, information was a vital key. Dr. Bryant furnished the information in a manner that not only was most ingenious for the period but would eventually become a national model. He presented the Kansas City urban area on the basis of a system of "areas of similarity."[8] The basis for the analysis was the then-existing pattern of U.S. census tracts—geographic subdivisions of the area for data collection and presentation. Twenty-one social characteristics or variables were selected to describe the characteristics of population in the tracts. Later, in connection with the development of the master plan and its components, these same areas would be related to traffic zones and would serve as a major source of information required for various forecasting programs. The data compiled for this first round of analysis included the usual socioeconomic statistics, such as population, age composition, race and sex, school years completed, and housing data. Also included, and more important for the evolution of a rational planning process, were a complete analysis of land form and subsoil conditions to estimate future potential for new development in terms of holding capacity and an analysis of probable replacement of existing development where obsolescence and decay had reached levels requiring probable removal in the normal land-economic process. That part of the basic research and survey work was to become invaluable in the planning process, when new federal programs called for swift assessment of slum-clearance needs on which allocations of federal housing and redevelopment funds depended.

This fundamental work represented a penetrating analysis of the city, its strengths and its weaknesses. In moving from community to community and relating the elements not only to the municipal entity, Kansas City, but to the broader metropolitan community, which began to identify itself as Greater Kansas City following Harry Truman's earlier initiatives, the researchers laid a perfect foundation and framework for the subsequent work of the physical planners. Immediately after World War II, a series of reports was issued by the City Plan Department that addressed such topics of concern as transportation, neighborhood facilities, parks and recreation, the Missouri riverfront, the downtown area, housing, the need for municipal expansion, industrial development, and utilities. In 1947, a formal master plan was published and adopted by the City Plan Commission, clearly enunciating the objectives and goals to be accomplished eventually under the vigorous planning program initiated by the Cookingham administration.

In addition to the city-planning staff and the Welfare Department's social-planning programs, the city manager had obtained city council permission to establish a fiscal-planning office known as Research and Budget. All three units were effectively staffed with competent young professionals, whose idealism would carry them through the ups and downs of municipal management and planning, long hours, and poor pay, under the brilliant leadership of Perry Cookingham, who had given hope and promise to city administrators everywhere. It was Mr. Cookingham's management style to attract outstanding professionals who would accomplish their creative work and then move on. These people were not his deputies. Department heads under Cookingham were average people, whose loyalty was unquestioned and who would keep matters on an even keel. This style of administration has the advantage of fostering stability without jeopardizing creativity. Mr. Cookingham was a master of giving credit where it was due and of allowing the younger, talented staff to deal directly with the business community and the political leadership, as appropriate, of course, under his tight management. But there was nothing more exciting and exhilarating for a young planner, engineer, or sociologist than to be invited to a dinner at the Kansas City Club for the purpose of presenting to the city council, other dignitaries, his department head, and Mr. Cookingham the fruits of many weeks of his labors, which had produced a possible solution to an issue that had Mr. Cookingham's approval. And Perry Cookingham knew well what was quality work and what was merely for show. He made it a point to pick specific people for specific jobs and to work closely with the principal individual. This administration was truly democratic, in the sense that the men and women responsible for specific tasks were allowed to see them through and get all the credit, but also to be fully accountable. Equally important was Mr. Cookingham's commitment to his staff. Once committed to a course of action, he would back the staff all the way. If withdrawal was indicated or the staff would fail—as people will—he would fail with them and, in his gracious and polished manner, find a way out that would leave no one embarrassed or dragged into the inevitable power play of complex institutions.

The Critical Thrust

Although the full spectrum of planning activities blossomed, for both the short and long terms, four elements deserve attention in retrospect because of the enormous impact they were to have not only on Kansas City but on urban planning throughout the United States. These elements were (1) plans for annexation and their implementation; (2) plans for urban freeways and other arterial streets; (3) urban redevelopment; and (4) current planning administration, particularly the effective use of development districts—a most innovative technique.

This is not the place to discuss the politics of annexation in Kansas City. It was complex, reviving memories of the Pendergast system and its power base. But in the end, the soundness of appropriate urban planning for annexation prevailed and, under Missouri's system of annexation, earned the required judicial consent and approval. In 1947, the planning commission issued the "Metropolitan Area Report." In that study, the planners pointed out where and how the then-undeveloped suburban fringe related to the central city of eighty square miles. The underlying physical-planning theory was the notion that drainage basins must be given serious consideration in determining political boundaries, because drainage-related facilities are costly and require complex infrastructures for upkeep and maintenance. Scale and land requirements flow from socioeconomic analysis. Based on the theory that reasonable expectation of growth and a discernible relationship to the services provided by the central city are the principal considerations for justifying annexation, this study laid the foundation for the legal steps that followed. In fact, it represented a compilation of a series of annexation monographs for areas located in Clay, Platte, and Jackson counties, which presented a complete review and analysis of the trends and conditions in each area under consideration. The final result of this effort was the annexation of 240 square miles of suburban land in carefully arranged and timed stages that would attempt to coordinate, as well as possible, the legal effective dates of council action with the city's actual ability to render services. The planning of this important and politically sensitive program was directed personally by Cookingham. Principal technical input was provided by the City Plan Department, the Water Department, and the City Engineer. The Water Department's role, under Melvin Hatcher, was particularly significant, as was that of the Finance Department, under Rollin

Agard. As is true for many cities, over the years Kansas City had become accustomed to serve as a water utility, through the sale of water to unincorporated communities. Negotiation for these water contracts typically included negotiation for certain concessions that are concerns of the planning administrator, such as standards of platting and specifications for elements of the physical infrastructure, particularly the water-distribution and sewage-collection networks. Legal relationships of this type made a powerful argument for ultimate annexation, particularly where a subdivision had waived any future right to oppose such city action.

The annexation program, carefully planned and executed with all due consideration to the political realities of the period, was successful. Only one countermove occurred, producing Gladstone, a suburban city north of the Missouri River. With that exception, the program was a resounding success, because it incorporated suburbia with the central city in Jackson, Clay, and Platte counties in Missouri. However, the program could not penetrate the most powerful of all American lines of political demarcation—the state line, in this case between Missouri and Kansas. The question of managing suburban development and avoiding the ill effects of unguided, mindless sprawl were resolved well on the Missouri side, with Kansas City as the central metropolis. On the Kansas side, not much was going on at that time; consequently, it was not an issue. Kansas City, Kansas, had always been the "poor cousin" in the area, and Johnson County, the southwestern section of Greater Kansas City was then only a relatively insignificant rural county, with a few subdivisions for rich people who liked to keep horses on the premises and with Mr. Cookingham's favorite social group, the Saddle and Sirloin Club.

To those who subscribe to the maximum centralization of local government, the state line and the fact that political and legal planning always comes to an end there represents the nemesis and the soft underbelly of the growth-management program for Kansas City, Missouri. Many years later, Johnson County would emerge as the new retail center of the metropolitan area, accommodating nearly one-fourth of its total population. If Kansas City, Kansas, and Wyandotte County are included in the comparison, half the people of Greater Kansas City now reside in Kansas. To those who argue that there is merit in versatility and political choice, Kansas City demonstrates the benefits that can flow from the existence of a state line as an institution fostering two distinct political mechanisms with their attendant loyalties. The situation also serves as an example of the fact that intergovernmental coordination of vital services and of physical infrastructures, especially for transportation and utilities, is more than a textbook figment of wishful thinking. It can and will occur on two conditions: that the public demands it and that leadership capable of implementing the will of the public in this regard can be provided.

That was accomplished in the Kansas City situation in a most remarkable and dramatic manner in connection with its plans and programs for urban transportation. This phase of planning produced three benchmarks: the 1951 report, "Expressways—Greater Kansas City"; its 1956 supplement; and the 1975 "Long Range Transit Plan."[9] The most significant achievement was the 1951 expressway study. Walter Blucher, famed past executive director of the American Society of Planning Officials (a predecessor to the American Planning Association), was elated when the report came out and expressed his delight in a personal letter to Phil Geissal, who had so diligently directed the effort. Mr. Blucher's enthusiasm is easy to understand. Here was America's very first urban-freeway plan, produced not by consulting engineers or highway departments but by a well-recognized, bona fide municipal-planning agency, which had become a viable element of the model of municipal administration in the country. In addition, a report approved by state and federal highway authorities was in fact produced in closest cooperation with them. That was a milestone, and all concerned had every reason to be proud of their accomplishments. Thirty years after the fact, they can be even prouder; almost all of it has been constructed and otherwise implemented. Robert Kipp, city manager of Kansas City since 1974, considers the "excellent planning of Kansas City's interstate freeway system" to be one of the most significant accomplishments of the Cookingham era. "The freeways in use today do not differ materially from the original plan of Cookingham's day, yet those plans were formulated in World War II and shortly afterward."[10] This opinion is shared by Robert Hunter, long-time chief engineer of the Missouri Department of Highways and Transportation, who called the Kansas City planning effort the first "integrated and most successful" program based on the work of "cooperating and coordinated" city and state teams of planning and engineering professionals. Hunter stated in a recent telephone interview that the report "Expressways—Greater Kansas City" was immediately acclaimed by the profession as a first-rate study. Looking back over thirty years of successful implementation, the facts speak for themselves.

Further, George Satterlee, district engineer for the Missouri Highway and Transportation Commission in Kansas City, whose outstanding management of the highway program for the metropolitan area has contributed much to its success, reports that the total investment in urban freeways on the Missouri side of the urbanized area as of January 1981 totals $199,409,143. This includes some $87 million for roads that were not in the original 1951 plan. The interstate highway engineer for the Kansas Department of Transportation in Topeka, F.T. Reed, finds that the public investment for urban freeways on the Kansas side was $172,418,204. These investments were made over more than a quarter of a century. Considering the rising cost levels of inflation experienced over that period, it becomes apparent that the investment in terms of present-day dollars, conservatively estimated, would be around a billion dollars.

Expressways—Greater Kansas City

Highway planning and construction in the United States matured during the 1920s and 1930s from pork-barrel politics to top-level professionalism. At the insistence of the old federal Bureau of Public Roads, a nearly insignificant organization in terms of engineering, administrations emerged at the state level to direct government-funded highway programs. This movement ran parallel with the state programs for the registration of professional engineers, sponsored by the American Society of Civil Engineers and other groups. Although the movement was temporarily disrupted by World War II, by the late 1940s the United States could boast of an outstanding system of capable highway administrations throughout the land, intellectually guided by the very ably managed Bureau of Public Roads.

In Missouri, chief engineers Rex M. Whitton and Carl Brown had made major contributions to that trend, as had Ross C. Keeling and Gayle Moss in Kansas. These men were keenly aware of the need for an integrated approach to highway development between rural and urban areas and believed that the time had come to move aggressively into programs that would relieve the large metropolitan areas of ever-increasing traffic problems. They welcomed the federal government's concern with the need for high-speed urban arteries, which in some form had to become integral parts of the national system of regional and defense highways. European lessons, too, were vividly on the minds of the engineers when they set out on their new task, which, after all, represented a substantial change from the former mission and preoccupation with rural highway networks and the old farm-market programs that had done so much to "get rural America out of the mud."

The Road Act of 1916 introduced a system of federal financial assistance for highway construction and legally recognized a national system of highways. This act was further amplified in 1921. However, it was not until passage of the 1944 Regional and Defense Highway Act that a more refined classification of highway types was written into the law, including the concept of a primary and secondary highway system (Sec. 7) and authorization for a national system of interstate highways not to exceed 40,000 miles. Unfortunately, that act failed to provide for the funding of such a system. Nevertheless, the Congress had now served notice that, sooner or later, the federal government would become seriously involved in highway funding. With the highway legislation of 1956, this was to become a firm commitment. Mr. Cookingham, with other alert administrators, acted confidently in anticipation of federal assistance, knowing very well not only that such highway programs were vital for the obvious transportation purposes to be served but that, traditionally, highway construction has been a major tool of government in combating unemployment. With the end of World War II in sight, programs had to be considered to provide work for returning veterans. Highway construction and housing production would accomplish that objective well. Although the federal government would provide the financial input, it would be the responsibility of local government, at state and municipal levels, to manage the projects prudently. Kansas City set out to do just that with remarkable success.

By and large, there was little field experience with urban highway planning in this country—or anywhere else for that matter. Largely as a result of Mr. Cookingham's confidence in the technical competence of his physical planning staff, the Missouri State Highway Department contracted with the City Plan Commission of Kansas City for a preliminary engineering report on the feasibility of an urban expressway system for the Kansas City metropolitan area.

The Greater Kansas City Metropolitan Highway Committee, originally formed in 1943, was activated and charged with the responsibility of providing political and citizens' input for the work from all parts of the area, not only from Kansas City, Missouri, proper. It should be noted that a *state agency* provided the funding—partly federal, of course—for a municipal planning agency to accomplish an objective that was, at the time, state and municipal policy within the framework of what eventually was to become a congressional mandate. It was a fine example of effective government interaction at the key levels.

Financial resources are only part of the pattern. Technical manpower constitutes the other, equally important element. It was agreed that city-planning staff, highway-department personnel, and top-level research engineers of the Bureau of Public Roads would constitute the production team, with specific tasks assigned to evolving component work groups. This process worked admirably. By that time, the federal agency had established its standards for what might be considered an adequate research data base on which significant decisions ultimately requiring substantial competition for federal funding could be based, if and when Congress would see fit to provide it. Consequently, there had to be an equitable basis on which to judge need and to set priorities, nationally and within each state, as the state was viewed as the ultimate consumer of the funds on behalf of that state and its respective political subdivisions.

The Bureau of Public Roads required that each jurisdiction interested in the development of urban expressways should first undertake comprehensive traffic surveys and produce appropriate forecasts of probable future traffic requirements. Construction cycles for major public works traditionally ran twenty to twenty-five years. Accordingly, it became general practice to attempt traffic forecasts for such a time span. How was this to be achieved?

Traffic Analysis, Custom-Made

A mere technical projection of statistical traffic data might yield useful results in some respects—for example, the order of magnitude of automotive traffic or transit patronage for a given universe—provided, of course, that there is enough historical data available to construct appropriate trends. However, such data will not tell us much in regard to the probable future distribution of traffic within our study area, nor will it give us many clues regarding traffic fluctuations and composition. It becomes necessary, at the outset, to consult the city's plans and programs, especially the element of the comprehensive plan that attempts to systematically analyze and utilize the available land area. The holding capacity of the various communities, existing and anticipated, and the probable timing of development will surely give some insight into transportation requirements, just as these indicators give us a measure of utilities needed to sustain residential and nonresidential land uses.

For Kansas City, the careful analysis of various social, economic, and land-development conditions and their interpretation in terms of areas of similarity, as discussed earlier, allowed us to refine the data further by arranging the information on the basis of some 250 zones and external stations. In the process of evaluating available variables, it was determined that the most convenient and effective method of determining zonal changes would be on the basis of population and employment, as both values were on record for existing and past conditions. Future population and employment would be derived simply from the calculation of the comprehensive land-use analysis by taking into consideration the amount of available developable or redevelopable land, its land-use designation, and the probability of timing in view of assumed access to roads and utilities. The planners who undertook this analytical effort were intimately familiar with the area and did, in fact, produce a custom-made plan.

Eventually, the results of the zone-by-zone analysis was expressed in form of a simple index: population and employment for each zone were added together for the base year (1950) and for the forecast year (1970), and the percentage change was determined. That factor would be considered a zone-expansion factor, as an indicator of growth or decline. To account for the probable change, especially anticipated growth, in areas that were then vacant, a pattern was developed, which became known as the hypothetical pattern. Values were assigned to these vacant zones to resemble a plausible base had there been growth at the time. With this accomplished, it was again merely a matter of judgment and arithmetic to develop the zonal factor of future behavior.

The planners then had a base for their traffic analysis. With care, skill, and imagination, what might be called soft data were converted to a solid, hard base describing the socioeconomic conditions that were considered the cause of traffic generation, with respect to both the generation of trips and the attraction of them by various destinations. Although it may be argued that traffic does not necessarily grow in direct proportion to population and employment, considering the crude nature of estimating at the scale of system design, one can readily point to the absurdity of traffic-forecasting refinements under laboratory conditions, which add very little to the end result other than some satisfaction with a statistical quirk. The managers of the Kansas City project would not stand for that. They had to produce results promptly, and they did.

Under the fine guidance of Darrell Trueblood, senior research engineer for the Bureau of Public Roads, it was agreed that the factors developed by the planners not only adequately described the probable future of the various traffic zones analyzed but would be equally reliable as expansion factors of trip interchanges between each two zones or of external-station and intrazone travel. One could apply the factors either to people or to vehicles and thus produce person-trips or vehicle-trips. A further refinement was added by so-called overall traffic-expansion factors, which were to measure major changes anticipated between sectors of the metropolitan area. Eventually, it was agreed to express the entire travel pattern in terms of twenty-four-hour and peak-hour vehicle trips, as the treatment of transit trips was managed separately. In order to obtain future travel factors for each zone-pair trip interchange, the geometric mean of each applicable pair of zonal-expansion factors was determined and applied to the reported trip interchange. Actually, the process was duplicated to test the method and its results. The first projection was from the original survey year to the analysis base year (1944 to 1950), and the second forecast was to the target year, 1970. This enabled the planners and traffic engineers to check results against actual patterns and to calibrate the system where necessary. This checking required, of course, an assignment of the zonal-traffic interchange to some network.

That network consisted of the entire arterial street system and a new system of urban expressway, called the "assumed system," which was superimposed. This assumed system was the result of initial diagnosis of the traffic conditions and future plans by planners and engineers during a two-year period preceding the actual formal planning program. Preliminary diagnosis, now sometimes referred to as sketch planning, often proves to be as important as the very refined planning that typically precedes action, or more so. Trips were traced manually from origin to destination through the entire system of intersections and interchanges, and the travel time was read off the network. In the case of alternate-route options, especially options involving the assumed expressway system, diversions were calculated to produce a simulated travel pattern that would resemble, as closely as possible, the actual traffic patterns. Since there were no comparable situations to examine at that time, it was simply assumed that travel-time savings resulting from expressway use would induce a proportionate number of trips to select that route. Travel times had been determined by field survey and by a further assumption that all limited-access facilities would be traveled at an average speed of 35 miles per hour. By dividing travel time on the route, including expressways, by the alternate city-street travel time, the proportion was determined and a stratified assignment was secured. Since the intersectional movements were also recorded, the long-range transportation study produced interesting by-products for traffic-engineering purposes. In later studies, of course, actual field experience with freeways became available gradually, allowing the analysts to prejudge probable traffic distribution by use of diversion curves that were derived from field observations in comparable cities.[11]

Manual traffic-analysis operations forced the engineer and planner to rethink every prior assumption repeatedly, thereby becoming intimately familiar with all critical situations in the study area. Moreover, the process provided many opportunities for revision and refinement and, in this sense, moved the entire planning process much closer to ultimate implementation and operation. Conversely, testing of alternatives became more cumbersome, if not impossible, on a large scale. The computer has become a powerful and effective tool in the planning process, and the technology that has emerged is useful. However, there are limitations to the use of computerized, canned programs in lieu of human judgment, as there is no substitute for the results of knowledgeable, painstaking analysis and planning. The key to the issue lies simply in the objective. If a mere overview is called for—to give some indication of order of magnitude of available alternatives—the statistical, computerized systems will do splendidly. If, however, planning leading to construction is at stake, then the creative human mind is indispensable if we are not to produce more mindless monuments to empty technology. The thoughtful analyst will find a good balance between new technologies and professional judgment. The decision maker would be well advised to ask whether the proposed operation is really necessary and what will be learned from it that is not already known.

The Kansas City planners had carefully determined development and redevelopment potential of the communities throughout the metropolitan area, and they then transformed this growth potential into travel patterns—interzonal, intrazonal, and external. The resulting trip interchanges were then assigned to the transportation systems—first to those that existed, then to the proposed systems. A traffic-engineering statistic was thus created that would give a clear indication of the order of magnitude required to solve existing traffic problems and to serve anticipated demand. It is at this stage that the typical transportation-planning process ends. Experience shows that that is a fatal mistake, which fortunately was not made in Kansas City at that time. The agreement between the city and the Missouri State Highway Department provided for a second element in the planning process: a preliminary engineering study of location, alignment, and overall design of the limited-access urban highway system that had emerged from the analysis of the probable impact of the assumed test system on the metropolitan area. Figure 2-5 shows that system in the 1980 context.

Freeway Location and Design

The analysts had laid the foundation. Now the designers could bring their talents to bear by transforming quantitatively expressed planning objectives into physical form. There was, of course, some overlap between the work of the planning analysts—Frances I. Gaw, Adolph Rice, and myself—and the designers—Robert K. Maiden, C.M. Cushing, and Phil Geissal, as project director. But the logical interaction was as impeccable as was the interaction with our counterparts at the Bureau of Public Roads—Clifford Shoemaker and S.W. O'Brien—and the State Highway Department's C.P. Owens, Myer Ableman, Harold Brush, and N.F. Tammahh, ably assisted by Dan Watkins. The planners on the team were more concerned with location and the engineers with highway design, of course. The engineers gave freely of their knowledge, and the planners learned from their diverse viewpoints. It was here that a keen awareness emerged of the enormous impact of the urban freeways on the urban scape and environment and of the unique opportunity to utilize this gigantic public-works effort not only for moving traffic but as a critical instrument of urban development.

From the beginning, the Kansas City team viewed the urban highway as an integral element of the urban pattern that would offer opportunities for the shaping of land development. The emerging freeways were just another part of the comprehensive planning process, integrated across state lines, municipal boundaries, and county jurisdictions. Conceptually, the system followed well-established notions of railroad planning. It had long been recognized that, in many respects, the modern urban highway system resembled a gigantic railroad, one, however, in which each car operated on its own initiative. The railroad principle that such a system requires careful consideration of feed-in and acceptance of traffic for local distribution became a highway-design principle. In the Kansas City program, great care

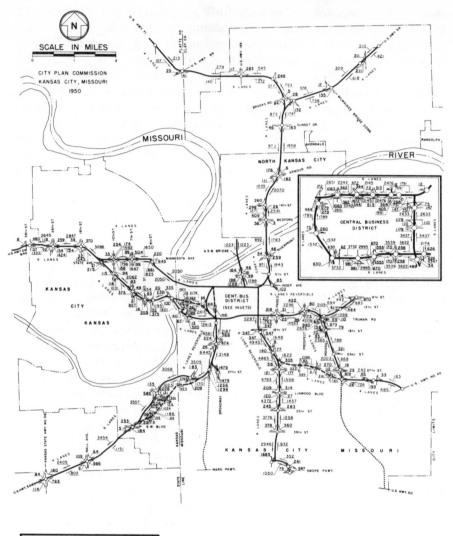

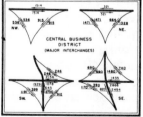

1970 TRAFFIC VOLUMES
ON EXPRESSWAYS & RAMPS
AFTERNOON PEAK HOUR

NUMBER OF LANES RECOMMENDED

Figure 2-5.   Assumed Freeway System

was taken to provide effective feeding into and acceptance from the freeways through an updated thoroughfare system, as it was clearly demonstrated through traffic analysis that no freeway system could work without a well-functioning secondary-support system.

Another principle of railroad planning—that main lines serve major movement from traffic production to attraction and that, in making location decision, these production and attraction centers themselves are shaped and sometimes even eliminated—resulted in a system design that clearly favored the Kansas City downtown area. A loop, patterned after the loop of the Chicago Elevated Transit System, was laid out, with multiple connections across the Missouri. From the loop emanated radial routes east, west, southwest, southeast, and north. Where appropriate, these urban freeway sections would connect directly with midtown and suburban boulevards and other thoroughfares. In this composition, the freeway emerged as the element of the metropolitan arterial system that would have the capacity to carry the increasing volumes of traffic of the inner city. Within the city's annexation and growth-management programs, the routes to the north were particularly significant, as were the new Missouri River crossings. Although it was not justifiable by existing or even clearly foreseeable development in 1949-1950, policy flowing from the comprehensive plan was allowed to override statistical data, laying the foundation for substantial growth and, as an unforeseen by-product, the opportunity to construct Kansas City International Airport, eventually, in a perfect airport environment, the remoteness of which was more than offset by freeway accessibility.

Wherever possible, the location of freeways served as an instrument for correcting improper land use and decay. A deliberate effort was made to eliminate slum housing through freeway location and to bring about systematic relocation of the slum occupants into new standard housing. In fact, the immediate reason for Kansas City's slum-clearance program, initiated at about the time the urban highway program was completed, was that relocation had to be municipally managed in order to provide standard housing to the poor. Last, but by no means least in priority, was the concern of the designers to produce not only functionally acceptable solutions but solutions that, by themselves, would be aesthetically pleasing or would create a framework of aesthetic quality. The entire downtown design, the airport entrance, and numerous other features attest to the success of this design policy. Figures 2-6 and 2-7 dramatically illustrate the point.

It should be noted that the initial urban limited-access highway plan for Greater Kansas City did not include the circumferential routes, I-435 and I-635. These routes were added in 1956-1957, in accordance with federal guidelines, as the result of a supplementary study by Wilbur Smith and Associates. The timing of their construction was paralleled by suburban explosion, which was to shift the focus of growth from Kansas City,

Figure 2-6. Downtown Kansas City, 1950-1980

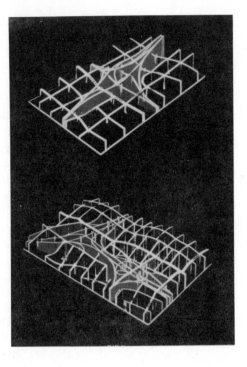

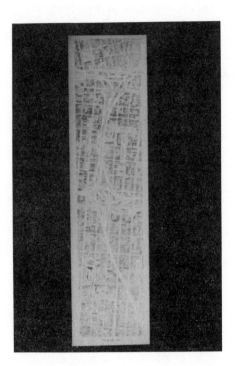

Figure 2-7. Plan and Action: Kansas City

Missouri, to Johnson County, Kansas, in the 1970s. Of course, these circumstances did not cause the decentralization. In an urban area with thoroughfare systems as well organized, developed, and maintained as those of Greater Kansas City—with superb traffic management by transportation director Delbert Karmeier—that development was feasible even without the freeways. However, it is correct to state, categorically, that the existence of the circumferential freeway systems in both Kansas and Missouri aided substantially in the process of suburbanization, particularly commercial and industrial, and certainly became a significant instrument in organizing the suburbanization. Coupled with generally excellent municipal land-development control throughout the area, suburbanization in Kansas City remains an outstanding example of American urbanization in general, of our culture, and of our technical ability.

Any access to transportation systems can induce development if there are development catalysts in the area. The scope and effectiveness of such development will depend on other factors, such as economic conditions, legislation favorable to enterprise, consumer preference, perceived social problems, permitted land uses, and corresponding productivity of land.

The transportation system that Kansas City created for itself over some twenty-five years of concerted effort is a statement of competence and leadership. As such, it is a worthy continuation of the planning and construction initiated by the era of William Rockhill Nelson and George Kessler. And both periods, in retrospect, make even the Pendergast years plausible, because, even then, the civic center, the auditorium, and the further improvement and extension of several boulevards were done in accordance with the old plans, which had produced so much for the city.

More than a billion dollars has been invested in the metropolitan freeway system since 1949. Much more has been attracted by land development along all the urban highway routes, and local taxation, authorized by the state legislature for transportation, has kept up with the most critical demand. The results are testimony that comprehensive urban planning works well, indeed, in the United States. In the Kansas City case, the results are a living monument to competent men and women, whose professional talents were mobilized and who were given every opportunity to do their very best by managers and administrators at the municipal, state, and federal levels, and by a civic leadership that set the tone of ambition with discipline and restrained goal orientation. The success of urban planning lies in the effective interaction of all these forces on a common base.

Public Transit

In 1972, the transportation issue was raised again, this time by Kansas City's two-term mayor, Charles Wheeler, who, in response to public demand, requested a careful analysis of public-transit potentials for Greater Kansas City. During the late 1960s, diligent political planning—with substantial federal financial aid—had led to the creation of a bistate Metropolitan Area Transportation Authority, which was given authority to acquire the financially defunct Kansas City Transit Company. I was privileged to submit the first transit improvement program under the 1964 Urban Mass Transportation Act to the Urban Mass Transportation Administration. As a direct result of this effort, the Kansas City Area Transportation Authority (ATA) was awarded an additional $1 million in federal transit funds. The transit improvement program was practical, candid, and result-oriented.[12] Robert McManus, urban mass transportation's intellectual and spiritual leader, was instrumental in this first effort of agency-municipality cooperation, as was William Icenogle, ATA's able legal counsel. The noncapital aspects of the program were gradually implemented by Red Jennison, general manager for the system. However, there was no base for longer-range considerations. Charles Wheeler promised in his campaign that he would act, and the Chamber of Commerce concurred. A team of three consulting firms was formed (Howard, Needles, Tammen and Bergendoff; Parsons, Brinckerhoff, Quade and Douglas; and W.G. Roeseler, Consulting City Planner); and that team, known as Kansas City Transit Associates, won the contract for a comprehensive transit plan from the Mid-America Regional Council, the now-formalized successor to the several regional planning commissions and Greater Kansas City regional transportation committees. A three-year program produced an interesting and significant further element of the ongoing transportation and comprehensive-planning process, which is carefully implemented by the agencies concerned under the sensitive direction of a responsive Council of Governments and its key professionals, Pete Levi and Hampton McDowell. Relying fundamentally on the corridors that by then were so well established as a result of the study, "Expressways—Greater Kansas City," in 1951, the principal recommendation of the effort was intensification of bus transit. Also recommended, however, was consideration of right-of-way acquisition for possible future exclusive busways, which, in time, might be converted to light or commuter rail service. It is unlikely that significant demand for such intensive transit will occur in Kansas City in the near future, except that the old streetcar linkage from the Country Club area to Plaza and downtown might be revived as an experiment for light rail, the modern version of the streetcar used so effectively in all the reconstructed major urban areas of Germany, Holland, Belgium, and elsewhere (see figure 2-8.)

Busways

The Kansas City planning process produced, as an almost unnoticed by-product, the concept of an exclusive busway. It emerged in connection with a

Figure 2-8. Kansas City Country Club: Old Streetcar Right-of-Way Could Be
Reclaimed for Light-Rail Transit Use

1967 study of passenger ground transportation from and to the international
airport.[13] After testing a number of options, I conducted a penetrating study,
with the assistance of the late airport director Frank Pittenger, of the
characteristics of passenger origin. It happened that a majority of the
passengers had a common base of origin—in fact, two bases: their homes in
the southwestern part of the metropolitan area and an intermediate stopover,
their downtown offices. The delays occurred at certain interchanges and
Missouri River bridges during peak hours. It appeared reasonable to find a
method for buses to bypass these congestion points. Later, an entire busway
could be constructed. If circumstances required, that busway could, of
course, become a rapid-transit link. Matters were aided by the fact that an old
suburban transit right-of-way, which had been abandoned years ago, was still
intact. Unfortunately, the Federal Highway Administration of that period
did not have the means to assist in the implementation of the idea in Kansas
City, but the Virginia Highway Department did. Through Howard, Needles,
Tammen and Bergendoff's efforts, the idea was transferred from me and
Kansas City to Virginia, and thus was born the Shirley Highway Express Buslane program, which has been a resounding success. Figure 2-9 illustrates the
buslane concept.

Coordination and cooperation comes easily to the midwesterner. There

Figure 2-9. Buslane in Urban Freeway: A Sensible and Cost-Effective Solution

exists an atmosphere of sincerity and result orientation that represents the very best of enlightened conservatism and self-interest. This applies to major issues as well as to the many little things that can make life so much easier. For example, Greater Kansas City has a fully integrated, uniform street- and house-numbering system, crossing all political jurisdictions, and zoning and subdivision regulations bear some rational resemblance to one another. Midwesterners have their share of irrational quirks, too, of course. On balance, however, the positive and constructive wins, and that is perhaps the real secret of their success in urban and regional planning and public administration. Success in planning is also to the credit of business and the professions, their restraint and constructive critiques, and time and again, to the helping hand of the *Kansas City Star*. Figure 2-10 presents an interpretation of interlocking transportation and development systems for downtown Kansas City by Charles Goslin, noted Missouri artist.

Urban Reclamation

There is no better example of the intricate relationship of urban transportation to land values in modern times than the story of the redevelopment of

Figure 2-10.   Transportation Systems and New Town-in-Town: Kansas City

Kansas City's skid row along North Main Street. It is my favorite example of effective planning for renewal and refurbishing, which had such a bad name because of the incompetent management it suffered in the hands of the old Housing and Home Finance Agency (HHFA) and its successor, the U.S. Department of Housing and Urban Development (HUD)—a department of hundreds of useless documents. This incredible bureaucracy notwithstanding, competent planners and administrators in the cities of America, despite the federal government, were able occasionally to make good use of the funds Congress had provided, and they produced interesting results.

HUD had a good and substantial beginning with the old Housing Finance Administration, which, with the Veterans Administration, provided the financial means for building the United States we all now live with—the infrastructure of our cities, established since 1945. After much political maneuvering, a recommendation that was dear to the objectives of

President Franklin Roosevelt's National Resources Committee—slum clearance and urban redevelopment—finally found its way into the package of federal urban-assistance programs with the National Housing Act of 1949.

Kansas City wasted no time and moved swiftly into the urban-redevelopment program. With President Truman just reelected for a second term, applications for funds were certain to get prompt attention. The initiative for this phase of planning predictably came from the downtown interests. Under the effective leadership of Louis S. Rothschild, the City Plan Commission sponsored a series of urban-renewal studies, which all led to early implementation under Title I of the Housing and Urban Redevelopment Act. However, while taking advantage of the federal program, the commission was aware of its inherent shortcomings: that the entire decision-making process was tightly controlled by Washington and that the inevitable delays might work at cross purposes. How right they were! As we will see in connection with other city programs, that eventually destroyed the program.

Missouri had a better answer to urban redevelopment—its own Redevelopment Corporations Act, put into effect after an amendment to the state constitution in 1949. Redevelopment under this statute required only two prerequisites: a comprehensive city plan with which any redevelopment project had to comply and demonstration of financial capacity by a redeveloper. The initiative to redevelop was entirely within the discretion of private enterprise. The incentive to go into slum clearance and redevelopment rather than working in open suburban areas was derived from a form of direct tax abatement. For the first ten years of the project's legal life, no taxes were due on the new structures, and for the following fifteen years, only 50 percent of what otherwise might have been due was charged. This tax abatement became, in fact, a capitalizable asset, which allowed the redeveloper to negotiate from relative strength for his financing. Moreover, land assembly was accomplished under eminent domain. Since its inception, some thirty-two redevelopment projects have been carried out; all but two have been very successful.

North Main Street was Kansas City's skid row for years. The occupants were generally good-natured alcoholics, who really bothered no one and lived their lives according to the style they had themselves carved out. Occasionally, some well-meaning person or organization would have them all gathered up and would attempt to settle them in what the sponsor considered more appropriate environs. The results were predictable; they would run away and find another place to congregate. I recall vividly that the old HHFA made us prepare relocation plans and rehabilitation programs for the occupants of skid row. After setting aside various bureaucratic objections to the redevelopment of North Main Street, however, HHFA allowed the area to become a redevelopment project, following the city council's declaration of blight for that part of the central business district (CBD).

To the planners and the downtown interests, North Main Street was one of the key entrances to the CBD. Accordingly, a major access point had been provided to and from the freeway loop in this location, as well as an overpass to facilitate access to Kansas City's old municipal airport on the Missouri River. Our theory was that this land would become so valuable that development was just a matter of time. In a way it was, but we all learned a lesson we never forgot. During the entire planning phase, when alternative highway-design and redevelopment options were discussed publicly, absolutley nothing occurred with respect to the land we considered so precious. No one made any attempt to assemble land, and the wild speculation the planners and realtors had fully expected did not take place.

After months of planning and programming, the day finally came when the highway department's contractors moved in with heavy equipment. As if flood gates had been opened, people began to compete for the land in the North Main Street section. Although assembly had been partly accomplished under the federal program, construction of redevelopment was induced under the redevelopment corporation's act. The results are shown in figure 2-11. It was a spectacular transition from skid row to a truly magnificent entrance to the CBD. It is interesting that the renewal had an orientation that was new for downtown—banking and offices, no longer retail and service—heralding the beginning of a new era of decentralization of the old power base of local commerce. Although CBDs were reduced in stature throughout the country, alert cities were able to keep abreast of the trends through effective urban redevelopment, carefully coordinated with planning and construction of transportation facilities and building of needed government office structures. With that, the downtowns were given a new and meaningful lease on life, as it allowed them to find their proper place within the metropolitan community of the second half of this century. The initial loss of tax revenue, in all instances, was made up during the first few years, when partial taxes became due—in addition to the earnings and income taxes generated by the developers and their tenants.

Although the constitutionality of slum clearance had been previously confirmed by the Missouri Supreme Court—following precedents in other states that viewed the public actions of slum removal to be within the broad police power of the state and its subdivisions, including acquisition of private property under threat of eminent domain—confirmation of the constitutionality of the redevelopment corporation came in 1965.[14] The court confirmed its previous position regarding the taking issue, ruling that, in the absence of fraud, the city council had legislative and discretionery powers to declare an area a blighted area and that the use of eminent domain is incidental, as is the subsequent reuse of the property by the corporation.

Figure 2-11.   North Main Street Renewal, Before and After

Tax abatement was viewed as a matter of public policy, particularly justified in view of past experience with other redevelopment corporations—their success and their ability to pay more in taxes over the first two or three years of tax liability than was lost during the tax-abatement period.

Not much redevelopment is in progress today. The market is no longer there, because the previous projects have effectively exhausted it. Also, the incentive is no longer there, because real-estate taxes have been relegated to a much less significant position in the total tax pattern of business than they held in the 1950s and early 1960s. Tax incentives today would have to be derived from the abatement of state and federal income taxes to get the attention of investors. For the period when redevelopment was attractive, Kansas City's planning and the initiative of developers and financiers there paid off handsomely and, indeed, was in the public interest. Figure 2-12 shows the basic urban renewal plan for that area.

Current Planning: Challenge and Opportunity

Too frequently, the popular image of urban planning is the grand plan. Actually, much is accomplished in urban planning through everyday decisions and actions by numerous people and organizations, whose efforts are coordinated and sometimes stimulated or shaped by the planner as a consultant or in public office. That function is generally called current planning to distinguish it from the longer-range programs typically initiated by a public agency. As we have shown in the preceding sections, there is, of course, good reason for planning's image of far-reaching designs. Major arterial street or public-transit programs, civic centers, schools, parks, and so on, are the result of such planning and become reality through major public investments, typically in the form of massive issues of general-obligation or revenue bonds. These public debts are retired from tax receipts or from income derived by the public entity from a specific enterprise—an auditorium, for example, or an airport.

The full benefit of planning as a function of general-purpose government at the municipal and county levels is realized only if a finely tuned relationship exists between the creative long-range plan making and the day-by-day current planning, which also must be creative but in a different manner. Its creativity lies both in seeking compliance with plan objectives that are not detrimental to the entrepreneur and in finding administrative solutions that avoid undue bureaucracy and stagnation. Kansas City had the benefit of several outstanding administrators in planning, who devoted their lives to that responsibility. Perhaps no one stands out more in this regard than the late Colonel G.G. McCaustland, who guided that work for over two decades beginning in the mid 1930s. Meticulous record keeping

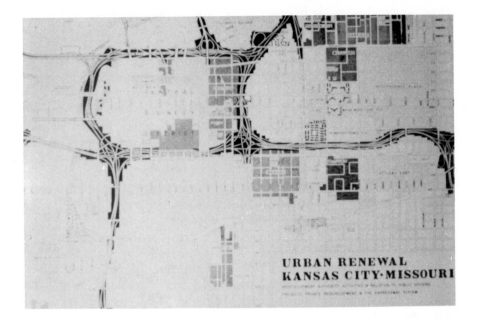

Figure 2-12.   Urban Renewal: Kansas City, Missouri

and management of the business of the City Plan Commission and of the Zoning Board of Adjustment, careful preparation of ordinances for council action, and general coordination of private action with proposed public improvements are among the principal responsibilities of the current planner. The change of zone application and the subdivision plat are the crucial instruments of that daily business.

If competently staffed and reasonably well equipped with the latest in public records—from well-coordinated city and county records of tax assessment to planning-data files and computerized or microfilmed public-works records—planning administrative procedures are possible that require considerable talent and flexibility beyond the normal routines. Such a procedure was established with a concept known as development districting.

Development Districts: The Kansas City Experience with Growth Management

Any large regional airport has substantial impact on the use of land in its vicinity. Any transportation facility of that magnitude requires effective environmental planning in order to take full advantage of the facility as a tool in shaping the urban form.[15]

The city of Kansas City, Missouri, in cooperation with the Administrative Court of Platte County and the Mid-America Regional Council—the local council of government—prepared a comprehensive plan guiding development in the area likely to be affected by the new $300 million international airport. Following adoption of this plan, the city council also adopted an ordinance that combines zoning and subdivision procedures into a logical single-design control system—or development district—which was both innovative and effective. The process was swift and was executed in the spirit of cooperation by all—to no small measure due to the tireless efforts of former Councilman Donald Stubbs (now president of the Citizens Association), the political leadership of Mayor Ilus Davis, and the enlightened support of the *Kansas City Star*.

Implementation of the comprehensive plan for the area adjacent to Kansas City International Airport (KCI) is as complex as the airport itself. It requires a full complement of local governmental resources and powers on the basis of a concerted, well-integrated system of development guidance and control and public-improvement programs. This objective necessitates acceptance of certain practices that combine functions usually carried out separately and often in an uncoordinated manner.

Over several years, the public, through the Kansas City municipal government, had made an investment of a magnitude never before attempted in this region. This investment—the acquisition and construction of the Kansas City International Airport—created a wide variety of development opportunities in the general vicinity of the airport, as well as requirements for additional supporting public facilities, including major highways and municipal utilities. The original investment of several hundred million dollars is viewed as a continuing process, calling for mobilization of public and private resources to assure the effectiveness of this regional transportation facility, which is designed to serve national and international trade and commerce. KCI is the gateway to a vast midland empire and serves the same functions as traditional seaports throughout the world. The federal government recognized this function by granting free-trade-zone status to a section of the airport.

Local government agencies entrusted with administration of the facilities are committed to a public policy assuring maximum return for the tax dollar invested. This concerns not only the airport elements that are directly under public control but also lands adjacent to the airport, which have become valuable for private development. Through systematic development planning, compatibility of private development with public investment will be assured. Goals and objectives have been appropriately stated through various planning documents. Many of these objectives—such as construction of roads and utilities—will be implemented under capital-improvement programs of city, county, and state. The development of private land, however, can be channeled in the desired direction only through a comprehensive guidance system that is designed to convert the present agricultural lands and wastelands to urban development.

This guidance system is justified by the comprehensive plan, which presumes to attain, to the highest degree, objectives furthering the public interest, health, safety, convenience, prosperity, morals, and general welfare. Such plan implementation requires both good regulatory devices and public programming.

The Guidance System

The rationale of regulations for the KCI development system combines zoning and subdivision administration. The comprehensive land-use plan and the comprehensive plan for highways, thoroughfares, and other major streets, with the plan for utilities, constitute required reference documents for the application of the regulatory measures. They also relate the development controls to the public-improvement programs of the city, county, and state. Goals and underlying policies of the development guidance system are as follows:

Land development must be in accordance with the comprehensive master plan for the area, including the urban-design objectives and standards established.

Each land use must be compatible with the location, as measured by applicable standards of urban design and performance. Land development will be closely coordinated with provision of required public services and facilities and authorized only when these facilities are available, unless installed entirely at the expense of the developer. When public facilities are installed at private expense, design and construction must meet the standards and specifications of the city of Kansas City.

For nonresidential and residential areas, agricultural or conservation, minimum public facilities, which must be available before private development will be authorized, are an arterial or trunk highway or thoroughfare providing principal access to the development area, an adequate water-trunk line, and an adequate interceptor sewer.

The development-guide plan, designed at a map scale of 1 inch for 800 feet, was prepared cooperatively with the operating departments of the city and county. It shows the location of collector and pertinent minor streets in relation to the major street network and the location of public-utility systems. Private developments are to conform as nearly as practicable to the development guide plan. The guidance system does provide adjustment and modification procedures.

The development-guide plan and land-use regulations are supplemented in areas of particular public importance by more particularized urban-design-guide plans. Certain areas near the airport are severely affected by aircraft operations and are subject to extreme noise and hazardous conditions. Development in such areas is either prohibited or restricted to compatible uses. The airport and several related but required use areas will contribute to air pollution. It is also recognized that certain land areas are not developable, from an economic point of view, because of topographic conditions. Combining both considerations, it is possible to greatly offset air pollution by maintenance of large open areas at and about the pollution-generating centers.

Some of these open spaces are tightly controlled, purchased, and brought under public ownership for recreation-area development. Other areas remain in private hands. Open space remaining in private ownership is restricted generally to agricultural and recreational uses.

The policies and goals of the development guidance system are accomplished by two basic measures: (1) the establishment of a system of land-use-control zones and (2) the establishment of land uses in three distinct phases of development, beginning with the present unoccupied status and culminating in construction and occupancy of buildings and land. Figure 2-13 shows an artist's interpretation of this concept.

Control Zones

A district was established and appropriately called the Kansas City International Airport Area Development District (KCID). The boundaries of KCID encompass approximately one hundred square miles.[16]

KCID is subdivided into several land use control zones as follows:

1. Industrial uses, including airport and river transportation-oriented industrial uses;
2. Airport-related restricted commercial uses, including offices, hotels and motels, restaurants, and minor retail establishments within office or hotel buildings;
3. High-density residential uses;
4. Retail commercial uses;
5. Medium-density residential uses;

Figure 2-13. Kansas City International Airport: Concept of Growth Management

6. Agricultural and low-density residential uses; and
7. Agricultural and conservation uses.

Under certain conditions, zones 2, 3, 4, and 5 may be combined into an integrated development project. The zone system is viewed not as the conventional pyramid structure but as a system of exclusive geographic areas where only expressed, authorized uses may be created.

Within each zone, the uses permitted are regulated (1) by certain specifications expressed in concise terms of kind, quantity, or dimension, as may be appropriate; (2) by standards of performance regarding operating characteristics and maintenance; (3) by urban-design standards and criteria; and (4) by building and construction standards and specifications. The concepts for each zone are briefly described as follows.

Industrial Zone. With the exception of incompatible uses, any industrial use may be established in this zone that can meet the specifications, performance standards, and design criteria prescribed. Among incompatible uses are low-intensity uses; unsightly uses; all forms of residential and commercial uses, except certain industry-related services and the like. A list of these uses was incorporated in the ordinance. As an important subzone, an airport-oriented industrial area will be offered. This subzone would be used for those who depend on airport access directly for their operation.

Airport-Related Restricted Commercial Zone. This zone represents a carefully selected group of land uses, which, in the judgment of informed people, constitute services commonly desired by the traveling public at or near major air terminals. Common retail uses will be excluded as principal uses but may be authorized as accessory uses within large office or hotel buildings.

High-Density Residential Zone. This is intended to be a high-rise apartment zone, with a minimum building height of six stories. Its application will be limited but should be effective. Proposed maximum density will be thirty-five dwelling units per gross acre, with credits for open space.

Retail Commercial Zone. This is a somewhat conventional retail business area, tending to be more exclusive than the ordinary district because of severe design restrictions relating to structures and to outdoor advertising. Only relatively small areas within KCID will actually be zoned exclusively for this category.

Medium-Density Residential Zone. This zone will be used sparingly. It will permit all forms of dwelling units under four stories. Townhouses, cluster developments, and mobile-home parks are included. Densities will not exceed ten dwellings per acre, with credits for open space.

Agricultural and Low-Density Residential Zone. This zone will govern areas that will permanently remain open space. It will permit all customary agricultural uses and rural nonfarm residences on tracts of land that are not less than forty acres in area and are fully self-sufficient for water and sewer service.

Agricultural and Conservation Zone. This classification is to be used primarily in the flood plains and in areas characterized by steep slopes or other natural features, making urban or rural nonfarm development undesirable. Residential uses are prohibited. It is not anticipated that this zone will be changed, except in situations where flood conditions, for example, have been removed by public improvements.

Density, bulk, and intensity are regulated by combinations of ratios and dimensions, including floor-area ratios, direct or indirect height and set-back limitations, lot-area-per-dwelling-unit ratios, and the like. Construction is to be governed by the applicable building, housing, plumbing, electrical, fire-prevention, pollution, and related codes.

Stages of Development

The first phase, the process and the initial government action, was the adoption and establishment of KCID. This provided (1) that all existing land uses may be continued until replaced by an authorized use under KCID zone system; (2) that all nonconforming uses of land will be discontinued immediately on the effective date of the new district and nonconforming buildings upon establishment of any one of the land-use-control zones, except zones 6 and 7, but in no event would a nonconforming structure be permitted after an established cutoff date; and (3) that no new land uses or buildings can be established or constructed, except in accordance with the procedures prescribed for the second phase.

With the establishment of KCID, only zones 6 and 7, agriculture and conservation, are actually mapped, plus a small existing industrial district, in compliance with the concept. All other zones are considered floating zones, to be established and mapped on application either individually or in suitable combination—all, of course, in accordance with the objectives of the comprehensive master plan.

The second phase consists of development procedures. Whenever any person, firm, or corporation proposes to undertake the physical development of any part of KCID, it will submit to the City Development Department a series of documents, culminating in a final subdivision plat or plats for the area under consideration, together with the necessary zone plans. The documents contain the following elements.

1. A preliminary-sketch plan, showing how the proposal will relate to the official master plan and the official subdivision-guide plan of the city and county.
2. A more particularized site plan, at a scale of 1 inch for 400 feet, showing arrangement of streets and other public ways, utilities, building sites, and other germane features, which will vary substantially from case to case, especially in residential developments or combination projects.
3. A change of zone plan in accordance with the aforementioned plans.
4. Preparation of preliminary and final plats, in accordance with subdivision regulations and the specification of the KCID. This step will entail approval of construction of public facilities, posting of surety bonds, and other common procedures.
5. Specific sketches and designs regarding buildings, landscape treatment, continued maintenance, and so forth.

Building construction represents the third phase in the process. Following review and approval of these plans and authorization of construction, the developer will apply for building permits. Compliance with the codes is enforced through occupancy-permit procedures. In turn, utility services are contingent on securing occupancy permits in accordance with standard practice. The developer may offer for sale sites within his project. Third parties may then apply for building permits in accordance with the approved plans.

Administration and Supplements

Internal efficiency is crucial to the administration of the KCID. Upon application for development and rezoning, the coordinating agency will designate a contact officer. The contact officer will make sure the various documents, plans, and studies are circulated when the coordinating agency is satisfied that the proposal is compatible with the master plan. Agencies contacted include the Departments of Water and Pollution Control, Transportation, Public Works, Parks and Recreation, Finance (Assessor), and Fire and Police within the city government and, if they are concerned, the State Highway Department, State Pollution Control Board, and so on. Upon completion of all processing, the proposal is forwarded to the City Plan Commission, then to the city council.

Incidentally, the provisions of KCID apply not only to privately sponsored development but also to all public improvements. In connection with public buildings, the Municipal Art Commission is consulted.

In areas of particular prominence or public interest, such as the airport entrance, the City Development Department may prepare specific designs for locations, bulk, height, and appearance of buildings and for landscaping. There are few such situations. These designs are processed as a supplemental-control zone, superimposed on the basic zone classification. Precedents exist in San Francisco, Seattle, and Cincinnati. In all instances, the supplemental-district concept is applied to protect unusual views and exposure, which often constitutes a high percentage of the building value.

Supplemental restrictions are used also for enforcement of airport approach-zone restrictions as needed in addition to the provisions of the basic system. The master plan presents several typical design solutions as a guide. Closely related to the measures discussed herein is the preservation of various rights-of-way for future public use. Based on the proposed development plan, the ultimate taking lines for street and utility rights-of-way—including drainage channels and streambeds—may be established and protected by ordinance.

Regulatory measures enforced under the police-power concept have a fundamental limitation: they must never become confiscatory. Short of complete public acquisition of a particular site, it is often advisable to secure by purchase certain development rights in the land, thereby compensating the owner for obvious loss of rights, which might be considered confiscatory. Moreover, these regulations can only be effective within a meaningful framework of public-works programs. Without public facilities, private development is impossible. Conversely, coordination of public works with review and processing of private plans is a prerequisite to the concepts advanced here.[17]

The regulations adopted in Kansas City in 1969 will go far toward good development near the regional airport. Field experience over the years has been encouraging and indicates that the methods and techniques deployed here are effective and substantially superior to conventional systems. Although, in some respects, it follows the concept of the planned-units development that is now widely accepted by planners and zoning administrators and popular with developers because of its inherent flexibility, the development district designed for Kansas City International Airport allows for a far better area-wide correlation than the planned-units development district in most situations. The development district is firmly grounded in a particularized comprehensive plan, but the planned-units development district rarely has that advantage. Consequently, the constant threat to planned-units zoning—the charge of inconsistency—which is so dangerously close to a charge of arbitrary and capricious action, is essentially eliminated with the development district, because the key decisions concerning use of land and standards of development, location, and design of the infrastructure have already been made. With all its recognized advantages over old-fashioned specification zoning, the planned-units development system, for whatever use—mixed occupancy, shopping centers, industrial parks, and so forth—without well-defined standards of guidance in the form of a solid plan, can easily find itself on shaky grounds, leading to disputes and disappointments.[18]

It is important to remember that land-use controls in the United States are matters of states' rights and only rarely are a federal responsibility. Consequently, the effectiveness of land-use control and development guidance will vary regionally and, at times, from state to state, depending on statutory grants of power to regulate land use in direct relation (1) to the ability of the public to provide necessary services and (2) to the scaling or dimensioning of land-use areas so as to satisfy reasonable demand expectations without creating land monopolies. This entire, complex issue was first tested in the United States in the case of the *Provincial Development Company, Inc.* v. *Joseph D. Webb et al., Lexington-Fayette County Regional Planning Commission, Kentucky* (1960), which we will discuss later. It was confirmed in 1972 in the case of *Golden* v. *Ramapo,* ably managed by Robert Freilich of the University of Missouri Law School. These judicial decisions are consistent, of course, with the comprehensive-plan theory first enunciated by Alfred Bettman, as discussed in chapter 1.[19]

In Kansas City, the tradition established by George Kessler and William

Rockhill Nelson a century ago lives on. The French author André Maurois, after an extensive lecture tour in Kansas City made the following observations about the city:

> Who in Europe, or in America for that matter, knows that Kansas City is one of the loveliest cities on earth? The downtown section is like any other in the United States, the violent contrasts of skyscrapers and wasteland. But the residential section is a masterpiece of city planning. The streets follow the curves of the hills or the winding of the streams. Flowering shrubs encircle the houses. The homes themselves, designed in the best of taste, are artfully grouped in an immense park whose trees unequaled in variety and luxuriance. . . . Few cities have been built with so much regard for beauty.[20]

In 1972, the American Institute of Planners bestowed upon the Kansas City Development Department the Missouri Planning Award for "Comprehensive Planning at Kansas City International Airport."

Notes

1. William H. Wilson, *The City Beautiful Movement in Kansas City* (Columbia: University of Missouri Press, 1964).

2. Kansas City Park Board, Report of 1893, p. 23.

3. Ibid.

4. "Results of County Planning, Jackson County, Missouri," Administrative Court, Hon. Harry S Truman, Presiding Judge, 1932. See also W.G. Roeseler, "Planning Enabling Legislation for Cities and Counties in Missouri," *Kansas City Law Review,* Summer 1956; George F. Nickolaus, "Annexation in Missouri," University of Missouri Extension Division, 1967.

5. An authoritative discussion of the era of bossism may be found in Alfred Steinberg, *The Bosses* (New York: Macmillan, 1972).

6. 47 Sup. Ct. Rep. 114 (1926).

7. Alfred Bettman, *City and Regional Planning Papers* (Cambridge, Mass: Harvard University Press, 1946).

8. "Patterns and People," Kansas City, Missouri, City Planning Commission, 1944.

9. "Expressways—Greater Kansas City," Kansas City, Missouri, Plan Commission, for the Missouri State Highway Department, 1951; W.G. Roeseler, "Methods for Traffic Analysis and Forecast" (Manual prepared for the Bureau of Public Roads, U.S. Department of Commerce, 1951); Wilbur Smith and Associates, "Kansas City Metropolitan Area Origin-Destination Survey," 1959; Kansas City Transit Associates, "Long Range

Transit Plan, Kansas City Metropolitan Area Transportation Study,'' for Mid-America Regional Council, 1975; U.S. Department of Commerce, Bureau of the Census, "Selected Characteristics of Travel to Work in Twenty Metropolitan Areas: 1977,'' P-23, No. 105, 1981; V.G. Stover, W. Foster and J. Benson, "Effects of Small Sample O-D Data on Traffic Assignment Results,'' Transportation Research Record No. 637, Transportation Research Board, 1977.

10. Bill Gilbert, *This City, This Man* (Washington, D.C.: International City Managers Association, 1978), p. 152.

11. Roeseler, "Methods for Traffic Analysis and Forecast.'' (Manual prepared for the Bureau of Public Roads, 1951).

12. W.G. Roeseler, "Transit Improvement Program'' (Prepared for the Mid-America Regional Council, 1971).

13. W.G. Roeseler, "Bus Rapid Transit to Airport,'' American Society of Civil Engineers Annual Meeting, Report 914, 1969.

14. AnnBar v. Westside Redevelopment Corporation, 397 SW 2d 635 (1965). Many similar projects were accomplished under this remarkable program of tax incentives. Crown Center, sponsored by the Hallmark Corporation, received nationwide acclaim, as did Mr. Kitchen's Quality Hill Apartment Complex, the first attempt to induce a return to the central city by residents.

15. W.G. Roeseler and David Runnels, "Kansas City International Airport and Vicinity Environmental Development Plan and Impact Study'' (Prepared for the Kansas City, Missouri, Plan Commission, 1970).

16. Kansas City Ordinances.

17. W.G. Roeseler, *General Policies and Principles for Prototype Zoning Ordinances and Related Measures,* (Bryan, Texas: EMR Publications, 1976), Appendix A-1.

18. Frank S. So, "Planned Units Development Ordinances,'' Planning Advisory Service, No. 57, May 1973.

19. Provincial Development Company v. Joseph Webb, Fayette County Circuit Court, C.L. & Eq. Division, Lexington, Kentucky, Order of Reference No. 7973, 1960. Golden v. Ramapo, 30 NY 2d 359, 285 NE 291, 409 U.S. 1003 (1972).

20. André Maurois, "From My Journal'' (1948), as cited in Don Roth, "Pioneer Work of George E. Kessler Recalled by City Planners,'' *Kansas City Times,* 31 March 1955 (during the annual conference of the American Institute of Planners, which was founded in Kansas City in 1917).

Dallas and Fort Worth: Products of New Technology

Opportunity Spurs Action in the Great Southwest: "Big D"

In every respect, the Dallas-Fort Worth metroplex region is a product of the new technologies that characterize the second half of the twentieth century—jet aircraft for military use and electronics. Distribution industries, women's fashions (successors to a rich cotton heritage), and numerous other activities round out the economic empire focused on these two urban giants. The population curves shown in figure 3-1 tell the story convincingly. Although they were regionally significant for about a century, into the 1930s—as rail centers, in the cattle trade, and in cotton, insurance, and banking—Dallas and Fort Worth were not spectacular cities. They were pleasant enough and offered opportunities to carve out a comfortable living, a condition amplified by the growing oil and gas industry and its spin-offs.

The advent of military aviation, especially jet aircraft, and the accompanying service industries, notably in electronics, brought wave after wave of talented people to the metroplex, causing a virtual explosion of population from the 1940s to the present. All this was made possible by the evolution of air conditioning, which made the scorching summers of the Southwest tolerable for industrial and intellectual production-oriented enterprises. However, at the end of World War II, the cities were defenseless and confused by the onslaught of massive inmigration and land development. Half a century earlier, both cities had embarked on ambitious urban-planning efforts, mindful of the same kind of activity in Kansas City. George E. Kessler had been retained by the park boards of Dallas and Fort Worth and had prepared two interesting plan documents between 1906 and 1912. Darrel Noe, long-term city planner in Fort Worth, recently observed, "If the people of the Kessler era had been as reluctant to act as their counterparts are today, neither Dallas nor Fort Worth would have any parks."[1]

It is interesting that the Board of Park Commissioners of Dallas, strongly supported by the City Plan and Development League of the Chamber of Commerce, considered its mission to go far beyond the traditional function of a park board and to include such issues as flood-control levees; a belt railroad to consolidate individual lines, after the Kansas City example; construction of Union Station, for passenger transport, and of several freight terminals; elimination of grade crossings; major street

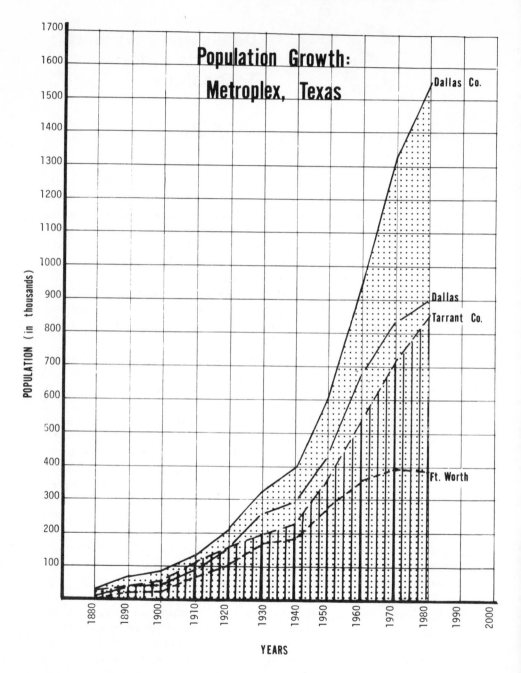

Figure 3-1. Population Growth in the Dallas–Fort Worth Metroplex Region

construction; a civic-center development program; design and ultimate construction of a comprehensive system of parks and boulevards similar to that designed by Kessler for Kansas City; and the acquisition and development of numerous playgrounds throughout the city. In other words, they wanted and ultimately designed a comprehensive plan for Dallas. In fact, in Kessler's 1911 plan, we find a major drawing entitled "General Plan for the City of Dallas."[2]

The city's population at that time was just over 100,000. Kessler's plans envisioned a much larger city, although he rarely concerned himself with the art of forecasting. Instinctively, Kessler knew that some day there would be a city of regional, perhaps national, importance and that such a settlement deserved the best that contemporary design and good judgment could produce. In his characteristic thoroughness, Kessler delineated the elements of the plan in great detail, yet with a clear concept of a fully integrated system, as so unmistakenly shown by his own schematic interpretation, reproduced in figure 3-2. As in his other urban plans, Kessler never tires of stressing the importance of the riverbanks for passive recreation, of the tributary streams for surface drainage, of the boulevards for land development and permanent aesthetic beauty, even of the need to control billboards in conflict with significant vistas, and of numerous other features that make the urban area livable.

Unfortunately, the Kessler plans for Dallas and Fort Worth were not to have the same immediate impact as the Kessler plans for Kansas City, which is attributable to a variety of factors, including the absence of the kind of dominant leadership that William Rockhill Nelson and his park commissioners provided in Kansas City. Nevertheless, key elements of the plans were implemented, and others came to fruition when planning finally came into its own in Dallas in the 1950s.

The growth of the defense industry had given Dallas a test of rapid urbanization during the war years of the 1940s. During Mayor Woodall Rogers' administration, the city retained the services of Harland Bartholomew and Associates of St. Louis, noted city planners of that era. Mr. Bartholomew produced a master plan for Dallas, which, however, did not stimulate much interest and was soon forgotten. In 1950, bewildered by development proposals, numerous subdivision plats, and countless zoning propositions, the city decided to build a strong in-house planning team. Marvin R. Springer was retained as director for that team and was to become one of the leading personalities in urban affairs of Texas. A native of St. Louis and an intellectual product of the philosophies of the Urbanism Committee of the National Resources Committee of the Roosevelt administration, Springer immediately set out to bring growth under reasonable management control. There was no time for longer-range thinking; there was a crisis to be met in day-to-day planning and zoning and,

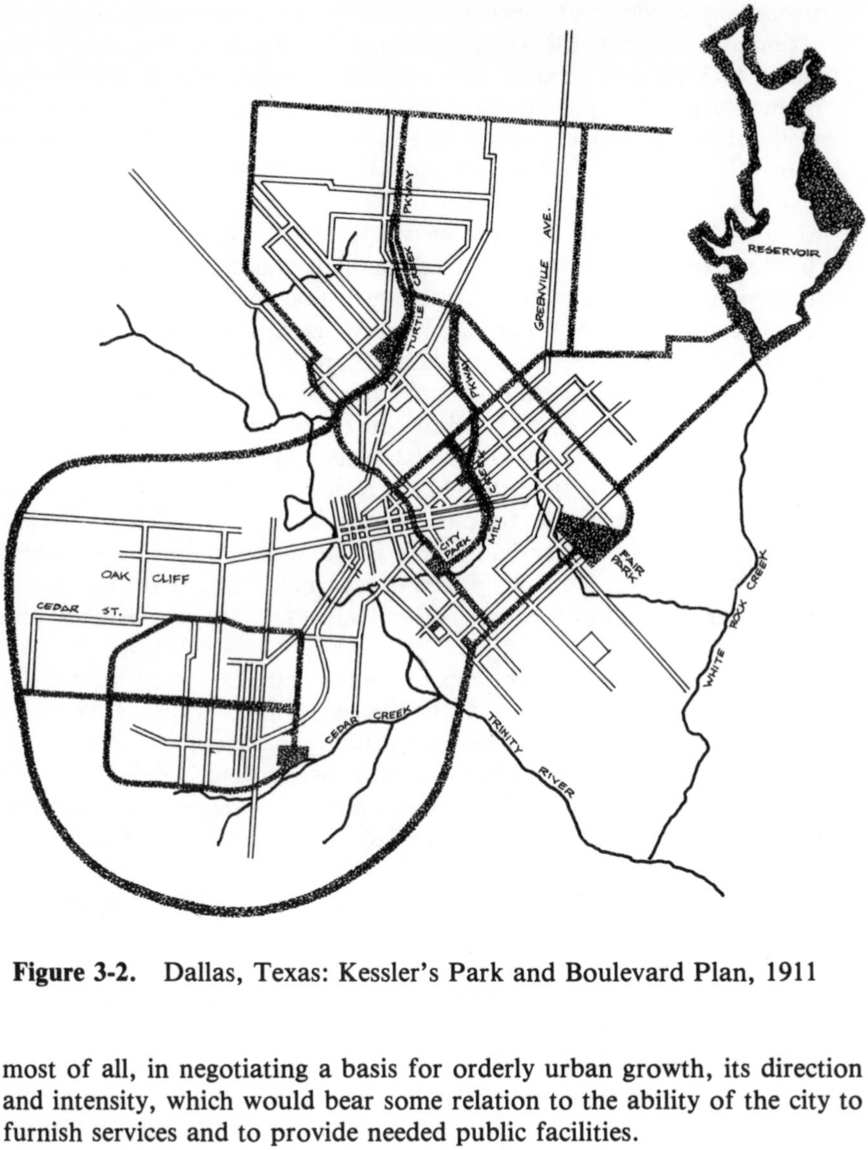

Figure 3-2.   Dallas, Texas: Kessler's Park and Boulevard Plan, 1911

most of all, in negotiating a basis for orderly urban growth, its direction
and intensity, which would bear some relation to the ability of the city to
furnish services and to provide needed public facilities.

The Springer Plan

Springer realized that the city's mission would fail unless it had sound support from the public at large and from the economic power structure of the
community. To gain such support, Springer had to convince leading citizens

beyond the municipal family that the planning process and the systematic management of growth would help and not hinder private initiative by assuring investors of stability and consistency in public policy and administration.

At the time, dynamic leadership was provided in Dallas by Robert L. Thornton, chairman of the board of the Mercantile National Bank and later mayor of the city. Mr. Thornton accepted Springer's concepts for the planning of Dallas and became the catalyst of public-policy shaping for a decade. That decade proved to be crucial for the metropolitan area, and the fruits of the combined efforts of civic leadership and able technical direction will be harvested for decades hence.

The intitial thrust of the Springer program was aimed at administrative consistency with respect to the processing of subdivision plats and zoning requests for new development. To achieve that, the city had to stabilize its growth. That, in turn, called for a consistent and enlightened policy of annexation of virgin territory. Here, the planners needed the help of the engineers in all fields, but especially the public-works people. Springer found enthusiastic supporters for his plans: Karl F. Hoefle, director of water utilities, and Harry Stirman, director of public works. Both became trusted friends and cooperators. Hoefle and Springer strongly advocated that drainage basins be considered primary elements of any annexation program and that development outside developing drainage areas or watersheds be discouraged as the pure concept of what was later to be called the urban-service-area principle. The engineer's reasoning, of course, was that tapping new drainage areas prematurely merely increases the tax burden of the property owner without marked benefit to the public at large. So long as there remains a reasonable choice of land and no land monopolies created in the process of development make development-site acquisition prohibitive, the city should direct new growth into areas where it already has the utility and road infrastructure to serve new subdivisions with only routine extensions. New areas should be tapped only when land runs out and investment in the trunk facilities of the urban infrastructure would be justified, unless these trunk facilities are essential for the economic development of the urban area.

The political and civic leadership of Dallas was ready for such measures. Under the generally liberal annexation laws of Texas, Springer and his staff staked the city's future territorial interests and implemented, through the city council, an effective step-by-step program of progressive annexation. This program was further complicated by the fact that annexation to Dallas would add to the service area of one powerful public utility company while reducing that of a suburban competitor, though both were actually owned by the same holding company. Nevertheless, Springer's annexation program eventually enlarged Dallas from about thirty square miles in 1950 to over three hundred square miles ten years later—a development

and procedure very similar to that carried out by City Manager Perry Cookingham in Kansas City during the same period. Parallel with that program,
Springer's staff produced a new comprehensive-zoning ordinance and updated subdivision regulations and procedures, with the assistance of the
Department of Public Works. The initial steps of Springer's planning administration had moved away from the city-beautiful notions of the Bartholomew plan and the concepts of Mayor Rogers, although Springer took
great care in preserving the significant and valid aspects of that period.

In fact, he went beyond that and rediscovered the timeless genius of
George Kessler and his turn-of-the-century plans for Dallas. Having put his
administrative house in order, Springer prevailed upon R.L. Thornton to
support a comprehensive-plan program that would be the guide for the
numerous public works and for the longer-range use of private land in the
metropolitan area. Thornton obliged and became the prime mover in the
appointment of the Dallas Master Plan Committee, under the chairmanship
of D.A. Hulcy. The City Planning Commission was so overworked with the
daily routines of development that it could not take on the task of oversee-
ing the preparation of a comprehensive plan, which was to become not
merely an exercise but a genuine instrument of municipal management and
resource allocation. Springer's idea of a separate entity was appropriate; it
gave him a committee with no other obligations to distract from its principal
mission, and it provided a significant opportunity to involve the city's power
structure directly in a venture that would be undertaken with great pride.

The Master Plan Committee produced a series of technical reports that
were to constitute the city's comprehensive plan. It is significant that all the
reports addressed topical issues of the Dallas metropolitan area, not merely
those of the city of Dallas proper. Here, as years earlier in Cincinnati, Kansas City, and elsewhere, professionals and political leaders readily
understood that the central city not only had an obligation to the entire urbanizing area to give direction and leadership to the development process,
but had, indeed, no alternative if it was to survive the new era of growth and
expansion. Metropolitan areas could simply fall apart and produce
numerous impotent towns surrounding an equally incapacitated central
city, or the central cities would attempt to act cooperatively with determination and prudence to create, ultimately, a basically unified metropolitan entity capable of providing the kinds of services and facilities that make the
difference between a cultured, civilized existence and primitive survival, in-
capable of the spiritual uplift that flows from the opportunities of the
metropolis. The leadership of Dallas organized and lined up solidly behind
an enlightened program of vision and realistic progress that was to bring
about another powerful and magnificent city of the great American West.

Perhaps the most significant of the master plan series was a report entitled "Thoroughfares—Dallas Metropolitan Area," issued in December

1957.[3] The study follows very closely the methods and techniques established in Kansas City seven years earlier, which were sanctioned by the Bureau of Public Roads and endorsed by the National Committee on Urban Transportation, chaired by Glen Richards, Detroit's director of public works. This interdisciplinary committee was effectively managed by W.A. Rusch, now executive director of the International Tunnel, Turnpike and Bridge Association. The committee was active from 1955 to 1960. It formalized the kind of experience Kansas City had with the first generation of transportation plans after World War II and outlined the procedures that are now known as the transportation-planning process.[4] The committee's effort was effective and must be considered to be the closest the United States has come to formulating a generally applicable transportation-planning policy based on nationwide technical representation. Dallas, too, produced its plans for urban road systems within the context of comprehensive planning, not merely as an engineering extrapolation. One is immediately struck by the thorough analysis of the metropolitan area from a demographic, general economic, land-use, and traffic point of view and by the skillful manner in which these and other critical elements of the urban fabric are carefully woven into interlocking systems, which allow policy governing future events to be related to immediate deficiencies of the transportation infrastructure.

Marvin Springer's overriding concern for preservation of open spaces and rights-of-way at the right time for future public use is clearly in evidence throughout the work.[5] The plan itself is presented in considerable detail, both graphically and by narration, leaving the reader with a concise picture of the intended program—a physical plan in the finest tradition. Plan making requires that kind of expression. One cannot make plans on the basis of vague policy. (The so-called policy plans that show up here and there are no more than a "cop-out", and in a way represent a fraud: the public is teased, the politicians abdicate their responsibility, and the professionals might as well have stayed home.)

At some point, the planner and the political leader working with him have to "stand up and be counted," and so does the public. There is no law that says every city in America must be efficiently operated, livable, and beautiful. Conversely, there is no excuse for the typical American city, with its wealth and opportunities beyond the wildest dreams of most cities around the world, not to be efficient, livable, and beautiful. It is all up to the people and their leaders. A public that tolerates corrupt and inept leadership deserves it. The image of the city is an unmistakable expression of its spirit—an expression of fair play, opportunity, and reasonableness.

It is thus not surprising that the reader of the Dallas thoroughfare plan is exposed to utility issues, topographic and soils problems, questions of future land requirements and probable population distribution, and very careful presentations of the types of street and road networks to be designed. As in "Expressways—Greater Kansas City," the actual location of the urban freeways is superimposed on aerial photographs, allowing close examination of location and design in relation to existing and future potential use of land. The guiding hand of Frank Cawthon, then district engineer for the Texas Highway Department in Dallas and a member of the Master Plan Committee, is very much in evidence throughout the report. Again, the ability of the planner, Springer, and the engineer, Cawthon, to collaborate at the local level within the context of a committed civic leadership was prerequisite to ultimate success. That success was nearly complete implementation of the ambitious thoroughfare plan within less than a quarter century—another remarkable achievement of American planners and engineers and their political counterparts (see figure 3-3).

Figure 3-3. Dallas Skyline and Convention Center

Energy and Transportation: Key to the Future

The era of the 1950s and 1960s in urban-thoroughfare planning in the United States is crucial to present economic productivity and anticipated urban growth over the next several decades because of the importance of the automobile in our national economy. Much confusion and discussion has been sparked by the several petroleum crises of the last decade. Reactions to natural crude-oil shortages have ranged from calls for abandoning private transportation to total mobilization of synthetic fuels. We now have a convincing overview of the situation and can pass judgment with considerable certainty regarding the future shape and form of the American urban area and the modes of transport that will be efficient and cost-effective.

Mass transportation will have its position in the future city. Surely, there will be rubber-tired transit in most cities over 100,000 population. There will also be fixed-guideway rapid transit—in high-intensity corridors of the very largest metropolitan regions. However, the workhorse of urban transport will be what it has been for decades: the private, efficiently powered automobile.[6] We will find marvelous opportunities for rapid transit in various situations. At best, these situations will accommodate 10 to 15 percent of the total work trips in a very large city—not including New York in this context, of course. Higher densities will, in time, occur around transit stations, which, in turn, will increase ridership and introduce segments of our population to new ways of life. This well be a very slow and limited process, because even with a doubling of urban population in a few decades, the process of nucleated development in the urban regions will allow people to live at relatively low densities for a long time to come. The argument of land and construction cost, I believe, is invalid, for it will again find a more reasonable level—as it has under comparable conditions in the past.

The urban street and highway planning and subsequent construction since about 1950 will continue to pay handsome dividends in this country.[7] Systems have been developed that can be expanded and augmented by other modes as the need arises. Development of rapid transit must be viewed as an evolutionary process in response to demand. Only the experience of shortage of specific urban space and discernible time loss will induce the public to call for a different mode of transport. Such demand will, in time, be coupled with the public's readiness to adjust its own lifestyle to transit, because transit is not capable of adjusting to individuals. This is the cardinal difference between an urban community whose daily activities depend largely on mass transportation—as for example, in the large cities of Europe and Japan—and transportation at will in the typical American urban area, where the only constraints are the infrastructure of the road system, the traffic-control devices, and the means of the driver. The level of investment in capital structure and operations is not materially different in the two situations: neither system can exist without substantial ongoing subsidies from taxation, in whatever form. In industrialized countries, it is either a matter of choice or a matter of necessity because of space limitations, as, for instance, in Germany and Holland.

Whatever the future holds in a given situation, the planning efforts of the last three decades and the gigantic national and regional investments in transportation-plan implementation have given the successful cities a solid foundation on which future generations can build with confidence. Some solutions might have been improved upon and some resource allocations might have been made differently. No one claims that these programs were perfect. However, they were "perfect enough" to last for centuries and serve us well.

Fort Worth Catching Up

In contrast to Dallas, Fort Worth has had an affinity for grandiose beginnings without discernible results. Over the last several decades, a tendency to out-do Dallas often induced decision makers to employ "big-name" consultants who had little or no genuine interest in this western city and no understanding of its spirit and aspirations.

Not unlike Kansas City, Fort Worth is a friendly, outgoing community, which, unfortunately, forever sees itself in the shadow of Dallas. It, too, experienced spectacular growth with the advent of jet-aircraft manufacture and air conditioning, but it was rather late in organizing its municipal operations to cope with growth. Until the late 1950s, Fort Worth had no planning department, merely a planner on the staff of the Public Works Department. Eventually, this was changed, although it was not until 1979 that the city finally employed a professional planner as its planning director. Superficial measures were taken to give the impression of progressive management. The downtown plan by Gruen and Associates is a good example of that failure. An architectural exercise was presented to the people of Fort Worth that bore no relationship to the realities of the central business district, was entirely overdesigned, with a building volume greater than Manhattan's, and had absolutely no consideration for the numerous historic landmarks of the city. The plan was soon forgotten. However, the city did not stand still.

Under generally effective city management, key elements of formal planning were developed, including major thoroughfare and land-use plans. Moreover, the business community made a concerted effort to redevelop downtown and to provide modern, attractive convention facilities. Construction of the attractive convention center seems to have spurred an intriguing renaissance. Numerous older buildings of good architectural quality are now undergoing major refurbishing and modernization. Main Street has become a feature of urban design—an axis extending from the quaint Tarrant County Court House south to the Convention Center—in which practically every old building of historic interest will soon enjoy a new lease on life.

Beyond this most noticeable transition, the planning staff is in the process of developing sector plans and overall plan elements to cope with the issues of the next two or three decades, which likely will push the Fort Worth metropolitan-area population over the one million mark.

The metroplex of Fort Worth and Dallas is a fine example of effective urban planning and stands in sharp contrast to the pathetic urbanization of Houston, one of the fastest growing urban areas in the world.

Following World War II, Houston had a good beginning. Ralph Ellefrit, as planning director, and Vernon Henry, as chief of long-range planning, provided excellent technical solutions to the problems of the growing metropolis. It certainly was not the lack of professional competence that ultimately caused Houston's dilemma but the blatant failure of the economic power structure, the bankers and merchant princes, to do their part in the democratic process. In practically every major U.S. city of that era—Dallas, Kansas City, Cincinnati, Minneapolis, and Boston, to name but a few—the post World War II period brought about a resumption of public responsibility in reform government by the power elite. In Houston, they forfeited their right and responsibility and allowed the affairs of the public to drift into the hands of opportunists and fast-talking salesmen. It is hoped that recent events in that world city, with all of its opportunities, will spur a new beginning there, too, and a return to enlightened self-interest for the good of all.[8]

Notes

1. Interview with the author, January 1981.

2. George E. Kessler, "General Plan for the City of Dallas" (Prepared for the Board of Park Commissioners, 1911).

3. City of Dallas, Texas, "Thoroughfares—Dallas Metropolitan Area," Master Plan Committee, 1957.

4. Public Administration Service, "Better Transportation for Your City," National Committee on Urban Transport (W.A. Rusch, executive director), 1958, and seventeen procedure manuals for traffic surveys and analysis: D.L. Witherford, "Urban Transportation Planning," chapter 12 in *Transportation and Traffic Engineering Handbook,* Institute of Transportation Engineers (Englewood Cliffs, N.J.: Prentice-Hall, 1976).

5. Updates of earlier open-space plans by Mr. Springer include Springer

and Associates and Schrickel, Rollins and Associates, "Dallas County Open Space Plan" (Prepared for Dallas County Commissioners Court, 1980); Marvin Springer and Associates, "Coordinated Planned Open Space Development Trinity River System in Dallas, Texas" (Prepared for Dallas Park Board, 1969).

6. Aspen Institute Report, "Fueling," Washington, D.C., 1981; Midwest Research Institute, "Economic and Environmental Evaluation of Alternative Transit Plans, Kansas City Metropolitan Region," 1975; Kansas City Transit Associates, "Long-Range Transit Plan, Kansas City Metropolitan Area Transportation Plan" (Prepared for Mid-America Regional Council, 1975). Kansas City Transit Associates was a joint venture of Howard, Needles, Tammen and Bergendoff; Parsons, Brinckerhoff, Quade and Douglas; and W.G. Roeseler, Consulting City Planner.

7. D.A. Maxwell and J.P. McIntyre, "The Texas Vanpooling Program" (Presented at the Transportation Research Board annual meeting, 1981). The Texas program, organized by Dr. Maxwell of Texas A&M University, would be unthinkable without the extensive urban-freeway systems in the major cities of the state. It includes 120 privately financed, industry-sponsored van pooling programs in Texas alone, serving 21,000 persons daily, with 2,000 vehicles. It is estimated to save more than 30,000 gallons of fuel daily.

8. David McComb, "Houston, the Bayou City" (Austin: University of Texas Press, 1969); Berry J. Kaplan, "Urban Development, Economic Growth and Personal Liberty: The Rhetoric of the Houston Anti-Zoning Movement, 1947-62", *Southern Historical Quarterly,* 84, no. 2 (1980); W.G. Roeseler and C.W. Smithson, "The Impact of Technological Change in Transportation Networks on Regional Productivity and Development" (U.S. Department of Transportation, Office of University Research, 1981). This was an econometric study of urban highways and railroads in the Houston-Beaumont region since 1950.

Part II:
The Major City

Within the large region dominated by the megapolis, we find the major city that influences our lives either in a manner similar to that of the megapolis or by performing a very specialized function, for example, as a center of government or higher education. More often than not, the major city is the home base of an industry whose raw materials are found in the area. I have selected for discussion Shreveport, Louisiana, an example of local resource-based industry; Lexington, Kentucky, home of the distinguished University of Kentucky and of significant state agencies; and Butler County, Ohio, an urban county with a heavy industrial base, performing a variety of functions. All three jurisdictions have distinguished themselves over the years through effective urban and regional planning and implementation.

Shreveport, Louisiana, Comprehensive Urban-Transportation Study: A Second-Generation Prototype

Opportunities and Project Organization

In compliance with the requirements of the Federal Highway Act of 1962, comprehensive urban-transportation studies were initiated in all metropolitan areas with a population of 50,000 or more. In many cases, the execution of these studies was left to local or metropolitan planning agencies. At that time, the councils of government that later were to carry this responsibility had not been established.

Regional Planning by the Highway Department

In Louisiana, a different approach was used. Administratively, Louisiana may be considered a rather centralized state, reflecting to this day the programs and policies of the late Governor Long. Accordingly, the Louisiana State Highway Department (LSHD) carried out practically all significant highway planning in the state, with little effective input from the cities, except, possibly, in a reactive manner.[1] By and large, however, there have been few serious objections to the operations of LSHD, which for many years took great pride in high-level professional performance by its key personnel.

It is not surprising, then, that LSHD immediately took the initiative when the federal government—at the time through the Bureau of Public Roads of the U.S. Department of Commerce—established a mandatory urban-planning process. Under the able direction of its former chief transportation engineer, Grady Carlisle, it initiated required transportation studies for each of the state's eligible areas at its own discretion and financed these efforts with federal funds flowing to the states for research under prevailing highway-aid legislation, Title 23 of the U.S. Code.

It may be noted here that Mr. Carlisle and his equally distinguished colleague, W.T. Taylor, had pioneered in many of the transportation, traffic-planning, and engineering systems of the post World War II era and were no strangers to urban-transportation planning. On the contrary, unlike some jursidictions, the leadership of LSHD welcomed the federal mandate, as it provided a formidable base and defense against arbitrary political decision making in the state highway development.

The planning staff of LSHD, though highly competent, was nevertheless too small to undertake the task of preparing the urban plans themselves, nor did they have the expertise in such areas as land development and land-use planning, socioeconomic forecasting, urban drainage management and general utility development, provision of the vast array of community facilities the urban areas had become accustomed to at that time, the municipal financing process, and the urban growth-management techniques essential to assure compliance with basic policies on which transportation systems were to be based.

It was decided to turn to multidisciplinary consulting firms to fill the gap. Howard, Needles, Tammen and Bergendoff (HNTB), consulting engineers of Kansas City and New York, was commissioned to undertake the Shreveport study. Despite its meticulous record in the highway and bridge field in Louisiana and elsewhere, HNTB had no expertise in urban and regional planning. To remedy this deficiency, Mr. Bergendoff, then senior partner of HNTB, invited me to join the firm and to establish a department within HNTB that could carry out the Shreveport transportation study and other similar planning projects. I accepted and proceeded to undertake several such studies, which were part of an era that may be described as the second generation of urban-transportation-planning programs in our metropolitan areas. The first generation is represented by the major transportation-planning projects of the immediate post World War II period through the 1950s. Highlights of that experience were the Chicago, Detroit, and Kansas City studies, among others, discussed earlier in this book.

I have selected the Shreveport study in this context because it represents not only one of the most successful programs of that period but urban-transportation planning in general. It was a prototype study, and it also offers several interesting lessons in planning within the framework of general-purpose government at the local and state level.[2] Perhaps the most significant aspect demonstrated by this study and its effective implementation is the fact much stressed by the late Dennis O'Harrow—for many years executive director of the American Society of Planning Officials—that the planning function must be an integral element of government or of the *power to carry out plans*. Otherwise, the planning process deteriorates into a civic debating society of the garden-club variety: they all mean well but have no mechanism of implementing the simplest resolution. Consequently, it is reasonable to state that planning that operates outside the legally defined framework of general-purpose government serves no useful purpose except, perhaps, to stimulate thought. Moreover, when the subject matter of planning extends beyond the jurisdiction of a particular municipal corporation or county, a higher level of public authority must take charge. In most situations, that higher level should be the state.

Under the U.S. Constitution and those of the several states, proper authority for such action is vested in the state. When more than one state is involved, those states may band together by a formal treaty or compact, duly ratified by the U.S. Congress. Substitutions for that constitutional authority by makeshift entities have generally failed.

The Louisiana case demonstrates that the states are capable of performing meaningful regional-planning functions within the framework of traditional, constitutional concepts and that no substitution will be required if management at the state level is progressive, professional, and responsive. LSHD demonstrated that these conditions can, indeed, be met.

The experience of Shreveport also repudiates the notion that urban-planning studies must be done by in-house staffs, as has been periodically advocated by some agencies, notably, the U.S. Department of Housing and Urban Development. On the contrary, it will become apparent that the expertise required in major urban-planning projects is not available in the United States in adequate numbers to undertake these efforts competently, but that a combination of a local core staff and a consulting team represents the most practical mix of talent to be mobilized in most situations. The overriding consideration remains the fact that the entire effort is directed by a unit of general-purpose government that is fully able and legally competent to implement the plans and proposals effectively and expeditiously, because the timing of implementation of plans and programs is as significant a consideration as is their conception.

Study Organization

Having been given the responsibility to carry out the Shreveport Urban Transporation Planning Study and the necessary authority to discharge my assigned task, it was most fortunate that I was also given the opportunity to participate in the negotiations pertaining to the specific scope of the work as well as to the study organization. There was general agreement among all parties, except that I had recommended a 20 percent higher budget than the partners of HNTB thought advisable. As it developed, that produced no problem for the team but a lower profit for the firm.

My early participation in the discussions with LSHD laid the foundation for an outstanding and close working relationship with Mr. Carlisle and his staff. In my judgment, this was a major contributing factor to the ultimate success of the entire undertaking, one that cannot be overemphasized in the planning process. There must be mutual confidence and respect for each other's strengths as well as tolerant appreciation for everyone's weaknesses. The team has to stand up against numerous pressures, and it cannot cope with excessive internal friction. (For this reason, I have always been very firm with troublemakers in any situation but lenient with those who tried to do their best even if they would sometimes not be up to desired levels of performance. It is the team leader's job to find ways to make up for occasional deficiencies.)

In contemporary practice, any planning effort may be divided into *three principal tasks*. Task one's first and most basic aspect concerns the existing state of affairs. It is a fundamental research effort aimed at developing a clear understanding of natural and man-made conditions in the subject area, thus covering a wide range of activities. Physical constraints and characteristics of the study area must be inventoried, clearly understood, and interpreted, with particular emphasis on topography, drainage, and geology to determine suitability of the various components of the microcosm for urban development. Man-made modifications are related to this analysis through land-use studies, and the entire process is molded into a comprehensible schematic overview of given conditions. This process is appropriately described as the *environmental assessment*.

The second aspect of task one is an understanding of social and economic conditions and of the established political mechanism for public action. The microeconomic and social analysis serves as the basis for forecasting probable future changes in the study area that will underlie the programming phase for public works. To reach pertinent conclusions, it is necessary to understand the goals and aspirations of the body politic and to enter into an ongoing dialogue with the political and civic leadership and with the public at large. This is accomplished through conversations, interviews, meetings, committee work, systematic sociological surveys, and presentations. The purpose of these efforts is to lay a foundation for the scale and form of the solutions to be presented as results of the studies. It is important to keep this objective in mind, for it is not the planner's job to undertake these research efforts for their own sake or for resolving national, social, or political issues.

In the case of categorical plans, such as plans for transportation facilities and utilities, it is required to proceed beyond the master-plan level of socioeconomic studies to determine facilities demand. In other words, we are adding to the analysis process carried out for the purpose of forecasting overall growth or decline, a particularized dimension through analysis of market and of consumer behavior. In the transportation sector, this requires intensive studies of travel behavior and trip generation in order to ascertain whether or not new transportation facilities will be needed in the foreseeable future to assure the functioning of social, economic, and political activities in the area.

Task two of the planning process will develop responses to the issues and problems identified through inventory and analysis of prevailing conditions and circumstances. It is the problem-solution phase, which will ultimately lay before the political decision makers a number of technically feasible options, as perceived by the analysts and planners. This element of perception is likewise a critical one and must be reconciled with parallel perceptions of the public and the decision makers, as these may not necessarily be in agreement. In any event, the end product of the second phase of planning is a draft statement of solutions that will constitute the basis of negotiations with the decision makers at the various levels of government involved and with the ad hoc representatives of the public, who are called in for advice and consultation as part of a public-involvement process required by law.

From this effort will flow the third task, the determination of costs and priorities for public works and the development of regulatory measures needed to implement non-capital-related parts of the plan and to protect the facilities to be constructed under the plan. Seen from this perspective, it will be readily apparent, once again, that the planning process is a formidable management tool. Problems are systematically analyzed and solutions are developed that appear feasible and desirable at that point from a responsible public-administrative point of view. In the light of the American judicial tradition that can be conceived of in the sense of the celebrated case of *Lawton* v. *Steele:* "To justify the state in interposing its authority in behalf of the public, it must appear—first, that the interests of the public require such interference; and, second, that the means are reasonably necessary for the accomplishment of the purpose and not unduly oppressive upon individuals."[3]

From time to time, this fundamental principle of representative government appears to be lost in political action. Not so very long ago, into the 1920s, public works at the municipal and state level were largely pork-barrel decisions by the politicians in power. The governmental reforms brought about in part as a result of antidepression programs of the 1930s— ably articulated by the Urbanism Committee of the National Resources Board—correctly fell back on the classic American concepts of law with respect to general-purpose government and laid down rules that would assure compliance with these notions. Without strict adherence to these principles of public interest, alienation of the public from its own government is inevitable, and with such alienation rises unrest, if not revolt or revolution.

Consensus regarding needed public works and other measures was soon conceived as the necessary basis for objective resource allocation in the public-works sector. Such consensus negotiation requires procedures that are open and accessible. Decisions for or against a public improvement would have to be documented in technical reports, and these would have to be accessible to *all citizens*. Moreover, once a decision was agreed on, there had to be a means of holding subsequently elected officials to that policy to avoid arbitrary deviation from the approved policy. This had to be accomplished so as to avoid locking decision-making bodies into courses of action that were no longer appropriate.

The planning process was rediscovered as an effective means of accomplishing both purposes. First, the planning process, through its periodic issuance of formal documents, would establish a communications base, which would advance new ideas and submit the necessary documentation, strictly from a professional technical viewpoint, to the public so that it could understand the reasoning behind the planning proposals. It would also lead to commitments of construction and to regulations that could not be arbitrarily removed. Changes in the officially adopted planning process had to be submitted to formal amendments, as were those originally advanced for the initial program. Consequently, the process and the plan become tools for the public and its representatives to agree on a course of action for the management of public works and regulatory measures, accompanied by a mechanism to adjust to the ever-changing conditions in the city or region.

The execution of such an enterprise requires adequate staffing. The key persons are the executive director of the program and his immediate chief of staff, the *project manager*. In the Shreveport assignment, I was most fortunate in securing the assistance and service of James Stinson, a dedicated professional engineer and planner, with substantial experience in urban street and highway design but—most important—with a talent for establishing and maintaining outstanding working relations with all concerned levels of federal, state, and local government. It cannot be overemphasized that the ability to keep everyone informed and in a cooperative spirit is key to the success of public planning. Suspicion of ulterior motive or political objectives or questioning of ability and competence will destroy the effort. Sincere differences of opinion of a technical nature will surely arise. If a positive atmosphere prevails, with mutual respect and confidence in the integrity of the participants, negotiation will lead to solutions in a form that is ultimately acceptable to the majority. If that ingredient is missing, the process will fail.

As is typical for the execution of projects of this type, Mr. Stinson was placed in residence in Shreveport and was given the authority to assemble a staff suitable to collect pertinent survey information and to establish required liason with municipal, parish (county), and state agencies, especially with the client agency, the Louisiana State Highway Department. He was greatly assisted in his efforts by Shreveport's planning director, Rhett

Parker. The executive director, at company headquarters in Kansas City, organized several teams of specialists to carry out specific tasks and routines in accordance with a carefully developed critical path of performance and a corresponding program-evaluation and review system, agreed upon by the client. Gary Alstot was placed in charge of traffic forecasting, including modeling of trip distribution, networks, and traffic assignments; Don Woodard was given the responsibility of directing field surveys; and the director reserved for himself the responsibility of socioeconomic analysis and, most important, the design of future transportation systems with alternatives. I have always considered this element of the planning process to be my prerogative and, from a very personal point of view, the only reason for me to be in this field of endeavor. Figure 4-1 is a schematic overview of the entire planning process.

Problem Identification

Systematic analysis of human settlements requires (1) the division of the universe in question into comprehensible units of reference; and (2) a synthesis of the components into a reasonable representative working model of the entity as the casual observer perceives it. This model must be sufficiently accurate to serve as a basis for decision making, even though it is only an abstraction of the real world.

In the physical-planning process, it has become customary to divide the study area into two basic entities. For socioeconomic analysis, the census tract is the most practical unit of reference, and for physical design, the drainage basin and subbasin. They should relate to one another with a minimum of incongruous boundaries. From these divisions flow others, such as traffic zones and districts, benefit-assessment districts, and so forth, which will be either further subdivisions of the basic units or fully coterminous with them. Once established, these units will remain essential references and will allow convenient recalculation of variable factors as needed in the future for plan-relevance testing or revision.

As one designs the scope of the several work items considered necessary to achieve the desired information, one will discover swiftly that the notions of distinguishing between various levels of planning may become somewhat irrelevant. Those who maintain that a strict line must be drawn between the so-called general plan and all other more particularized or categorical plans and attempts to transform such highly theoretical notions into practice may find that they lose not only whatever momentum may have been there initially but any hope for operating effectively under such a system. Conversely, there may be situations that lend themselves to the purist's point of view. In my own practice, I have paid little attention to these thoeretical

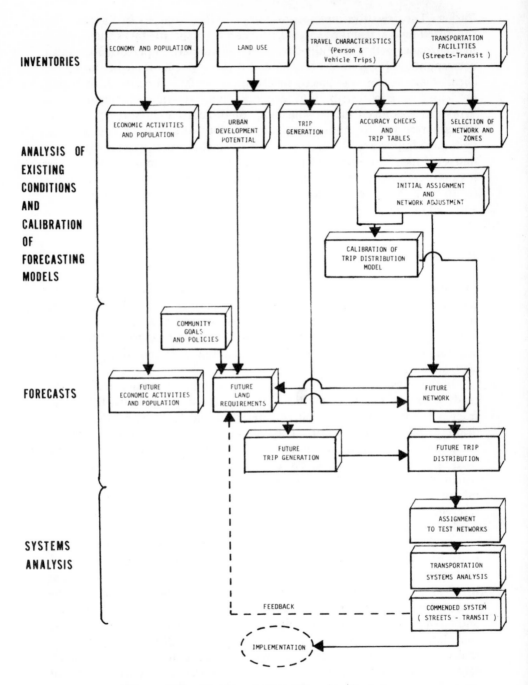

INVENTORIES

ANALYSIS OF
EXISTING
CONDITIONS
AND
CALIBRATION
OF
FORECASTING
MODELS

FORECASTS

SYSTEMS
ANALYSIS

Figure 4-1. Transportation-Planning Process

distinctions and have generally followed the pragmatic concept that Ladislas Segoe applied so effectively throughout his creative lifetime: to do what seemed to be in the best interest of solving the problem at hand. Consequently, one would go farther in some situations than in others, and the focal point of the planning strategy would vary. If transportation is the objective, then that would obviously be the focal point; if the schools are primarily at stake, they would be moved to the center of attention, and so on. The art in all these strategies lies in the project team's ability to think and plan comprehensively, which means no more and no less than to analyze each component holistically—in relation to every other component—and to assess adequately the consequences of action on the entire entity in any one of the subject categories. A highway serves more than traffic movement. It may become a land-use barrier deployed to advantage in community organization and stratification; its interface or node points may occasionally lend themselves to extraordinary land-development efforts, and steps must be taken to facilitate interaction between the public and the private sector, and so on.

Similarly, a high school and its accompanying open space is much more than a secondary educational facility. It can also serve the community at large as a community center for civic events, as a sports center for all ages, or as a cultural center. At times, one must prepare the client for such a comprehensive view of the community. In the case of the Louisiana State Highway Department, my task was made easy in this respect, because Mr. Carlisle was a man of broad vision and comprehension, who had little trouble accepting the planner's reasoning once its logic had been made clear. Moreover, the times were favorable. Everywhere criticism was voiced against mindless categorical programming of this or that facility, and enlightened administrators were looking for meaningful counteraction. In the design of the studies to be conducted, we were able to apply, by and large, what we had previously learned from similar programs. Important studies included from the first generation of post war American urban plans are represented by such reports as "Expressways—Greater Kansas City" (1951), discussed earlier, and "Cincinnati Metropolitan Master Plan" (1948).

These models had in common total community design rather than one specific categorical element. Kansas City, in particular, surpassed all others in producing a true plan for a metropolitan area without regard to political boundaries. One of its most remarkable achievements, as pointed out earlier, was the negotiation of political consensus, which we considered essential in Shreveport as well. A similar organizational infrastructure was established. A joint body of representatives of the parish and of the citizens of Shreveport and Bossier City would provide the liaison with the highway department and the planning team.

Within this framework, the team began to evaluate systematically prevailing conditions in the metropolitan area. The cornerstone of the programming that would follow was a thorough economic base study in the form of a sector analysis, which produced a comprehensive statement of existing and potential characteristics of the local economy.[4] This study was also used by others—notably, the Chamber of Commerce—for community-development activities. The economic study was complemented by a thorough analysis of social conditions, and these were carefully related to geographic entities in the area through the process of recognizing *areas of similarities* reflecting various social indicators.[5] The study and analysis of land-use and development conditions rounded out the basic socioeconomic fact-finding effort. This activity was followed by inventories of public facilities and corresponding analyses of their respective capacity. Included were sewer and water systems, police and fire facilities, recreation and cultural area and facilities, schools, and health-care-delivery systems.

The inventory and survey element of the transportation study consisted of four parts: (1) interrelated inventories of the existing street system by classification, intercity bus, rail, air, and pipeline operations and facilities, a public-transit inventory and a corresponding analysis of school-bus service; (2) existing traffic conditions and travel characteristics developed from origin-destination surveys and motor-vehicle inventories; (3) a comprehensive parking study; and (4) an analysis of traffic-control systems and accidents. The origin-destination survey was conducted in accordance with the federal procedure manuals, using a 5 percent home-interview sample.[6]

Analysis of Needs

In 1965, the Shreveport-Bossier City area consisted of 252.5 square miles of developed land. Some 119.9 square miles remained undeveloped in the geographic expanse delineated as the urbanizing area. The developed land was composed as shown in table 4-1.

It is important to distinguish between developed and undeveloped land, because the determination of future land requirements finds its statistical base in the careful analysis of the development potential of the currently vacant areas within the service area of the cities and of the replacement or redevelopment potential of existing developed but obsolete or blighted areas.

From a land-economic point of view, and in the light of municipal or county service capacities, both categories must bear a functional relationship to the urban-service area. This concept was first suggested by Ladislas Segoe and Associates and has achieved general acceptance in planning practice. Typically, the planner defines the urban-service area as that geographic

Table 4-1
Land Use, by Major Categories: Shreveport Area

Land-Use Category	Bossier Parish	Caddo Parish	Total Acres	Total Percentage[a]
1. Residential	11,425	28,951	40,376	25.0
2,3. Manufacturing	206	911	1,117	0.7
4. Transportation, communications, and utilities	1,437	3,524	4,961	3.1
5. Trade (wholesale and retail)	1,186	1,976	3,162	1.9
6. Services	14,368[b]	3,161	17,529[c]	10.8[c]
			(4,090)	(2.5)
7. Cultural, entertainment and recreational	283	1,200	1,483	0.9
8. Resource production and extraction	2,403	4,344	6,747	4.2
9. Undeveloped land and water areas	26,972	49,787	76,759	47.5
Subtotal	58,280	93,854	152,134	94.1
Streets and public rights-of-way	—	—	9,520	5.9
Total	58,280	93,854	161,654	100.0

Source: LSHD, "Profiles of the Shreveport-Bossier Area, Vol. I," 1968.

[a]The percentage figures for each land-use category would be significantly greater for the urbanized area than those shown for the study area, because of the large amount of undeveloped land in the study area.

[b]Includes military land and Indian reservations: 10,997 acres of military land in the urban area, 11,045 acres of military land in the study area, and 18,701 acres of Indian reservations in the study area.

[c]Includes Barkdale Air Force Base, which totals 13,439 acres in the study area.

expanse within which existing urban settlements are expected to grow over a tentatively assumed period of time, and where required municipal services can be effectively and economically provided.

The delineation of this urban-service area is a critical step in the planning process. It is accomplished by reconciling the constraints identified through physical-environmental analysis with socioeconomic requirements, both those existing and those anticipated to occur at some future time. It is as simple as that; yet it is at this juncture that the planner's imagination and competent judgment pass their critical test. At this level, decisions will be made that either will create opportunities of growth and desirable development or will place unrealistic and often costly constraints on the city for many years hence, perhaps for decades.

The procedure followed in Shreveport is characteristic of the technique commonly applied in the comprehensive-planning process, whatever the specific categorical-plan emphasis may be. The physical planner will obtain from the economist several series of data that represent probable growth or decline patterns of the area. Concurrently, and independent of the economic analysis, the sociologist will produce population forecasts and projections. The distinction lies in the methodology. Projections are purely mathematical abstractions based on quantifiable parameters and trends; forecasts are projections modified by unquantifiable observations and judgmental decisions. Projections give us technical indexes; forecasts represent analyses of the fundamental components of social and economic change. Both the economic and sociological forecasts must be reconciled by deductive methods.

In the Shreveport-Bossier study, we selected the sector method of economic forecasting and relied on a combination of step-down and cohort survival techniques for the population forecasts. Generally, I prefer the sector method to mere mathematical abstraction in economic research. It is also superior to the input-output model, which attempts to describe the interdependence of commerce and industry in a given area. It should be readily apparent, however, that such interdependence, while actually existing in any area, can be conceived of effectively only in the context of a very large economic universe—such as the western United States, the nation, Western or Eastern Europe—but rarely within the context of a single metropolitan area. To the extent that the interdependence within the study area does occur, the sector analysis will adequately describe it.

It is easy to become overwhelmed by economic theory and microeconomic modeling, for the subject is indeed a fascinating one for the theorist. It seems to hold convincing promise to satisfy man's insatiable drive to venture into the unknown and to predict with certainty the future by "indisputable" mathematical clarity. Unfortunately, mathematics by itself is not all that factual and, when applied to the realm of human behavior, cannot be taken as a substitute for human judgment based on perception, which escapes quantification. The quantitative analysis is a fine tool, but it is for the analyst and the planner to determine to what extent credence may be given its results. The planner cannot afford to follow scientific procedures blindly. It has been said many times that planning is both a science and an art. In fact, the pendulum swings back and forth, and the wisdom of planning enters the scene whenever it becomes necessary to decide between these two forces.

For the planning team, the objectives are all-important. Insofar as economic and population growth is concerned, the planner will look at the level of action of quantity and impact. The study of economic conditions and of population composition will produce data describing, in the final analysis, land requirements. The kind of economic activity expected to grow and the stratification of the population by such criteria as age and sex or occupational composition will give the planner a basis for the determination of required raw land likely to be converted into productive urban land during the planning period. Moreover, the public facilities and services needed to support this converted land in the form of roads, utilities, schools, fire stations, and so forth, will allow the planning team to calculate the probable cost of that new growth and, accordingly, to make pertinent recommendations with respect to the most cost-effective methods and the ultimate scheduling of construction of these facilities. This effort will go hand in hand with rational regulatory measures, which will guide private land-development initiative and assure consumer and investor of the kind of stability that is necessary for civilized life under urban conditions.

The Shreveport-Bossier area has two principal sources of income or basic, spending-power-producing industry: the petrochemical industry and the military. The sector analysis of microeconomic research requires statistical analysis and firsthand contact with industry. Using the organization of industry groups of the Standard Industrial Classification Manual, of the U.S. Department of Commerce as a base, the economist has three essential sources of information from which to draw his ultimate conclusions: the periodic U.S. census reports for trend analysis of employment and level of investment; the vast number of private industry reports and trade publications; and personal interviews with knowledgeable people in the planning area. The first two categories of source material will allow the economist to become reasonably competent in exploring the all-important third source, personal contacts. Competence must be established, but again only to the point of satisfying the planner's immediate objective—*dimensioning the plan* and tentatively allocating available public resources.

Equipped with some basic understanding of a given industry group, the analyst will tap the important resource of personal experience and judgment, which is available for the asking from local industrial management. It is at this point that the planning team will gain substantial insight into the economic and political affairs of the city and will soon appreciate that they go hand in hand. Through this process, the planners will invariably earn the respect and confidence of the local leadership group; or they will fail miserably. A competent and sincere effort by the planner, making it clear that he is there to be useful to the metropolitan community, will be well received and rewarded handsomely through loyal support by the informed public. The planner must take care never to violate that trust once it is established. If he does, he will never regain it.

Having established rapport, it is then equally important to inform *the general public* and to solicit its input in due course, a problem to be treated in some detail elsewhere in this discussion. Once the team understands the economic system of the study area well, it will proceed to analyze with equal thoroughness the social issues of the citizenry. We accomplished this by dividing the study area into subareas of socioeconomic similarity. The data used were taken from the latest available federal census and included such items as family size, age composition, family income, race and sex composition, median number of school years, and housing conditions. It may be noted here that this census information was later compared with results of the traffic origin-destination home-interview survey and updated as appropriate. On this basis, the information developed primarily for transportation-planning purposes could be used with equal validity in connection with housing and redevelopment planning of the two cities.

Two comprehensive reports were issued on the economy and population characteristics that constituted the foundation for the entire planning process. Three series of forecasts were discussed and the most likely series, the middle range, was considered to be the most reliable quantitative base for anticipating probable development and redevelopment in response to normal market interaction and to policy measures introduced for humanitarian reasons, such as slum removal and senior citizens' housing.[7] From these quantitative indicators, gross land requirements for various categories of urban land use were estimated, as presented in table 4-2.

This estimate of land requirements must be related to the physical, geographic study area by moving from the more abstract economic and social *order-of-magnitude* concepts to the existing man-made and natural environment, with all its constraints and opportunities. While the economists and sociologists prepared their studies, environmental specialists took a hard look at geography, topography, and soils. They would identify problem areas, such as flood channels, and delineate those

Table 4-2
1985 Land Requirements, by Major Categories: Shreveport Area

	1965 Square Miles Existing	1985 Square Miles Required	1985 Square Miles Provided
1. Residential	63.1	90.0	99.0
2,3. Manufacturing	1.8	3.3	7.0
4. Transportation, communciations and utilities	7.8	16.3	23.0
5. Trade (wholesale and retail)	4.9	7.6	8.5
6. Services[a]	27.4	32.1	37.1
7. Cultural, entertainment, and recreation	2.3	5.0	5.0
8. Resource, production and extraction	10.5	15.0	15.0
9. Undeveloped land and water area	119.9	59.3	30.8
Subtotal	237.7	228.6	225.4
Streets and public rights-of-way	14.9	24.0	27.2
Total	252.6	252.6	252.6

[a]Includes 21 square miles of Barksdale Air Force Base.

sections where urban development was considered eminently feasible by reason of topography, geology, and micro-climatic conditions. Man-made constraints are related to these natural features. Among those of foremost importance are the utility and road systems and the ease or complexity with which they may be extended. Other significant services include schools, police and fire protection, and administrative services of general-purpose government. On this basis, potentially developable vacant land is identified on maps and rated—an operation that cannot be relegated to computerization except for rough initial estimating. Typically in America, there will be substantially more suitable land in any given situation than is required by the area economy. Since the potentially required land will be subject to land-use controls in order to assure its continued desirability and the city's ability to keep up with services and facilities, it is clear that the market will respond swiftly to any artificial curtailment of available land. The plan must therefore safeguard against land monopolies inadvertently created in the planning process.

Experience shows that this can be accomplished if there is approximately twice as much land available for residential development as is actually justified by statistical indicators. In the case of commercial land, 10 to 15 percent over demand is a reasonable ratio. Industrial reserves are in an altogether different category. It is more important to protect the land suitable for that purpose from undesirable preempting by nonindustrial uses than to be overly concerned with surpluses. The reason is that only industrial land, when developed, produces revenue surplus, from the city's standpoint, and wealth to its citizenry. Future industrial acreage cannot be as readily anticipated as can residential and commercial land.

Commercial land generally pays for services it receives but depends on orderly residential development for support. Residential land is clearly a deficit element in the city system, with the exception of adult high-density development. But, of course, it is the residential development that constitutes the only real reason for the city's existence: a place for human habitation. This is not to say that the city's location finds its justification in the desire to house people. To the contrary, its is always an economic reason that provides that element.

With these and other tools, the planner begins to design. Prior to design, the reconciling of socioeconomic data requires subservient, secondary inquiries pertaining to the particular demand for the categorical plans to be produced and intermediate decisions with respect to development standards. As it developed, the most likely trends were the most reliable. As a result of the national recessions of the mid 1970s, growth was somewhat slower than might have been with continued prosperity. However, this was not significant enough to modify the plan execution and implementation during that period.

The transportation-survey technique that was specified at the time by the former Bureau of Public Roads of the U.S. Department of Commerce (now the Federal Highway Administration of the U.S. Department of Transportation) progressed from a 5 percent home-interview sample survey of trip making to a series of synthesized trip-distributed and assignment models. By this procedure, the field surveys are conducted principally for the purpose of calibrating the synthesized ultimate models, which, in turn, are based on a series of equations describing trip-making potentials by relating observed socioeconomic variables to each other and to trip attractions for a variety of trip purposes. The attractions are mathematical expressions of the land-use distribution and development intensity stated in the comprehensive plan at given levels of growth. These levels of growth are customarily expressed in terms of population and some reference of a future year with the planning forecasts.

Accordingly, plans are referred to as 1990, 2000, or 2020 plans, which is to say that certain facilities and services will be required whenever the population reaches a certain level, and that it is anticipated that this level is most likely to be experienced at some certain year. The time estimate is less important than are the systems required to do the job at a certain level of growth, which may happen sooner or later than indicators now suggest. Changes can be anticipated by appropriate monitoring.

The obvious limitation of all human activity dealing with the future is the simple fact that we have no idea how people will live and what their requirements may be in the distant future. We know some aspects with certainty, such as the food that must be provided. But we have no idea what sources of energy may be available or desired in the next century and how people will move about. There are fundamental human requisites and limitations, and, within these parameters, the planner must find judgmental answers that will be reasonably pertinent.

River towns are often handicapped by the lopsidedness of the original settlement. The early period of a river community experiences growth, travel distances from and to the central business area become unduly cumbersome, and disjointed satellite development tends to distort the original order. Shreveport managed to overcome that problem some time ago with the development of Bossier City and its extensive military establishment. At the time of the Shreveport-Bossier transportation study, the urban area had assumed the shape of a wagon wheel, with radial roads extending from the central business district. The pattern was imperfect, of course, particularly with respect to circumferential arterial streets.

At the time of the surveys, some 240,000 persons resided in the Shreveport area. Including through trips, these people produced some 650,000 person-trips on a typical workday. All but 17,500 of these trips were accomplished by private automobile or truck, the remainder by public transport. In their daily travels—carefully analyzed with respect to travel time, congestion, accidents, traffic devices, and so on—the people produced considerable deficiencies in arterial roadway space and were frequently forced to accomplish their travel objectives in an indirect, sometimes awkward travel pattern because of lack of facilities. Keeping these findings in mind, the planners decided to continue and further strengthen the wagon wheel and a system of "new rims" in the form of major circumferential arterial streets. A conceptual plan was drawn up and subjected to rigorous testing through the traffic-analysis process.

Systems, Plans, and Programs

Any good metropolitan comprehensive plan is both a composite of various functional, categorical plans and services and an integrated urban-design concept. The Shreveport-Bossier metropolitan plan, shown schematically in figure 4-2, clearly follows the established concentric-circle pattern of a

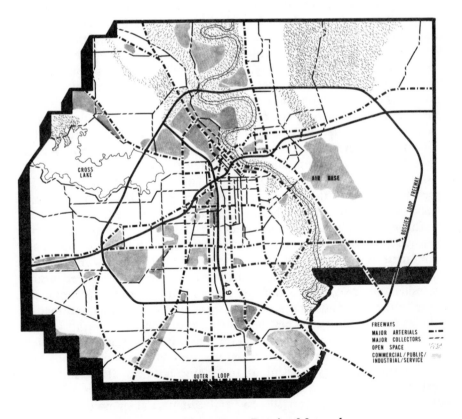

Figure 4-2. Shreveport-Bossier Metroplan

near-perfect wagon wheel. Commercially and aesthetically, the hub of the wheel is the central business district of Shreveport and its cultural civic center. Moreover, an effort was made to provide, for each component part of the metropolitan entity, a design that would be appropriate for its particular function and would compose harmoniously with adjacent land-use concentrations and the overall development pattern.[8]

In the residential communities, adherence to the eminently practical and aesthetically pleasing neighborhood principle of design was observed where feasible (see figure 4-3). The elementary school provides a natural focal point in residential areas, and the attendant district can be accommodated within approximately one-half to two-thirds of a square mile. That is, within such an area, a sufficient number of dwelling units can be accommodated to sustain and support the school population required for a well-operated elementary school. In addition, the elementary-school grounds and assembly rooms provide adequate and desirable facilities for various neighborhood activities. Regarding transportation, through traffic is kept out of the neighborhood whenever possible, and access to the minor residential streets is provided by a means of a minor collector street, which does not continue beyond the boundaries of the neighborhood. Arterial streets skirt the area so as to avoid any unnecessary conflict of through traffic with local traffic. This, of course, works to the advantage of both the residential occupant of the neighborhood and the intercity or intracity traveler. One of the most undesirable effects on the arterial street is the location of elementary schools on major streets, requiring elaborate traffic-control devices to provide for relative safety. Shopping facilities are provided at the perimeter of the neighborhood, usually at the junction of two major streets. Several neighborhoods are grouped into a subcommunity, whose focal point is normally a junior high school. Several junior-high-school districts constitute a community, or senior-high-school district, which together with the educational facilities at that level, normally provides extensive playfields for both youngsters and active adults.

The nonresidential planning areas are based on the same principle. Intensive-use areas, such as shopping centers, central business districts, and manufacturing areas, are designed for maximum efficiency within and for minimum interference by through traffic. Arterial streets are routed around nonresidential areas, just as they are routed around residential areas. But access to the nonresidential areas and their terminal parking and loading facilities is provided by the best means of transportation.

The third dimension of the urban form may be accentuated by the high-rise building. As a commercial structure, the high-rise building has long been considered a key element of the major business districts. People, organizations, and entire areas are identified with the skyscraper, which is a symbol of accomplishment, success, and commercial or political power.

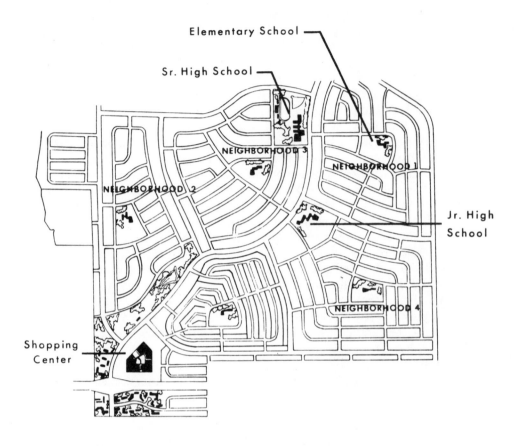

Figure 4-3. Typical Neighborhoods

Aesthetically, the high-rise structure offers an opportunity to break away from the low-rise sprawl of the undercity. Placed on hilltops of relative prominence, offering superior exposure, high-rise buildings scattered throughout the urban area will create focal points for functional orientation and pleasing effects. In this regard, the high-rise apartment building—or apartment and office combination—will blend in well with midtown or suburban patterns. However, it is all-important to provide ample open space around high-rise structures to optimize their setting and other environmental amenities and to maintain a rational gross density. If this is not done, the skyscraper will be harmful and will contribute to various forms of blight.

The transportation system constitutes the framework and the backbone of the entire metropolitan plan and gives it definition, shape, and life. The lifeblood of the urban economy flows through its transportation facilities.

The location and alignments of arterial streets and highways is an integral part of the urban-design process. In some instances, the transportation network not only serves the immediate and primary objective of moving people and goods, but also provides amenities of great aesthetic or recreational value. This is so where arterial streets, in addition to optimum engineering design, receive parkway treatment through extensive generous landscaping. Outstanding examples throughout the world demonstrate time and again that such treatment not only would be aesthetically desirable but also would produce substantially higher land values and substantially better private land development than is otherwise the case.[9]

In general, before a planning team can initiate design, standards must be set. Standards of development may be reflected in public policies and goals as given to the planner by the local policymaking bodies, or these bodies may look to the planner for alternatives.

Density of development is as much a function of service capacity of the municipality or other unit of local government as it is the result of custom and tradition. It is essential to negotiate with those concerned and to determine which standards would be acceptable as well as feasible from the planning standpoint. Feasibility in this sense is always tempered by the ability of the public to pay for added costs, which is measured by past performance and calls for careful analysis of cost and tax-revenue relationships in the community.

Standards are neither absolute nor universal once civilization has advanced beyond elementary subsistence levels. Even within the same civilization or culture, expectations vary substantially. A person accustomed to a small-town environment situated in an attractive natural setting of mountains or seashore will make entirely different demands on design of municipal facilities and neighborhoods than will the New Yorker who is conditioned to living with an altogether man-made environment. Tradition has much to do with value. Accordingly, the citizen of Kansas City, with a tradition of over a century of effective city planning, will expect a great deal more from municipal and county government than will the person from an environment without such a tradition. The planner must carefully note these nuances and transform them into appropriate notions within the context of a planning effort.

Traffic Analysis: Testing the System

Traffic forecasts flow from land-use forecasts. Traffic is a function of the numerous economic interactions that relate to the manner and intensity in which urban land is utilized. As previously discussed, the process of forecasting traffic begins with the collection of data in the various surveys and inventories. The origin-destination (O-D) survey provides the basic trip data for the process. The survey sample is expanded by statistical methods, and traffic simulating existing conditions is assigned to the existing street network. In this manner, the traffic pattern of automobiles, taxis, trucks, and transit vehicles on a typical weekday in the metropolitan area is portrayed for analysis.

Determination of deficiences is based on comprehensive analysis of network capacity. To this end, all elements of the existing and future street systems are described or coded, link by link. This description includes type of route; intersection controls; link length and width; surface type; turning lanes; zoned and actual speed; area type, where located; average daily traffic; land use; and jurisdiction.

In the testing and model-development process, assignments of traffic are first made in the form of free assignments, without capacity restrictions. Once a good pattern of traffic distribution is achieved, the assignments are refined by adding restraining factors to the network elements, which describe more realistically the probable capacity of the systems. Forecasted traffic is assigned to this refined system following established capacity-restraint procedures.

Various factors are applied to establish restraint capacities or levels of traffic service. These are based on recognized technical standards. Among the control factors considered are green and yellow time distribution, load factors relating to area types, population and peak-hour factors, factors regarding trucks and buses, and turning-movement factors.

Freeway capacities were based on highway-design speeds of 50 to 70 miles per hour. Level of Service D—a term denoting an acceptable traffic-flow tolerance level—was considered satisfactory under certain peak-hour conditions. On this basis, at 60-mph design speed, the service volume of a freeway lane would be approximately 1,120 vehicles per hour. The effect of ramps was calculated, and lanes adjacent to ramps were considered to have correspondingly less capacity than other lanes. The average daily capacity of a four-lane freeway was estimated to be between 18,000 and 19,000 vehicles in each direction; that of a six-lane freeway between 28,000 and 30,000; and that of an eight-lane freeway nearly 40,000.

Existing trips (in 1965) were assigned to the coded existing street network in order to calibrate the network so that assigned trips on each link closely approximate the actual volume counts made during the O-D survey. Calibration consisted mainly of adjusting travel times on various links to obtain the desired assignment. Using the existing trip data and various socioeconomic data obtained in inventories, trip-generation equations were developed through multiple linear-regression analysis. Equations were developed for trip productions and trip attractions for ten trip purposes. These equations, which relate trips produced and attracted to various socioeconomic data, were then used to forecast future trips by substituting the forecasted variables. Standard statistical methods were applied to determine the reliability of the equations, and checks were made to assure that variables were logical. In order to distribute the forecast trips between O-D zones, it was necessary to develop and calibrate a trip-distribution model. By calibrating the model on the basis of existing trip distribution, a synthesized model was developed of the distribution of the 1985 forecast trips.

The gravity model was used for this purpose. This mathematical model was so named because of its similarity to the gravity equation in physics. Briefly, the theory states that the number of trip interchanges between zones is directly proportional to the relative attraction of these zones and inversely proportional to some function of the spatial separation. Travel time is used to express this spatial separation.

Separate models were developed for each trip purpose. The models were calibrated by adjusting travel-time factors that express the spatial separation, until the existing trips were distributed in approximately the same proportion as those of the O-D survey. Travel-time factors were adjusted by comparing the O-D survey and gravity-model trip-length frequency-distribution curves. Through trips without origin and destination in the study area were projected and distributed by a simple method of growth factoring. This method is known as the Fratar system.

After a model has been adjusted so that the trip-length frequency distribution agrees closely with that of the O-D survey, it still may not distribute trips between O-D zones in the same proportion as in the O-D survey. This may be caused by peculiar social or economic conditions in certain zones or by physical barriers, such as a river. Zone-to-zone adjustment factors (K-factors) are used to account for social or economic adjustments. Physical barriers are given consideration by adding time penalties to all trips crossing the barrier. In Shreveport, such a time penalty was used for trip interchanges crossing the Red River. Travel-desire lines for 1985 were produced from the gravity model for internal, internal-external, and through trips. These patterns reflect probable changes of the metropolitan-wide interchanges caused by land development, reflected in the comprehensive metropolitan plan.[10]

Following analysis of shortcomings of the existing and committed network—which adds road improvements legally committed for construction to the existing system—1985 traffic was assigned to a test-plan network and eventually to the recommended plan. After final adjustments, this system was considered adequate to handle Shreveport's travel demand in the foreseeable future.

The proposed circumferential system will provide improved access to the major employment centers and will relieve congestion in the central core area. It will also serve a proposed turning basin on the Red River in the southeast section of Shreveport. The outer loop will serve primarily the developing residential areas. The north-south freeway will accommodate very heavy movement from the central and southern residential areas to the central business district, providing relief to various arterial streets that are currently utilized at capacity. The analysis of the 1985 assignment to the existing and committed network indicates that, in due course, north-south automotive transportation will bog down unless relieved by the facilities that seem to suggest themselves.

Effect of Transportation Facilities on Urban Environment

Goals and objectives are formulated on the basis of a clear understanding of existing problems and a desire to solve them. The principal objective in the case of a transportation plan is the movement of persons and goods as an element of the daily routine in the economic life of the city. Such a plan must be well integrated with the pattern of urban land uses in the area it is to serve. To accomplish this, it may be well to recall briefly the land-economic effects that major urban freeways have had in principal cities of the United States in recent years.

Several years ago, the Texas Transportation Institute of Texas A&M University undertook an exhaustive study of the effects of the Dallas Central Expressway on land values and on land use.[11] The Dallas Central Expressway is a major urban freeway that passes through low- and medium-density residential areas and industrial areas and skirts the central business district. It is designed generally to interstate standards, consisting essentially of two six-lane roadways and frontage roads. Texas Transportation Institute based its analysis on three bands: Band A, the land immediately abutting the highway; Band B, the next zone on either side, approximately two to three blocks wide; and Band C, a third zone of similar width. Conclusions of the inquiry were as follows:

1. Prices of abutting land were substantially increased because of expressway influences. For example, land that sold for $0.23 per square foot prior to construction of the five-mile test section immediately abutting the freeway was found to have increased $1.06 per square foot. Productive benefits attributable to the facility also occurred in the second and third bands but were smaller. It was found that measurable influences seemed to terminate six to eight blocks from the facility.

2. The same findings were reflected in the tax valuations, although, as would be expected, tax valuations lag behind land prices.

3. During the period of initial uncertainty regarding the nature of the expressway, the marketing of land was affected. This was more than offset, however, by the gains after establishment of the route.

4. Land use was altered substantially in the band abutting the freeway, resulting in a substantial number of new buildings, often at substantially higher density. Vacant land in Bands A and B disappeared swiftly.

5. An attitude survey was made, which indicated that both residential occupants and businessmen were highly satisfied with the facilities provided. In fact, practically no adverse opinions were viewed. It is to be remembered here that the freeway lies in areas of both good and moderate to poor residential areas.

6. It was noted that principal factors affecting the influences of the expressway on land values were prior land use and, to a large measure, zoning. Areas previously used for good dwelling and zoned for such received minor influences. Conversely, underused tracts or tracts occupied by inadequate or poor housing were replaced by standard and superior accommodations in many instances.

Garrison and Marts, in their study, *Influence of Highway Improvements on Urban Land,* note that, in every section of the Edens Expressway in Chicago except the west side between Harrison and Dempster Streets, residential property values within half a mile of either side of the expressway increased faster than for all properties farther removed. They increased, on the average, 18.6 percent annually, compared with an increase of 14.1 percent for real estate located two miles away.[12] The same holds true for the Calumet-Kingery Expressway.

Other examples are the Atlanta Expressway (land value change before and after highway improvement for combined improved and vacant land immediately abutting the highway, 134 percent to 159 percent) and the Houston Gulf Freeway (259 percent). The greatest increase in land values occurred when the freeway caused conversion in the use of property, particularly from vacant or agricultural land to some highly productive urban use. One of the most spectacular examples in this regard is, of course, Massachusetts Route 128, with its incredible industrial development around Boston. The Boston Chamber of Commerce and the Massachusetts Institute of Technology calculated for 1957 that investment along Route 128 amounted to two-fifths of all investment in all the Boston metropolitan area. The east-west toll road in Indiana has been described as breathing new life into the surrounding area. Some 44 percent of 400 industrial plants established in Indiana from 1961 to 1964 were located within 45 miles of the Indiana Turnpike. It may be said, generally, that very significant industrial investment has taken place along the nation's toll roads and freeways in all major urban centers, most in the form of generously developed industrial parks.[13]

Thus, the history of freeway and fixed guideway public transit construction in major U.S. cities in recent years indicates, that, in every instance, land prices and taxable property values have increased substantially as a result of the highway construction, and land-use changes that have been induced have either good, bad, or indifferent effects, depending on the effectiveness of city-planning efforts as implemented under zoning and related controls. We find it confirmed time and again that major transportation facilities will stimulate land development, and conditions have not changed at all since Homer Hoyt's brilliant analysis, *One Hundred Years of Land Values in Chicago,* in the 1930s, in which he demonstrated that every change of modes of transportation in Chicago resulted in skyrocketing land values along the transportation routes.[14]

Urban-Design Opportunities

What should be an urban-design objective on which plans could be based for the integration of development concepts for transportation facilities and land uses? The facts seem to suggest that the principal urban-design objective should be provision of the best possible transportation system in a corridor. This requires (1) that any freeway design be of the highest attainable standard, and (2) that a complete transportation system be designed.

Concerning land use, the market will create a framework within which to mold the future land-use pattern. Increased land values will, in time, produce greater tax revenues and more job opportunities. The public's concern should be the implementation of goals and objectives established under the metropolitan plan, which represent tested urban-planning principles through effective zoning and other land-use controls. In doing so, it will be extremely significant for the effectiveness of the transportation system to avoid creation of unmanageable high densities that cannot be serviced by the transportation facilities. Thus, achievement of a balance between the transportation-system capacity and land-use intensity is a prime design objective.

Finally, the need for open space should be recognized and, where appropriate, a wedge of open space should be created, preferably in conjunction with the redevelopment of residential areas in the corridor, which might be accomplished as joint development.

Joint development of highway and other transportation facilities with the development of abutting lands is an interesting concept. In historical perspective and broad present-day application, there are, of course, numerous examples of land-development coordination with the development of transportation facilities, ranging from fullest, most intimate integration to an occasional or coincidental occurrence, in some sequence. The concept advanced years ago by the old Bureau of Public Roads—acquiring slightly more right-of-way than necessary—has much merit inasmuch as the public agencies often have to pay nearly full market price to

compensate for damage to abutting property. Returning this land to productive use could be a powerful tool in the general urban-development and
redevelopment process.

Utilization of urban-renewal funds for the renewal of blighted areas in
connection with the construction of transportation facilities is common and
can be brought to bear again where appropriate. As reported, Kansas City,
in its downtown-redevelopment efforts, has successfully carried out several
projects that are comparable to the joint-development concept and have
created incredibly high land values. Its central business district core area has
benefited as a direct result of well-coordinated planning of private projects with the construction of freeways and execution of public-rede-
velopment programs. In Seattle, an opportunity presented itself several
years ago to consider the development above an interstate tunnel section of
I-90 for housing and open space, primarily for the benefit of people to be
relocated from the right-of-way area. However, the fact that a well-
designed transportation facility invariably generates substantial increase in
land values makes it somewhat academic to speculate on the manner in
which land abutting the freeways should be specifically developed. This
would seem to be a matter of private concern, requiring only that the urban-
planning agencies involved have a clear understanding of objectives and can
guide private development toward these objectives through zoning, capital-
improvement programming, and other means. It is for this reason that it is
emphasized again and again that urban planning is a process and not a
single event in the history of the metropolitan area. It does not lend itself to
a rigid form of preconceived, detailed designs or statements, but can only be
successful through a continuous decision-making process, which would rely
on sound technical principles and good judgment. Uppermost among these
principles are (1) the need to attain a workable balance between intensity of
land use and the capacity of the public facilities to support the land uses;
and (2) the need to give definition and stability to the general urban pattern,
to maximize functional relationships, and to enhance aesthetic values.

Postscript on Traffic Surveys

Among the various surveys of the transportation study was a comprehensive parking survey of the Shreveport downtown area. Such routines are
hardly worth discussing, but in this case, an incident that placed the
engineers in the position of detectives is of interest.

Parking surveys have two principal objecties: (1) to ascertain the total
number of vehicles that use parking facilities on a typical business day; and
(2) to obtain a reasonably representative indication of duration of parking
in given spaces. The spaces counted are primarily metered spaces; how-

ever, illegally parked vehicles are also counted to ascertain total actual demand. In any event, the survey was conducted in the usual manner, and parking data were developed for planning evaluation. As a matter of routine, revenues were estimated from the accumulation checks and were reported to the client.

Much to everyone's surprise, this simple aspect of the study led to the discovery of a major scandal in Shreveport. Finance officials discovered that the amount the surveyors estimated as typical revenue was substantially above that reported in the past by the director of public works, who was legally responsible for meter-revenue collections. An investigation disclosed that the director had the collected funds deposited in a room next to his office for which he alone had the key. Rather than depositing the funds immediately upon counting, deposits would always be made the next day. It was established that funds were removed prior to deposit by the director—in fact, stolen. The man was convicted—a tragic situation, because he was otherwise competent.

The incident shows, from an entirely different point of view, that the planning process is, indeed, a first-rate management tool if it is used prudently in the hands of a capable administrator. Even by-products of numerous studies can improve internal management functions. In the case of census-type surveys, such as a parking-accumulation study, the data constitute an excellent base for internal audits of parking-revenue collection. Similar opportunities present themselves regularly in connection with transit-patronage studies, toll-road traffic counts, and other operations research.

Community Facilities and Other Planning Considerations

Satisfactory conclusion of the transportation aspects of the planning program did not conclude the project. To the contrary, the transportation elements then had to be placed in proper perspective to other needed community improvements, and the ability of the local jurisdiction to provide required financial contributions for otherwise state and federally funded projects had to be tested. Accordingly, the plan addresses school needs; parks and recreation facilities; hospitals, fire stations, and libraries; water and sewerage improvements; and, in response to an ongoing public interest in the matter, central business district improvements. These plan elements were developed with the concerned operating departments and boards and were incorporated in the metropolitan plan with the full approval of these agencies. The plan elements were sufficiently detailed to allow for priority rating within each category and tentative, rough costing of every item.

On this basis, a fully integrated public-works program was developed by five-year planning increments. However, in order to portray a realistic impression of demand for community facilities and the metropolitan area's ability actually to accept a corresponding tax burden insofar as local shares and contributions to these various programs were concerned, an analysis of the financial capacity was made for each of the jurisdictions.

The total existing tax burden was compared with comparable other communities, and it was found that there was, indeed, a reasonable unused tax capacity in the Shreveport-Bossier area in consideration of then-prevailing household incomes. It was therefore reasonable to present voters with tax-increase options as an alternative to a do-nothing position. The team of planners, engineers, and other analysts had accomplished their task in a very short time—less than four years. The team had looked at transportation holistically and had fully satisified the principal assignment: what transportation must be improved in Shreveport and when. On 9 May 1968, the planning team made a final public presentation of the entire comprehensive plan and transportation study to federal, state, and local officials and numerous citizens. All proposals were very well received and carefully explained by the *Shreveport Times* and other news media, to no small measure thanks to the never-tiring efforts of Jim Stinson as resident project engineer. Formal adoption following the public presentation was a mere administrative formality by the boards concerned. There were no surprises in the presentation for them or for the public. Everyone was well informed and had participated in this four-year effort as interest and time allowed.

The state had performed admirably in the role of an enlightened, powerful regional planning and implementing agency. Finally, the federal government, through the Bureau of Public Roads, had accepted the holistic, comprehensive approach of classic urban planning, although the objective of the program was to improve transportation in the metropolitan area. To no small measure, the bureau's position was a result of the effective management of its part in the venture by Calvin Berge, at that time regional planning and resident engineer for Region V, Fort Worth. (Mr Berge is currently the Regional Administrator for the Federal Highway Administration, Region 7, Kansas City.) His positive response to the comprehensive-planning approach agreed on between the consultant and LSHD opened many doors for the technical team and for Mr. Carlisle and created a positive atmosphere for the entire team. It encouraged everyone to do their very best. Politics never entered the picture, and community leadership and staff were swept into a powerful stream of goodwill and progress. Fifteen years of plan implementation provided the ultimate evidence of success.

Plan Becomes Reality

The plan assumed that the various needs identified would be met by 1985. The comprehensive analysis of probable future needs in the Shreveport metropolitan area over the next twenty years or so indicated that the community would be severely deficient in all major public facilities. At 1968 cost levels, and measured by the standards prevailing locally at the time, these deficiencies were as follows:

Transportation	$175,000,000
Education	75,000,000
Utilities	30,000,000
Parks and recreation	10,000,000
Public buildings	10,000,000
Total	$300,000,000

Seen in this context, it surprised political leaders and highway officials that the relative share of funds needed for transportation purposes amounted to little over half the total estimated community requirements. If nonroad improvements are deducted from the total transportation cost item, only $140 million remain as a clear statement of road-building objectives under this plan.

As everyone knows, price levels rose dramatically in ensuing years, especially during the latter part of the 1970s, as inflation became a greater and greater threat to our entire way of life. It was fortunate, indeed, that LSHD had moved swiftly into implementing the Shreveport-Bossier plan immediately following its adoption by the agencies concerned. Major urban highway elements were almost immediately placed under preliminary engineering contracts with Howard, Needles, Tammen and Bergendoff. This prompt action allowed the department to schedule numerous construction projects on the basis of the transportation plan. As of this writing, over a quarter of a billion dollars has been invested by the taxpayer, through the highway authorities, in the implementation of the 1968 plan in about a dozen years—by any standard, a remarkable achievement in transportation planning.[15] The last element of the urban highway plan, the all-important north-south freeway, I-49, is now in preliminary engineering design.

Federal and state highway allocations were but one of the major sources of financing the implementation of "Metro Plan, Shreveport-Bossier Area" of 1968. Carl Conley, long-time executive assistant of the Shreveport Department of Urban Development, reports that downtown urban renewal along the Red River has also generally achieved its objectives. The project, Louisiana R-12, was initiated in the 1960s. It consisted primarily of removal of blighted and obsolete commercial buildings for various public purposes. The Civic Theatre, Convention Hall and Annex, and the Barnswell Arts Center are principal occupants of the former blighted area. Together with the attractive, relatively recent Red River Bridge, a fine example of HNTB design, and greatly improved access to downtown in general, the riverfront program has made a significant contribution to central-area reclamation. The Barnswell Center, incidentally, was the result of private and public efforts: the Barnswell family donated some $500,000 toward the project and the city of Shreveport invested $350,000 in public funds.

Another major achievement of the planning program was the construction of a parkway along the Red River. This was accomplished, among other means, by use of approximately $800,000 in federal revenue-sharing funds. The attractive boulevard—with divided roadways and center mall—is appropriately named Clyde E. Fant Memorial Parkway, in memory of the late Mayor Fant of Shreveport. Mayor Fant was the decisive political force in the area during the critical planning period of the 1960s, and he deserves much of the credit for its ultimate success. The parkway itself was augmented by additional parkland between the road and the Red River, acquired with substantial financial aid from the federal Bureau of Outdoor Recreation.

Mr. Conley attributes much of the success of the Shreveport planning program to the fact that key people of the original design team are still involved in the planning process, lending stability to the implementation programs. Moreover, the Shreveport Area Council of Governments, as custodian of the plans, provides periodic updates of basic data, which allows for modifications and revisions, as may be required from time to time, to adjust to changing conditions.

Notes

1. The LSHD is now the Louisiana Department of Transportation and Development. Its jurisdiction includes all matters pertaining to highways, public transportation, urban development, coastal-zone management, and such other related responsibilities as the governor may assign to the department.

2. LSHD, "Profiles of the Shreveport-Bossier Area, Vol. 1," 1968; "Metro Plan, Shreveport-Bossier Area, Vol. II," 1968; "Vol. I and II Supplement," 1968; "Technical Manuals," 1964-1966; all prepared by Howard, Needles, Tammen and Bergendoff, Kansas City.

3. Lawton v. Steele, 152 U.S 133 (1894).

4. LSHD, "Shreveport Metropolitan Area Transportation Study: Economy, Trends, and Forecasts," 1965, a sector analysis prepared by Howard, Needles, Tammen and Bergendoff, Kansas City.

5. LSHD, "Profiles of the Shreveport-Bossier Area, Vol. I," chapter 3.

6. U.S. Department of Transportation, "Origin-Destination Surveys," Washington, D.C. (revised periodically since 1944).

7. LSHD, "Profiles of the Shreveport-Bossier Area, Vol. I," chapter 2.

8. LSHD, "Metro Plan, Shreveport-Bossier Area, Vol II," chapter 3.

9. LSHD, Annual Reports, 1965 to date.

10. U.S. Department of Commerce, "Calibrating and Testing a Gravity Model for Any Size Urban Area," 1965; U.S. Department of Transportation, "Traffic Assignment," Washington, D.C. 1973.

11. William G. Adkins, "The Effect of the Dallas Central Expressway on Land Values and Land Use," Bulletin No. 6, Texas Transportation Institute, September 1957.

12. William L. Garrison and Marion E. Marts, *Influence of Highway Improvements on Urban Land: A Graphic Summary* (Seattle, Wash.: Highway Economic Studies, University of Washington, 1958).

13. Ibid.

14. Homer Hoyt, *One Hundred Years of Land Values in Chicago* (Chicago: University of Chicago Press, 1933). See also Homer Hoyt, *The Structure and Growth of Residential Neighborhoods in American Cities.* (U.S. Government Printing Office, 1939); Richard V. Ratcliff, *Urban Land Economics* (New York: McGraw-Hill, 1949).

15. LSHD, Annual Reports.

Lexington, Kentucky, Where Growth Management Began

The Circuit Court Judge

I thought it best to present some legal discourse for two reasons: to realize that, somewhere in the process, we are all accountable for our work and, because Judge Nolan Carter of the Fayette County, Kentucky, Circuit Court made such a splendid case for planning that no one could have said it better. Here, then, is the case of the *Provincial Development Company, Inc.* v. *Joseph D. Webb* (actually the City-County Planning and Zoning Commission of Lexington and Fayette County, Kentucky).[1]

Fayette Circuit Court
C.L. & EQ. Division

Nolan Carter:

Findings of Fact. Plaintiffs, William F. Wallin and Lillian Bagby Wallin, are the owners of a farm of approximately 282 acres lying in Fayette County, Kentucky, on the west side of the Lexington-Paris Pike, about four and one-half miles from the Fayette County Courthouse. The (LeMar) farm fronts approximately 1200 feet on the Paris Pike.

On December 15, 1959, the Wallins entered into a contract with plaintiff, Provincial Development Company, to sell this farm to said company at the price of $1,650.00 per acre. The contract is conditioned, however, upon obtaining a change of zoning for the farm from Agricultural-1 to either Residence-1 or Suburban-1.

Thereafter Provincial Development Company petitioned the defendants who constitute the Lexington and Fayette County Planning and Zoning Board for a change of zone from Agriculture-1 to Residence-1. Plaintiffs, Wallin, later joined in the petition.

A preliminary hearing upon the petition was held on November 19, 1959, at which time counsel for the plaintiffs presented to the Board their case for a zoning change.

A requirement of Resident-1 Zone is that the development be served by sewers. Petitioners ascertained that it was impracticable to install a sewerage system to serve the proposed development. Suburban-1 requires septic tanks for sewage disposal but does not require a sewer system. The LeMar farm passed the soil absorption test required by the Board of Health for septic tank installment on one-half acre lots. Both Residence-1 and Suburban-1 require one-half acre lots per residence.

At a meeting of the Planning and Zoning Board held on December 3, 1959, plaintiffs, through their counsel, Mr. Robert Houlihan, announced that plaintiffs were amending their petition to ask for a zoning change from Agricultural-1 to Suburban-1. At that time certain documents and plats were filed with the Board. In the center of the plats was the legend, "Change to Suburban-1".

At an executive session of the Board held on December 3, 1959, when neither petitioners nor their counsel were present, the Board members who were present voted unanimously (Mr. Wade Jefferson abstaining) to deny a public hearing on the petition. The minutes of the executive session state that the Petition for Zone Change from A-1 to R-1 was denied.

The value of the LeMar farm, if it is used for farming purposes, is according to the various witnesses, from $600.00 to $1,200.00 an acre; the sale price in the contract with Provincial Development Company being $1,650.00 per acre, the failure to grant the zone change will result in material financial loss to the Wallins.

The LeMar farm because of its location and because the land lies well, and because of the porosity of the soil, is well adapted for development in an S-1 zone.

The Planning and Zoning Board in 1958 adopted as a guide, the Master Plan Supplement which had been compiled by Ladislas Segoe and Associates, Planning and Consulting Engineers of Cincinnati, Ohio. The Master Plan Supplement supplemented the Segoe report of 1953 which had been previously adopted by the Planning and Zoning Board. These documents comprised the Master Plan for the development of the City of Lexington and Fayette County.

The Future Land Use Plan which is mentioned frequently in the evidence is a part of the 1958 Master Plan Supplement. An imaginary line, roughly in the form of a circle, is drawn through the environs of the City of Lexington and completely around the city, at a distance from the center of the city varying perhaps three miles at the nearest point to five miles at the most distant point. This line is not regular, but wavers as it follows the outline of some eleven sewage disposal areas which were previously ascertained by the J. Steven Watkins Engineering firm.

The area within this line is designated by the 1958 supplement as the "Urban Service Area" and is the area which the Land Use Plan designated as area which should be developed before development outside of the line, (with the exception of development under the provisions of an A-1 Zone), is permitted. The Board, in passing upon petitions for zone changes, has consistently denied petitions for zone changes from A-1 to R-1 or S-1 for properties lying outside the Urban Use Area.

In establishing the Urban Use Area, the planners have contemplated the accommodation of a population of 200,000 inhabitants at the rate of a certain number of inhabitants per square mile. A liberal allowance in acreage has been made over and above the acreage which would actually accommodate a 200,000 population, in recognition of the fact that if only the bare amount of acreage was included in the area to accommodate a population of 200,000 a land monopoly would be created; and in recognition of the probability that some of the land included in the area would not and could not be developed either because the owners did not want to sell or because the land could not meet the health tests or other requirements and regulations.

The present population within the urban service area is about 125,000.

Approximately 6,000 acres within this area, lying north of the city limits of the City of Lexington and between the Georgetown Pike and the Winchester Pike, is presently undeveloped. It has previously been impossible to develop this acreage because the soil would not meet the porosity test for septic tanks, and because no sewers were available to service the area.

At present a trunk line sewer is under construction along the Northern Belt Line and will probably be completed within a year. This trunk sewer will be available to service the 6,000 undeveloped areas, thus making this territory developable in the near future.

The LeMar farm is bisected by the imaginary line of the urban service area. The greater portion of the farm lies without the area. Various witnesses gave their estimates of the percentage of the farm lying without the area, one as high as 83 percent, others at a less percentage, but all agreed that over half of the farm was without the urban service area; the plaintiffs finally conceding that from 60 to 65 percent of the farm was without the area.

The members of the Planning and Zoning Board who testified gave several reasons why they voted to deny a public hearing, which is tantamount to a denial of the petition. Among the reasons given were that there was a possibility that a new United States Highway would be routed through this farm; that to permit this subdivision development would be to permit encroachment upon the race horse breeding farm belt, which is a tourist attraction. *But all members who testified gave as one of their reasons for denying the public hearing, the fact that the farm, or the greater part of it, was beyond the urban service area.*

Conclusions of Law. Section 100.004 KRS provides that it shall be the function and duty of the Planning and Zoning Board to prepare and approve a comprehensive plan for the physical development of the incorporated and unincorporated areas of the entire county; that the comprehensive plan shall include a master plan, and a zoning plan and regulations and restrictions. The Lexington, Fayette County Planning and Zoning Board has performed these functions. That section of the Statutes further provides:

> *"Such comprehensive plan shall be made with the general purpose of guiding and accomplishing a coordinated, adjusted and harmonious development of the incorporated and unincorporated areas of the entire county."*

The Master Planning Supplement with which we are concerned in this action was compiled by Mr. Segoe and associates after careful and comprehensive studies and surveys of this community, its problems and conditions.

That the plan is based upon sound planning and zoning principles and is reasonably good planning, both the witness Sheridan, a professional planner, who testified on behalf of plaintiffs, and the witness Roeseler, a member of the Segoe firm, who was instrumental in compiling the Supplement, agree.

Mr. Sheridan further testified that the perimeter of the Urban Service Area is not "an arbitrary line" for the reason that it is made to follow the topography of the land, so as to include the natural sewage areas as delineated by the Watkins Engineering Firm: that it is necessary to follow a master plan to achieve the purpose of planning and zoning; that the only way the plan can be implemented at all is by the Board adhering as closely as possible to the Land Use Planner under which the Board is working; and that to permit development within the area prescribed by the Land Use Plan is orderly procedure, though the Land Use Plan should not necessarily prescribe the absolute limit of development.

It must be remembered that the Court in reviewing the action of the Board will not substitute its judgment for that of the Board's; in which by statute the power to zone, or to make changes, is vested; and that the Court will not disturb the findings or rulings of the Board unless the petitioners, who must support the burden of proof, clearly show the unreasonableness of the Board's ruling.

Hatch v. Fiscal Court of Fayette County,
242 S.W. 2d 1018

Downing v. City of Joplin,
312 S.W. 2d 81, (Mo).

The Court is presented with this question for determination: Has the Board acted arbitrarily, capriciously or unreasonably, or has the Board discriminated against plaintiffs by adhering to the Master Plan and denying a public hearing in this matter?

Petitioners insist that they were being discriminated against for the reason that because of the line of the Urban Service Area, they are denied the right to develop in Suburban-1 category, whereas those fortunate land owners whose property lies within the area may do so.

As emphasized by Chairman Webb in his evidence, these petitioners are being no more discriminated against than all other land owners whose properties lie without the line, or whose properties are bisected by the line.

In the case of Michner, Appealed, 115 At. (2) 367, (Pa) the Court said:

"The law is well established that a variance may be granted only where a property is subjected to a hardship *unique or peculiar to itself as distinguished from one arising from the impact of the zoning regulations on the district.*"

The courts recognize that a line of demarcation must be drawn.

Smolon v. City of Philadelphia Zoning Board of Adjustment,
137 Atl. (2) 257 (Pa)

Plaintiffs contend that their constitutional rights have been invaded because by denying a zone change the value of the LeMar farm has been materially diminished. The evidence supports their contention that the farm is of substantially less value as it is presently zoned than it would be if the zone change were granted. However, as stated in the case of Shemwell v. Speck, 265 S.W. 2d 468:

> "It must be remembered that the purpose of zoning is not to protect the value of the property of particular individuals, but rather to promote the welfare of the community as a whole."

In the case of Hoskinson v. City of Arvada, 319 Pac. (2), 1090, decided by the Supreme Court of Colorado, *the Court held that loss of property value by the individual owner did not warrant setting aside a zoning ordinance.*

These decisions are consistent with the theory of Planning and Zoning, which is that the individual property owner must yield some property rights in furtherance of the general welfare.

To conclude, it is the finding of the Commissioner that the 1958 Segoe Supplement to the Master Plan for the development of this community is neither arbitrary, capricious nor unreasonable; that on the contrary, if followed, it should accomplish a coordinated, adjusted and harmonious development of the incorporated and unincorporated areas of the county; that in following this document, and specifically in refusing development in S-1 or R-1 category, of the LeMar Farm, of which the larger part lies without the confines of the Urban Service Area, the Board has not acted arbitrarily, capriciously or unreasonably, nor has it discriminated against plaintiffs.

It is, therefore, the finding of the Commissioner that the ruling of the Board denying a public hearing of plaintiff's petition should not be disturbed; and that plaintiff's petition should be dismissed.

Consistent Action: Major Impact

The Lexington, Kentucky, of 1960 is a classic case in the finest tradition of Alfred Bettman's theory of planning and zoning. By introducing the urban-service-area concept formally through the comprehensive-plan update of 1958—which followed a series of Segoe plans for the city and county since the early 1920s—a method was introduced to allow adjacent jurisdictions to collaborate in matters of land-use control. In the case of Lexington, a workable infrastructure had been created previously, but it lacked the technical methodology of carrying the comprehensive planning and zoning mechanisms beyond their respective boundaries.

The city administration was governed by that time by a Board of City Commissioners, which had all the common municipal legislative powers; and Fayette County was administered by a fiscal court. Under Kentucky law, the fiscal court has certain ordinance-making powers, including the power to enact zoning and subdivision regulations. Both entities had optional planning and zoning powers and, if they were exercised, were obliged to appoint planning commissions—one for the city, the other for the county. However, making use of intergovernmental cooperations powers, the city commission and the fiscal court accepted Mr. Segoe's suggestion of joint operations early in their program. A single staff was employed to serve both planning boards. Meetings were held jointly, but, for city matters, only the city planning commissioners voted, and, for county matters, the county appointees took action. Each such action would then be forwarded to the respective government body.

The impetus for a plan amendment actually stemmed from a shopping-center dispute. However, in analyzing the matter, it became obvious that the urban area had outgrown its 1952-1953 plan revision and that a fresh approach was indicated. My first task as project manager—to estimate reasonable area requirements for the next several years—was simplified by an excellent engineering study by J.S. Watkins, Consulting Engineers of Lexington, which had previously been commissioned to determine liquid-waste-disposal needs. We related these needs to other infrastructure requirements and were able to swiftly reach an agreement among the city and county officials of the physical characteristics to be considered in delineating the geographic area deemed suitable for urbanization in the foreseeable future. Since that would be the area where the normal urban services and facilities could be made available without undue burden on the general taxpayer, and since bond issues and other obligations had been authorized by the public for such facilities within that area, all of us came to call it the urban-service area (see figure 5-1).

With great care, the area was dimensioned and provided with the facilities needed to make urbanization possible in logical sequence. A comparison of table 5-1 with figure 5-1 will further illustrate this point.[2] The court took notice of the fine coordination between agencies and of the meticulous staff work by the engineers and planners of both the consultant teams and the city-county staffs; and the favorable ruling was to no small measure a result of that fact. In this context, it was not surprising that all of us, technical people and political people, began to think of the process more and more as a management process, and I believe it was one of the attorneys on the staff who coined the term *growth management* at a work conference in Mr. Segoe's office.

Based on planning commission records, Professor Charles Haar of Harvard University summarized the planning objectives as follows:

Lexington, Kentucky, has had an urban growth policy since 1958, when Ladislas Segoe & Associates proposed that the community adopt an "urban service area" concept. Its aim was to contain growth within a 67-square-mile area around the city of Lexington in order to achieve the following goals:

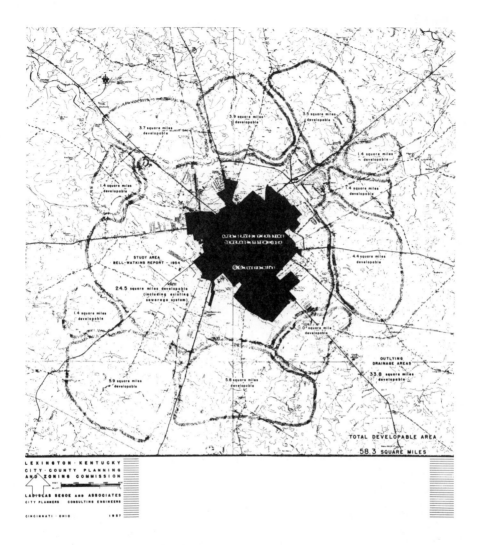

Figure 5-1. Lexington, Kentucky: Urban-Service-Area Plan.

1. delineate those areas which should be first developed in order that the most efficient use could be made of public tax money in providing necessary public service to developing areas,

2. provide sufficient area for the needs and growth of a population in excess of 200,000 persons in such a manner that the supply more than meets the demand, recognizing that some land can not or will not be developed.

Table 5-1
Future Land Requirements: Lexington Urban Area

Analysis Area	Acres per Population Level			
	125,000	175,000	200,000	225,000
Present developed area	4,800	4,800	4,800	4,800
Suburban density area	3,100	4,400	5,000	5,600
Urban density area	1,200	6,800	9,600	12,400
Total residential areas	9,100	16,000	19,400	22,800
All other urban uses	9,600	13,900	16,200	18,000
Total Land Requirements				
Acres	18,700	29,900	35,600	40,800
Square miles	29.2	46.7	55.6	63.8

Planning horizon: 200,000 population on 55.6 square miles of land

Source: City and County Planning and Zoning Commission of Lexington and Fayette County, Kentucky, "Master Plan Supplement, 1958," p. 13.

3. establish a limit beyond which only single-family residential and agricultural uses are permitted in order to help control urban sprawl;
4. promote the public health by requiring use of sanitary sewers in new developments, and generally permitting the use of individual septic tanks only in areas outside the urban service area;
5. provide for a minimum lot area for rural septic tank installations in order to allow adequate absorption of effluent over the years of operation;
6. provide a basis of progressive installation of sanitary sewer facilities as each drainage basin is developed and serve as a guide in assessing future neighborhood sewer needs; and
7. protect the agricultural area from urban encroachment, particularly the thoroughbred horse farm area which forms a distinctive crescent on the northwest side of the community.

As the policy has evolved, the following tools have been developed to implement the urban service area concept. Land ouside the urban service boundary is zoned Agricultural-Rural; multifamily, commercial and industrial uses are prohibited. All new developments are required by rule of the Fayette County Board of Health to have sanitary sewers, except single-family houses in the agricultural zones which are permitted to have septic tanks if they are on ten-acre lots which pass the soil percolation requirements. The urban service boundary itself coincides with the natural watershed divides around the community except along the county line to the south and along the interstate highway to the northeast. . . . In 1973, the boundary was adjusted slightly to follow property lines where they were in close proximity to the natural boundary, and a metes and bounds description was established. Finally, density guidelines were established for neighborhood development using existing population densities as the standard. The projected population capacity of the urban service area is 448,000 people.[3]

Conclusion

Technical excellence, fine administrative coordination under Bob Damerau—then planning director in Lexington—and consistent civic guidance through chairman Joseph Webb made this program possible. The planner never knows when one of his programs will become more than a local event and, as in this case, a milestone of national importance. City and county were ably defended by Armand Angelucci, county attorney (now Judge Angelucci), and Herbet Sled, his assistant. Both gentlemen vividly recall the case and believe that the foresight of planners and decision makers in this field did much to make the urban environment more tolerable. Years later, Bob Freilich accepted the theories laid down in Lexington in his brilliantly defended case, *Golden* v. *Planning Board Town of Ramapo.* In that case, the service-area idea was upheld by the U.S. Supreme Court. Coordinated planning, consistent enforcement of regulatory measures, and programming of urbanization while maintaining an open market, offering the public alternatives, was the logical conclusion of the American planning process as seen through the eyes of our judicial system from *Lawton* v. *Steele* through the great theorist Alfred Bettman to Lexington and Ramapo—all-told, an impressive record of successful urban planning. The fact that the case arose in the heartland of the finest American tradition, culture, and history makes the matter all the more remarkable.

I note with some, perhaps excusable, pride that the population forecast for 1980 was about 200,000, a level recently confirmed by the actual counts of the U.S. Bureau of the Census.

Another milestone was reached in 1974, when Lexington and Fayette County, Kentucky, merged into an urban county, a most progressive step for general-purpose government at the local level.

The comprehensive plan for Lexington and Fayette County was again updated in 1973 under the direction of William Qualls.[4] That revision confirmed the urban-service area of 1959, with approximately the same area total. In 1959, some 68 square miles had been incorporated in the urban-service area. Mrs. Quall's revision included approximately five additional square miles, for a total of seventy-three square miles. Dimensioning of an urban-service area, of course, is a function of population-growth expectancies. In this process, the forecasting of trends is viewed as an indicator, not a firm base of determining land requirements. Based on the general results of population forecasts, levels of population are related to required urban land and service facilities. The administrator will then monitor actual development and make such adjustments to the urban-service area as may be needed. In Lexington, this procedure has been followed effectively for twenty-three years.

Notes

1. Provincial Development Company v. Joseph D. Webb, Order of Reference No. 7973 (1960), Fayette County, Kentucky, Circuit Court, Equity Division. Emphasis is added by the author. Certain depositions were taken before the commissioner and filed with the report.

2. City and County Planning and Zoning Commission of Lexington and Fayette County, Kentucky, "Master Plan Supplement, 1958."

3. Charles M. Haar, *Land Use Planning,* 3rd ed. (Boston: Little, Brown, 1976), pp. 581-585.

4. Texas A&M University, "Effectiveness of Comprehensive Plans Survey" (Unpublished research records, Department of Urban and Regional Planning, 1976-1981).

Butler County, Ohio, Where City and Country Met

County in Transition

The Miami River meanders through Butler County from the northeast to the southwest on its way from somewhere north of Dayton to the Ohio River at Cincinnati. Over the years, it has periodically devastated cities and towns along the way when floodwaters have risen far beyond its normal banks. The Miami River gave city management in the United States a much-needed boost in 1915, when the good people of Dayton discovered that their honorable city commission was, after all, just a group of well-meaning citizens without the slightest technical competence to run a city. When flood disaster struck, civil order collapsed, and, after much suffering, it was decided to enact the city council-manager plan of government. Dayton was not the first city to do so, but it was the first major city in the then-new system. Hamilton and Middletown, Ohio, followed, as did Cincinnati and other cities.

For many years, Hamilton and Middletown were the only cities of any consequence in Butler County. More recently, Fairfield, in the southern part of the county established itself as a thriving municipality. Hamilton is the county seat and home of Champion Paper; Middletown is the headquarters of ARMCO Steel, among many other fine companies. Oxford is the home of Miami University. Under the leadership of the county's industry, the Board of County Commissioners decided in 1958 to undertake a comprehensive review of the county's development problems, which was to lead to the ultimate enactment of zoning and subdivision regulations based on a practical land-use and major road plan, which today would be called a sketch plan. At the time, the county population was slightly over 185,000, compared to an estimated 1980 level of 260,000. Situated between Cincinnati and Dayton, Butler County is part of the southern Ohio urbanizing corridor, which accommodates much of the country's heavy industry.

So long as its large, powerful neighbors were able to accommodate growth within their own counties, Butler County—with Hamilton and Middletown as focal points of its political and economic life—enjoyed a pleasant, somewhat detached existence. In the mid 1950s, however, it became apparent to the county people that a new era was about to begin, one that would bring economic advantages to Butler County. Demand for the fine farm land for urban subdivisions made land prices most attractive;

small contractors were easily induced to enlarge operations to take advantage of the coming building boom; young men and women no longer had to look for work in Cincinnati and Dayton, or elsewhere, but could find good jobs right at home; and the lending institutions, the retailers, the professionals, and all the people in the towns and on the farms sensed that their opportunity was about to change many things.

Unfortunately, with the positive came the negative. At times, it seemed that Cincinnati and Dayton had conspired to ship all the undesirables in the building business and other activities related to development into Butler County, which was very vulnerable without any kind of planning or land-use control. The situation was complicated in Ohio by its antiquated county-planning statute; in fact, there was no such legislation, and zoning had to be enacted township by township, by popular vote. I must admit that I was ready to throw in the towel when Mr. Segoe assigned the job to me. It was a real shock—nothing like Missouri or California, where I had cut my professional teeth. I will never forget Segoe's advice: "In such a situation one cannot afford to make mistakes." I don't know whether we did or not, but we learned that people make the difference and that law and politics will fall in place eventually anyway.

Planning with the Public

My first meeting with the Board of County Commissioners, chaired by Gordon Augspurger, with Ross Snyder and Ben Van Gordan as commissioners, was critical. The commissioners were hard-pressed for zoning, especially from the more sophisticated element of the population composed of professional and managerial personnel of major industry—represented by Robert Richardson of ARMCO and Ed Knapp of Champion Papers. At the same time, they were pressured by rural interests to resist zoning.

As had been our practice, we explained to the commissioners that zoning could only be produced on the basis of a plan that would set forth the county's real objectives, if such could be formulated. Mr. Augspurger immediately understood my strategy. We needed time to build support for the zoning, and the plan was as good a vehicle for him as any. He drew a parallel from his carpentry business and agreed that, indeed, nobody could build a house without a plan. So he was for the idea, but stated that it should not cost too much and not take too much time. We agreed that we needed at least a county road plan and a land-use plan to guide us in zoning. The land-use plan would give us the engineering data base, and the road plan would allow us to coordinate with Middletown and Hamilton. Thanks to the leadership of Mr. Verity, long-time president of ARMCO, Middletown had a prestigious planning program, which helped all around.

With the public endorsement of the county commissioners, we set out to draft the documents. It was particularly critical to satisfy the Ohio Highway Department with respect to rights-of-way and other road characteristics. With its enormous influence on rural jurisdictions, we devised a simple sketch-planning system for tentative location of roads and road extensions based on available topographic maps furnished by the highway department. As it turned out, the state was delighted with our timing, because the department was getting ready for a major transportation study in the Cincinnati-Dayton corridor. Anything we could contribute would strengthen the department's position in its dealings with the federal government.

Figure 6-1 shows the results of several months of careful study and negotiation with the county people and the highway department. When all was said and done, we had an acceptable planning base.[1] This plan was a sketch plan carried to a level permitting zoning regulations to be coordinated with road planning. Time was of the essence in the preparation of the document because of the urgency of presenting zoning regulations to the electorate. The effective use of available source material was demonstrated throughout the project. For road mapping, U.S. Geological Survey maps generally sufficed. In more critical areas, aerial and other surveys prepared

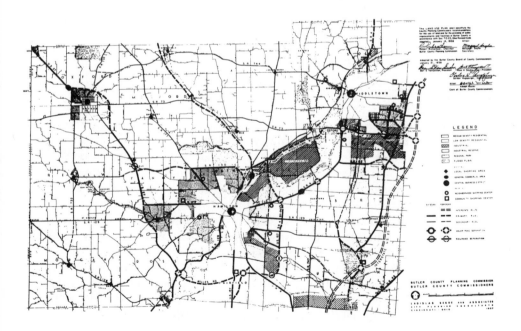

Figure 6-1.   Butler County, Ohio, Plan

by the state highway department for current road work were made available, as well as records of the participating cities. Personal suggestions by engineers and planners were equally important, as there is no substitute for first-hand knowledge of conditions and circumstances, especially in sketch planning.

The order of magnitude of traffic service for rural and suburban roads in this context was determined by carefully plotting observed traffic loads and by applying population and employment zonal-growth factors to existing volumes. The factors reflected areawide growth expectations. Through traffic was recognized by application of regional growth factors. It is interesting that traffic models synthesizing future traffic volumes throughout the Cincinnati-Dayton urban corridor, prepared in conjunction with various regional-transportation studies of trip generation, distribution, and network assignment, confirmed our simple and inexpensive estimates, further substantiating the validity of sketch planning and forecasting.

As a companion document, we had also laid out a land-use sketch plan and dimensioned it in the usual manner by calculating required urban space on the basis of population forecasts.[2] Having just dealt with the urban-service-area concept in some detail in Lexington, Kentucky, we took great pride in applying it in Butler County, but we didn't let anyone in on the secret that this was really an experiment that had not yet been tested anywhere.

Bold Moves and Ultimate Success

Zoning Battle Shaping Up

The planning commission, our staff, and the county commissioners were now ready to undertake the seemingly impossible task of convincing the people of thirteen townships that planning and zoning would be to their benefit and should be enacted, as required by law in Ohio, by simple majority vote of the township electorate. Conceivably, some townships would approve the plan and others would reject it, an intriguing problem concerning the legality of a comprehensive plan that is only in part operative. Commissioner and farmer Ben Van Gordon mobilized the farm community, and it was an impressive mobilization. It was an experience for us urban people to meet rural America at its finest: a well-informed, sincere group of people, who were determined to maintain the best of their traditions in the modern age. There was much give and take, but good sense generally prevailed, and, when all the votes were counted on that critical election day, 17 November 1956, ten of the thirteen townships had voted for zoning. This included all the townships directly affected by urban development—a *first for Ohio*.[3]

Key Issues: Flood Control and Mining

Aside from the fact that this experience has its own interest, the project pioneered in another area of concern: flood regulations. Since the 1915 flood, a state agency, the Miami Conservancy District, had been empowered to construct floodworks in a multicounty area of Southern Ohio and to assess benefited land for such improvement. Missing was zoning as a supplement to the capital investment. After much debate, we were able to convince the majority of the people that areas subject to periodic flooding along the Miami River and its tributaries should be taken out of urbanization, for they would not be suitable for that purpose. Invoking, once more, the public-interest clause from the standpoint of protecting the public health and safety, the planners, with the able assistance of the Miami Conservancy District, delineated the 100-year flood-prone areas. With the help of the county prosecutor, regulations were drafted for the zoning ordinance, which would, in fact, prohibit the use of these areas for human habitation, including mobile homes. Care was taken to allow a reasonable use of the lands so restricted for agriculture and certain types of recreation and storage. However, even these uses were subject to regulations, such as tie-downs, to prevent damage from floating or other hazardous materials in case of flooding.

As is so frequently the case, the prohibition of mobile-home parks in flood areas almost failed, had it not been for a most regrettable tragedy at the last moment before the election. In one of the areas where other accidents had occurred in the past, a mobile-home-park operator used every means, fair and often not fair, to secure defeat of zoning because it would have required the removal of his installation. (Nonconforming uses were recognized only for those housed in permanent buildings.) A few days before the election, another storm hit the area. There was much property damage and, tragically, a little girl fell victim to the irresponsible installation; she was killed in a trailer. There was no further argument.

The flood-control program has been effectively enforced through the county planning director's office since 1956. Because of its success at practically no cost to the taxpayer, the county commissioners declined to participate in the expensive and inefficient federal flood-insurance program.

Another interesting issue at the time was the mining of various substances and the problem of rehabilitation of mined-out areas. Again falling back on simple police powers—particularly safety—the county commissioners consented to include regulations pertaining to mining operations in the zoning order. The regulations required, among other provisions, that surety bonds be posted by the operator to assure the authorities of reconditioning of the property on completion of the mining and during operations. Enforcement and general administration of the procedure was accomplished by simply making all mining and other extractions conditional uses under zoning, rather than uses permitted by right, a well-established distinction.

Both the flood-control regulations and the mining procedures are good examples of simple solutions to complex issues, which the Constitution and our well-defined judicial tradition allow us to implement. Compare this realistic approach to flooding with the impractical and half-hearted procedures under the federal flood-insurance program. Obviously, not all flood problems can be resolved by police-power prohibition, but most of these situations are approachable on that basis. There is never an excuse for not trying to resolve as much of the issue through regulation as possible and leaving to capital-intensive and high-risk insurance only those problems that defy regulatory solutions. Moreover, only where regulatory solutions are effectively applied should the general taxpayer be called upon to underwrite insurance protection. It comes out of all our pockets.

Technical Problems in Rural Zoning

Were it only a matter of finding regulatory standards and procedures appropriate for urban affairs, on the one hand, and for rural situations, on the other, rural zoning would be a relatively simple matter. After all, agricultural land is easily defined, and the principal objective of a rural zoning code would be to keep incompatible urban uses out of rural areas. In part, that is, indeed, the objective. However, in an urbanizing county, complications arise immediately when it is realized that protection of the agricultural sections of the county is only one of the objectives of the zoning program. The other objective is the guidance of gradual urbanization through regulations that will neither strangle development nor create undesirable land-use conflicts.

Zoning regulations for a heretofore rural area that finds itself affected by urbanization inevitably must include both rural and urban regulations. In Butler County, consideration also had to be given to the existing zoning codes of the municipalities, notably, Hamilton and Middletown. In substance, city and county zoning should be compatible, so as to avoid outmigration of questionable uses from the cities to the county, and the reverse. It is particularly important that quantifiable standards, such as density standards, yards and other open spaces in residential areas, and standards of performance in industrial districts be appropriately attuned to one another in the cities and the county.[4]

In Butler County, it seemed advisable to include four residential classifications of varying density in the zoning measure, three commercial districts, two manufacturing categories, and two conservation districts—agriculture and flood plains. These classifications compared well with city regulations and allowed for a smooth transition from the municipal jurisdiction to the county administration. Within each of the zones, uses permitted by right constitute the majority of the use types and may be authorized by building or zoning permit procedure upon submission of appropriate plans. An occupancy permit serves as the key enforcement tool, as utilities cannot be connected until the required final inspection prior to issuance of the occupancy permit—a well-established standard procedure. The second group of uses in each zone consists of conditionally permitted uses that require authorization by the Board of Zoning Appeals. These are uses that conceivably could pose local problems and about which the public should have an opportunity to be heard prior to authorization. Moreover, if the board imposes conditions, such as installation of fixtures or time limits on operations, the board has the power to revoke the permit in case of failure to comply.

Beyond these points, the zoning code follows standard practice and provides for amendments, appeals, and other features, as required by statute and precedent.[5] For both zoning and subdivision purposes, the road dimensions of the major road plan are the basis of measurement for building locations. Care was taken to avoid confiscatory action on the part of the county and to keep all de facto reservations of future rights-of-way within the bounds of reasonableness.

The issue of potential industrial or heavy commercial development always arises in areas expecting substantial urbanization. The secret to attracting desirable, high-performance industry, with high real-property-tax yield, lies in (1) available services and infrastructure, such as utilities, highway access and fair taxation; (2) good, level land that is not preempted by residential and other incompatible uses; and (3) acceptable community services for employees. The first and the last of these items were available in Butler County. The land was also there—not plentiful, but nevertheless identifiable. It was impossible to scale future industrial-land reserves on the basis of market indicators. Over the years, I have always rejected economic projections for industrial-land needs because benchmarks of industrialization cannot be determined with any degree of certainty. However, applying all the common criteria for first-rate industrial sites, it usually becomes very obvious that such land is not abundantly available anywhere, while potential residential areas are plentiful. It is therefore reasonable to place all those areas that hold the industrial promise in zoning-district classifications that reserve the sites exclusively for that purpose. This creates, in fact, an industrial-land reserve, which will be activated by market forces when the time comes. The market will then be in a position to self-regulate and to produce maximum benefits for the industrial entrepreneur and for the community.

A perfect example of the appropriateness of this technique was recently given in Butler County. In 1956, we set aside several thousand acres of potentially prime industrial land in a part of the county known as the Trenton-Overpeck area, between Hamilton and Middletown. Despite its advantages in every respect, not much happened until the Miller Brewing Company decided to construct its largest brewery to date in that area. The plant will assume production in 1982, with an estimated initial work force of 1,800 people. This demonstrates clearly the value of longer-range land-use planning, which endeavors to protect the potentially high-return lands of an area against inappropriate preempting, viewing these areas as a vital economic resource. It is fully realized, of course, that not all such efforts are capable of implementation, for numerous reasons. However, the planner is well advised to be alert to opportunities and, in case of doubt, to risk the controversy that is always present in such situations. However, considering the county's present growth rate of over 14 percent, its location in Southern Ohio's metropolitan corridor, and an alert county administration, the odds are all in Butler County's favor.

Ongoing Process

In the course of the early efforts to establish planning, zoning, and subdivision regulations in Butler County, the commissioners also agreed to finance permanently a staff for planning and code enforcement. Francis Kosobud became their first director. After more than twenty years, he is still effectively administering the planning affairs of Butler County, Ohio.

Ten months of intensive work by political leaders, citizens, and professionals yielded handsome results. Not only was there now an effective planning program underway in the county, but the county's efforts and the staff's careful coordination with the planning departments of Hamilton and Middletown had induced these communities to take another look at their respective planning operations, resulting in major revisions of their comprehensive plans and in the initiation of successful urban-renewal programs.[6] An urbanizing area had come to grips with the realities of the times.

Notes

1. Segoe and Associates, "Butler County, Ohio Major Road Plan" (Prepared for the Board of County Commissioners, 1958).

2. Segoe and Associates, "Butler County, Ohio Land Use Plan" (Prepared for the Board of County Commissioners, 1958). Planning director Francis Kosobud has only recently found it necessary to initiate the

design of a new land-use plan, confirming the notion that a realistic plan should have a lifetime of about twenty to twenty-five years.

3. "Zoning Resolution, Butler County, Ohio," 1956; "Subdivision Regulations, Butler County, Ohio," 1956.

4. W.G. Roeseler, "Regional Planning in Butler County," *County News* (County Commissioners Association of Ohio), September, 1958.

5. Ohio Revised Code, Chapter 303.

6. "Master Plan, Middletown, Ohio, 1963," City Planning Commission, designed by Walter S. Newman and Paul Christianson under the general guidance of W.G. Roeseler and Professor Rudolf Frankel, Miami University. Paul Christianson and staff, "Master Plan for Middletown, 1975." The Garfield Urban Renewal Project involved clearance of some 300 dwellings and redevelopment for industrial use.

Part III:
Planning for
Medium-Sized
Cities

Planning requires the ability to respond swiftly and effectively to new events and situations as much as it requires comprehension of intricate relationships and foresight. At times, planning seems primarily to address grand strategy. It certainly does in the large metropolitan regions of the world. However, in the final analysis, the minutiae of the planning process—the particulars of design and construction and of regulatory measures and finance—determine the degree of success attained in that process. Nowhere does this fact come into sharper focus than in the planning for medium-sized or smaller cities. When I speak of cities in this context, I refer to those communities that had a population of 30,000 to 70,000 at the time the events related here occurred. The scale of planning is such that the community as a whole is involved, and the planner can ill afford to make too many mistakes. It is in this context that the planner almost instantly reaps the fruits of his labor, sweet or sour as they may be.

Cities of that size and smaller have become a matter of considerable national concern during the last decade or so. The surveys of the U.S. Bureau of the Census show an ongoing trend of population movement from the large, traditional metropolitan centers to communities under 70,000, a new American experience quite apart from the much-publicized move to the Sunbelt. Dissatisfaction with the metropolitan environment, physical and often political, as well as economic advantages are considerations, and no doubt are among the causes of this trend. It is interesting that cities in that category generally have responded to their new opportunities by strengthening urban-planning programs and by involving the public in the process as much as the public is willing to give time and effort to the challenge.

The medium-sized city, its characteristics, and its opportunities depend to a large extent on its regional setting. It may exist as a relatively autonomous urban entity, not directly related to any other larger complex. In this role, the medium-sized community may be a diversified industrial or trade center of regional, even national significance; it may function as a political center, as a state capital, or as the home of a major university. However, the medium-sized city also functions frequently within the context of a large metropolitan area, either somewhat autonomously or as a satellite. Satellite characteristics may be entirely or at least predominantly residential or industrial. In either case, such a community was probably the result of tension or general dissatisfaction, which caused it to break away from the central city. In other situations, the satellite city might have preceded the central city for reasons buried deeply in the annals of history. Whatever the circumstances, cities in that population range are a key element in the mainstream of American urban life.

Finally, the city of 30,000 to 70,000 population often offers the young, ambitious planner, with a few years of pertinent experience following completion of his formal professional education, the first chance to show what he or she can do in a position of final responsibility. Few, if any, mistakes go unnoticed, and the results of any planning effort in this environment will stand out for years to come. The following examples were selected to give an insight into this aspect of urban planning under widely varying circumstances.

Considered typical for the medium-sized city are Palm Springs, California; Norwood, Ohio; Council Bluffs, Iowa; and Zanesville, Ohio. This section will conclude with a look at suburbia.

7

Palm Springs, California: Resort of Renown

The Setting

Thirty years ago, Palm Springs was a town of some 35,000 in the winter and less than 10,000 in the summer. The summer exodus was prompted by the fact that there was no air conditioning in general use, except the so-called desert coolers, a crude evaporation-cooling device usually mounted on the roof, sometimes on the side of the house. The winters, of course, were magnificent and provided thousands of winter-weary vacationers from the Midwest and Northwest with welcome relief from rain and snow. The city became more widely recognized as a resort beyond the patronage of the Hollywood crowd, which by now had established itself in Palm Springs as a major constituency. Charles Farrell, celebrated star of the silent movies and owner of the Racquet Club, had become mayor, and in this role did much to strengthen further the city's ties with the film industry. Such film personalities as Bob Hope, Jack Benny, Ava Gardner, and Nat King Cole contributed time and effort to the city's betterment.

The new sometimes found itself on a collision course with the traditional, for Palm Springs had, indeed, a long and interesting past. It was once the sacred resort of the Agua Caliente Mission Indians, who came every winter to seek relief from illness in the ancient sulphur springs. Around the turn of the century, Judge McCallum acquired certain rights from the Indians, and Nellie Coffman founded a sanitarium, which was to become the Desert Inn.

Gradually, Palm Springs emerged as a white man's settlement and resort, first for tuberculosis and arthritis victims, later, under the firm leadership of Mayor Philip Boyd in the late 1930s, for all-around recreation. For a time, the decendants of that settlement resented the invasion by the Hollywood crowd. In time, however, each found their level.

When I arrived in Palm Springs as planning director in 1952, we still had to cope with a checkerboard pattern of land ownership of railroad-development days: every other square mile was Indian reservation, and normal real-estate ownership was only possible in the alternate non-Indian sections. The Indian sections were and still are under the jurisdiction of the Bureau of Indian Affairs, and any development proposal required the bureau's approval. In any event, development was possible only on the basis of short-term leaseholds, which fortunately were changed to ninety-nine-year terms in 1959. The approval process was cumbersome, involving tribal-council committees and the full gamut of the federal bureaucracy. The Palm Springs experience in dealing with that branch of the federal government left me with the conviction that drastic reforms were essential.

The council-manager form of government enabled the city to operate on a businesslike basis. The managers of that period, Russell Rink and Robert W. Peterson, attracted young, capable professionals for the key positions and gave them a free hand to work with the community. The period was, indeed, critical for the city. Development was just about to get fully under way, and steps had to be taken to assure quality as well as sensitivity to the particular requirements of the desert ecology. The city council was composed of businesspersons representing the old and the new community. There was tension at times, but, on the whole, the men and women in public office were able to reconcile their differences, thanks to the effective guidance and technical competence of key department heads, notably engineering, law, and planning.

Ecology

Man and nature posed their respective problems. Palm Springs' ecology is complex. A delicate balance exists between wind and water forces and the general climatic advantages and disadvantages of the desert region, provided man takes care in living with that environment. The Coachella Valley, widely known for its citrus, date, and fig groves and the Thompson seedless grape, accommodates several significant communities. Palm Springs is one of them, nestled into the foothills and canyons of Mount San Jacinto, an 11,000-foot wall of granite. Adjacent Palm Canyon, one of California's most beautiful natural features, with perhaps the oldest, most majestic forest of Washingtonian Filifera palm trees, creates a fitting setting for a resort. In fact, the Mission Indians thought so, too, and used it for that purpose, as a natural shelter from the summer heat.

The many beautiful trees, of course, could not exist in the desert without water. The water is provided by Mount San Jacinto run-off, which can sometimes be devastating, especially after a sudden snow melt in higher elevations. Flash floods are common in desert regions, especially where the desert abuts mountain ranges, with seasonally heavy snow accumulations in high elevations subject to sudden temperature changes. It can be difficult to reason with people who have just fled the winter world. Rarely will they accept the fact that their newly found paradise may have flaws and that one of those may, indeed, be destructive flooding.

As discussed in connection with the Kessler plans for midwestern cities, an old standby for surface drainage is provision of extra-wide rights-of-way for selected arterial streets so that these public thoroughfares not only will serve traffic but also will serve as channels for floodwaters. During dry periods, the channels can be used for recreation. After much debate, several streets were constructed with center malls of varying width around one hundred feet, inverted about eight to ten feet. In time, these systems would pay for themselves, as, in those areas of the city where they had been installed, flash-flood damage was minimal, while in other areas built in later years, damage was great. The system, designed by the Riverside Flood Control District, is far from complete. But it is a long-range plan that pays dividends as it is implemented.

Nature poses another water problem in the region. Although the mountains nourish a large subterranean freshwater lake under Palm Springs, the community's water supply, the Pacific Ocean and run-off also sometimes raise the water level of the Salton Sea, an inland salt lake, to the south of the city. A delicate balance exists between the opposing forces, as well as problems of contamination from waste disposal in the community. It became clear at an early date that wastewater treatment on a community basis was essential and that septic-tank operations would have to cease as the community increased in population. Thus, sewer systems were installed and treatment facilities were constructed.

Man-Made Issues

The man-made issues focused on development standards: zoning, subdivision requirements, and building codes. Business was in an up-beat mood, though cautious and cognizant of the vulnerability of the resort city. Yet a foundation was laid during the early 1950s that enabled several generations of planners to help shape one of the most beautiful communities in the country. Professionals such as David Hamilton, Dick Smith, Herman Ranes, and I were able to make contributions consistently, over more than a quarter of a century, through diligent, day-by-day work and appropriate larger projects, under enlightened political and civic leadership. Moreover, and most important, the public was receptive to planning and was prepared to give the kind of support that is essential to the entire process—constructively critical but firm once a course was charted.

It is interesting that, in this growth situation—the seasonal population more than doubled over forty years—the planners responsible for the program relied more on their own ability to react skillfully to growth pressure and to come forward with appropriate measures, which typically were quite bold under the circumstances there, than on written comprehensive-plan documents, except for the thoroughfare plan. This is not to say that the comprehensive-plan notion was disregarded; but it had little direct impact on events. I felt very strongly at the time (1953) that little was to be gained from the theoretical "what was good to do," but, rather, that the energies of my staff and myself should be directed toward solving issues at hand, while stressing ground rules that could expand with a fast-growing community. In retrospect, I am satisfied that we accomplished that very well, as did the planners who followed us.

Policy

In the early 1950s, Palm Springs wrestled with the problem of direction and orientation: should the city remain a relatively restricted resort, or should it become another Tucson, Arizona? Professionally, I was mindful of the elegant resorts of Europe, their persistence on development patterns fully compatible with the character of a resort. Many study sessions and debates focused on that issue, and, eventually, the city council agreed that there was nothing to be gained from copying Tucson, and certainly not Las Vegas. Palm Springs would be a resort appealing to sophistication and aesthetic values. Once this decision was made and had public endorsement—with much support from the *Desert Sun*, Palm Springs' daily paper, radio, and later television—numerous technical and regulatory issues arose and had to be resolved. The principal contribution of that period of planning was perhaps the very fact that it was feasible to resolve such issues. With the assistance of the architectural fraternity, architectural and land-development standards that could be enforced through the zoning ordinance were developed very deliberately. In fact, the real-estate board and the local lawyers also lent a hand in this process, and all agreed that Palm Springs would get its first modern zoning code, complete with performance standards, noise and dust controls, and many other features that were certainly not common in those days.

Techniques

Some examples of the pioneer spirit of planning commission and city council are in order. During those years, uses designed for automobile-type service sprang up all over the country: drive-in eating places, drive-in laundries, drive-in groceries, as well as automobile service stations. Typically, these uses tended to seek arterial-street locations. Lots on these streets were rarely more than 150 feet deep and abutted, at least in the rear, residential uses. These uses also could be disturbing to a hotel or other more sensitive occupant to either side, even though, from a business standpoint, each gained from the other. To remedy the conflict, we required construction of a four- to six-foot wall, with such ornamental features as seemed indicated. At first, there was much fuss by some oil companies, but eventually all complied without litigation.

Another example of controversy was off-street parking. The ordinance required parking and loading spaces based on the latest ENO Foundation recommendations. Noise was to be curtailed, and the city building inspectors were trained in the use of noise-level meters. At the time, noise was often an issue in connection with mechanical equipment and could become a serious threat to hotels. A new concept of resort development thirty years ago was the guest ranch, a hotel operation consisting of cottages and buildings for common usage, sometimes combined with certain athletic activities, such as horseback riding and tennis. David Hamilton, the planning department's gifted landscape architect, developed a sensitive concept for these facilities and translated standards into zoning regulations. Naturally, there was very strict control of outdoor advertising, so strict, in fact, that our helpful city attorney, Jerry Bunker, prayed he would never have to defend the regulation in a court of law.[1] He did not, because the public was clearly behind the law, and it was reasonable for the advertising people. It required merely a little consideration of neighbors and a little more thought than is sometimes given to that medium of communication. There was also some review by the planning commission of architectural features of buildings along major streets.

Perhaps one of the most critical issues then was building height. I thought it best to maintain a literally low profile for the desert oasis and to let nature to be the overriding feature. For one thing, no one can compete against mighty Mount San Jacinto, and any attempt at skyscraper mentality would be damaging. Bigger did not mean better, and the dinosaur complex fortunately had not become an affliction. Second, the local business community needed time and opportunity to find its own level. After all, this was still very much a period of testing. Finally, it struck me as significant to preserve an atmosphere of intimacy—amicably called the village image, to attract people from the major metropolitan areas who had money to spend on privacy and pure beauty, where all property could be assured of a reasonably unrestricted view of the magnificent landscape of Palm Springs. It was agreed that the building height would be limited to thirty feet, or two stories, and that only ornamental steeples and similar features would be exempted. In 1973, the height limit was further reduced to twenty-four feet. It is very much my hope that the concepts of thirty years ago will continue to guide the city policymakers (see figure 7-1).

As in all growth situations, traffic circulation and subdivision control are uppermost in the minds of developers, planners, engineers, contractors, and politicians. We addressed all these issues and were able to bring about major improvements on short notice. More important, we initiated a con-

Figure 7-1. Palm Springs Downtown: Low-Profile Delights

structive, ongoing dialogue with the California State Highway Commission and with the planners of Riverside County. Even then, the California Highway Department was years ahead of the country; to this day, it should be recognized as one of the foremost planning and construction agencies in the United States.

The city's first subdivision ordinance, adopted in 1953, required underground installation of all utilities and construction of all but community-wide features of the urban infrastructure at the expense of the developer.[2] It introduced the surety bond and other means of guaranteeing such construction and required that the land be suitable for urban development, a provision directed against the use of flood-prone areas or areas otherwise unsuitable and still mindful of the infamous era of California land sales by mail of the 1920s. (We had considerable trouble with some of those subdivisions featuring lots 25 feet wide and 500 feet deep, with much of the land tied up in impossible legal situations, making replatting nearly impossible short of public acquisition.) Moreover, sidewalks were introduced in the desert—carefully, and only under certain conditions—as was the rolled curb, which had proved to be so practical in many cities throughout the country. Figure 7-2 illustrates these regulations.

Once a Beginning—Now a Tradition

Within a few months, the planning commission and the city council received from the Planning Department and enacted, as appropriate, the following instruments:

Master plan for major thoroughfares

Comprehensive flood-control plan

Master plan for a desert museum

Master plan for a city hall

Zoning ordinance

Subdivision ordinance

Setback ordinance (for certain arterial streets)

Street-paving policy and design standards

Policy concerning the routing of trucks

Plan for noise and nuisance abatement[3]

In addition, the Planning Department initiated a design-assistance program for subdividers, which also would yield gratifying results. Public

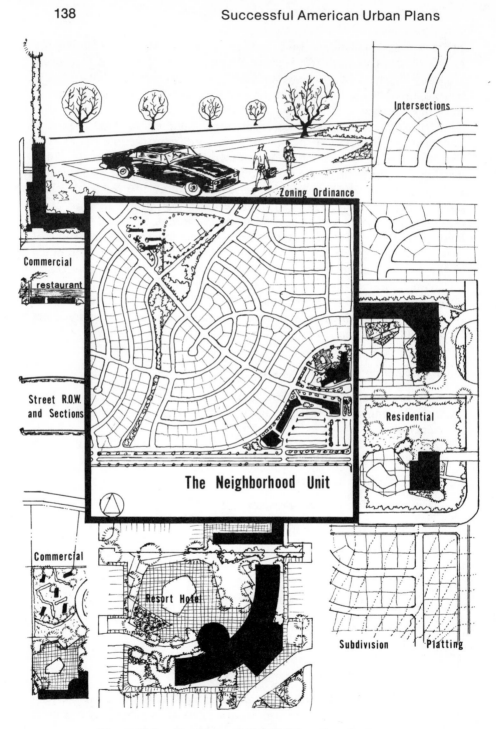

Figure 7-2. Zoning and Subdivision Standards

involvement became a never-ending process, including regular releases to the press and a weekly radio show, "This Is Your Planning Department." This show swiftly enjoyed considerable popularity because of participation by numerous community and motion-picture personalities.

As time went on, David Hamilton made major contributions, as a landscape architect-planner, to key developments in the city. The public projects he designed include the magnificent Tahquitz-McCallum Way boulevard, with its intriguing intersectional features composed of palm trees, silk oak, and fig trees against the background of a ground cover of annual flowers. The entire dual-roadway boulevard is flanked by palms, and the development alongside is skillfully coordinated—a masterpiece of urban design.

Many concepts have become reality, and most of the tools carved out thirty years ago are still serving their purpose in the zoning and subdivision regulations, broadened and extended over the years, particularly by Dick Smith and such able councilmen as William Foster, among others. All told, the planning program of America's foremost desert resort, Palm Springs, is a formidable one—speaking well, indeed, for the public at large, the political leaders, and the professionals involved.

Notes

1. Palm Springs, California, "Zoning Ordinance," 1953, as amended (notably, in 1973).

2. Palm Springs, California, "Subdivision Regulations," 1953, as amended.

3. Palm Springs City Planning Commission, "Annual Report—1953." John Mangione, community development director, and Marvin Roos, planning director, report that the city of Palm Springs does not have a truly comprehensive plan, although an attempt was made to adopt such a document in 1966. However, that report, prepared by Simon Eisner and Associates of Los Angeles, was apparently only acceptable at that time with respect to some elements, including streets and thoroughfares.

The Old Satellite

Norwood, Ohio: Working Man's Home and Castle

The location and alignment of the Norwood lateral, an integral element of the Greater Cincinnati freeway system, became the catalyst of Norwood's renaissance in the 1960s. The lateral originally had been proposed in the motorways plan of the Metropolitan Master Plan of 1948 and was subsequently included in several preliminary engineering reports to the Ohio Department of Highways.[1] For some reason, one of these studies contained a shift in alignment that would have caused the acquisition of an extraordinary number of sound apartment houses and other dwellings. Moreover, the highway would have constituted a major land-use barrier because of its elevated design in the center of town, further aggravating an undesirable condition caused by numerous railroad crossings. From a traffic-system planning standpoint, that solution would have committed the cardinal sin of traffic engineering: it would have concentrated all ingress and egress of Norwood on the one arterial street that could least afford to handle additional functions—Montgomery Road, which traversed the commercial area of the city, with intensive development on either side.

Urban freeway systems can function effectively only if an arterial street system interacts with the freeways and is capable of delivering to and accepting from the freeway system the heavy traffic volumes produced and attracted throughout the service region. If access points are constructed in already heavily congested areas and no provision is made for collection and distribution—or none can be made because of the prevailing crowded condition—the system becomes ineffective, and much of the investment value is lost. Accordingly, central business districts, shopping centers, and similar high-intensity uses of urban land must be near but not immediately at the freeway nodes, so that they can be seen but have adequate space for the service facilities that make or break both the highway system and the high concentration of intensive land uses.

Norwood, a century-old satellite community in the metropolitan area of Cincinnati, boasts one of the heaviest concentrations of highly productive automotive and other industries in Ohio. Its 35,000 inhabitants, predominantly Roman Catholic of Irish and German stock, traditionally have constituted a close-knit group, both politically and economically, with a keen sense of friendly rivalry with "big brother" Cincinnati. Much of

Norwood's industry is or was, for years, home-owned, and those of national standing, such as General Motors, made a concerted effort to fit themselves into the friendly town and were soon recognized as local. Business leadership was provided by a group of merchants along Montgomery Road. Political leadership at the crucial period of planning and building was in the hands of the Shea family and the Democratic Party.

The Ohio Department of Highways gave notice to the Norwood City Council that the Norwood lateral would be constructed in a certain location, running east-west through the city, immediately north of the central business district, and that it would have one access point at the CBD. The purpose of the notice was, of course, to obtain the approval of the city council for the grade of the roadways, a statutory requirement in Ohio. (This by itself is an amusing quirk of tradition. The highway department has superior condemnation powers under eminent-domain proceedings for the highways. However, it cannot construct a roadway through an incorporated city without the approval of the grades by the local legislative body.) Upon examination of the request, Mayor Joseph W. Shea, Jr., turned to Ladislas Segoe and Associates for advice. (Years ago, Mr. Segoe had been instrumental in the first plan for the town and in the drafting of a zoning measure.) I was asked to analyze the issues. An alternative solution seemed eminently feasible and, true to policy and practice, I proposed a new master plan for the city, as well as an examination of the most suitable specific location and alignment of the lateral.[2]

It took a little over a year to develop a plan that would resolve the immediate issues on the basis of intensive interaction with the Ohio Department of Highways and various community groups, notably, the merchants' association then led by Ben Youklis and John Porter—a jeweler and a banker. I noted in the plan issued in 1960 that public criticism of the previous alignment proposal was directed primarily at the heavy loss of dwellings and the barrier effect the highway would have. The business community and General Motors perceived the improvement as a direct threat to their operations. General Motors was particularly sensitive to the issue of access because of delicate negotiations with their union, which, among other considerations, included providing improved access and substantial parking facilities for their plant. Considering the tight conditions in the Norwood business area, it was almost impossible to achieve a good solution without some drastic measures, going considerably beyond the issue of the ill-located freeway, which only a resolute city government could undertake. The lateral, however, was a perfect test case. If the city could agree on a technically acceptable alternative that would be superior from a city-planning and development standpoint, and if it would be willing to stand up to the considerable pressures of the state to have matters resolved "immediately, or never," there was a chance to do considerably more than build just another urban road. A superior solution was produced—one that would have the road follow, in part, an old, abandoned rapid-transit right-of-way, which at this time was no more than an undesired monument to Cincinnati's days of the worst municipal corruption and bossism of the century. In this location, the Norwood lateral would be depressed and would unobtrusively skirt the central business district on the north, under the all-important Montgomery Road. The originally proposed interchange there was eliminated, much to the relief of the Ohio Department of Highways—which, in typical highway engineers' fashion, had assumed that this feature would be the price to pay for securing grade approval. Instead, it was agreed that two interchanges would be provided, with proper traffic controls for convenient ingress and egress control to the east and west of the bottleneck. Good access would be had to both, through an improved city-thoroughfare system. An anlaysis of costs indicated that our solution would be about $1.8 million under the highway department's line of $10 million. Some adjustments were made, and some good features of the highway department's proposal were salvaged. Eventually, about half of each route was agreed on at a meeting in January 1960, and the ultimate cost estimate came out about as expected. All concerned had cooperated splendidly, and engineers and planners once more had profited from one another's skills for the benefit of those who pay the salaries and fees: the taxpayers.

Urban Renewal Was the Answer

Encouraged by these events, the merchants became bolder and asked for a comprehensive parking program for downtown. In anticipation of such a request, the Master Plan of 1960 included a penetrating parking study. Under prevailing circumstances, the program called for fairly extensive property acquisition. Typically, when such a program becomes public knowledge—as it invariably will, from its inception, in a smaller city—land prices have a way of rising sharply, and the willingness to sell, let alone be the first to make a deal, diminishes at about the same rapid pace. Under the diligent guidance of George Kleb, former mayor and then planning commissioner, every path was explored and no stone left unturned to implement the parking program. Politically, it quickly became clear that the downtown interests would have to foot the bill in the form of special assessments and that the community at large was not interested in underwriting a partial solution to downtown problems. The public perceived downtown as becoming rapidly obsolete, in comparison with the new shopping centers that began to spring up throughout the Cincinnati metropolitan area. The price was too high, and downtown interests reluctantly accepted the bitter pill. It is to their everlasting credit, however, that they refused to give up.

National trends were in their favor. John F. Kennedy had just become president of the United States. The old Housing and Home Finance Agency (HHFA), after some stagnation under the Eisenhower administration, began to look forward to becoming the U.S. Department of Housing and became enterprising once more; people's attitudes were generally up-beat. The merchants and the city council agreed that urban renewal might be just the opportunity Norwood had been waiting for. Accordingly, we prepared a general neighborhood-renewal plan (GNRP), which, at the time, was the next step after the master plan—a more particularized program document leading directly to specific projects.[3] Issued in 1963, the GNRP set forth the following objectives:

> The General Neighborhood Renewal Plan for the Central Business District of this community shall accomplish, among other elements, the following:

1. Replace all obsolete or dilapidated buildings in the present central commercial area and develop in one of the sectors of said area a modern efficiently designed and attractive community or subregional shopping center;
2. Accommodate in suitable office and other commercial buildings those uses which are not normally accommodated in such a shopping center;
3. Provide an expansion area for Norwood's largest employer, the Chevrolet-Fisher Body Plant of the General Motors' Corporation which adjoins the business district to the northeast;
4. Provide for hotel and restaurant facilities of a high standard to serve business, industry and the community as a whole;
5. Provide for the expansion of the Cincinnati Branch of Miami University now operating in the Norwood High School which adjoins the business district to the west; and
6. Explore the feasibility of providing medium and high density low and middle income housing in certain areas adjoining the business district.

> The contemplated renewal effort shall be of such scope and magnitude that it will create an entirely new and improved image of the City of Norwood in general and of its central area in particular. Every effort shall be made to create through urban renewal a new focal point of business, public and community life for Norwood and for this part of the Greater Cincinnati metropolitan area (see figure 8-1).[4]

Under the no-nonsense leadership and administration of lawyer Joe Shea, Jr., and the meticulous, superb management of council affairs by city council president William Cosgrove, the city of Norwood moved to achieve these objectives with determination and dedication.

NORWOOD'S CHAMBER OF COMMERCE, CIVIC LEADERS, INDUSTRIAL LEADERS, URBAN RENEWAL CITIZEN'S ADVISORY COMMITTEE AND YOUR CITY ADMINISTRATION

Proudly Present **NORWOOD'S NEW LOOK**

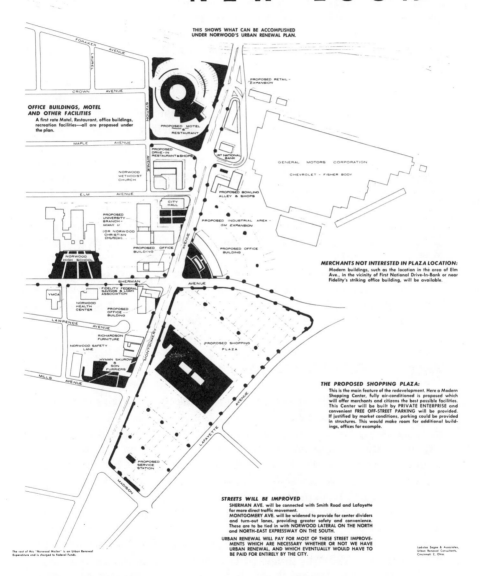

Figure 8-1. Norwood, Ohio: Renewal Plan

The CBD was well defined by major streets and land uses so as to provide boundaries sound enough to allow it to function as an independent unit, but not so formidable as to create an isolated area, which might thereby be prevented from being an integral part of the city. Of the sixty-five total acres in the CBD, fifteen acres, or approximately 23 percent, were roads and public rights-of-way. Commercial uses comprised thirty-four acres, or 50 percent; public uses, about three acres, or 5 percent; and residential uses, only two acres, or 3 percent. A large industrial district adjoins the eastern CBD boundary and further solidifies the nonresidential nature of the CBD, as opposed to the uses immediately to the southeast and west.

At the time of the initial renewal, many land uses typically associated with CBD functions had left the city and had given way to loan companies, clubs, and billiard parlors—generally marginal enterprises. There were noteworthy exceptions, as, for example, Mr. Steinberg's clothing store—a Norwood institution.

However, obsolescence and disorientation, lack of parking and good circulation, neglect, and decay were in evidence everywhere. A careful building-by-building structural analysis, required to qualify for federal urban-renewal assistance, revealed that most structures were severely deficient and unsafe or obsolete by reason of design. Many vacancies existed. Here and there, squatters passing through the city would temporarily occupy one or another building, just to be swiftly chased away by the very watchful Norwood Police Department. Prevailing environmental conditions reflected the structural conditions of the CBD. So frustrated were the remaining merchants and property owners that a dramatic showing had to be made to demonstrate that there might be hope yet.

Pappy Shea Builds a Hotel and Shopping Mall

Industrial management indicated to me repeatedly that their principal problem in Norwood was the complete absence of a modern hotel and accompanying eating facilities. Managers had to travel to locations in the Cincinnati area, distant and inconvenient, to attend to their frequent business visitors. A market analysis confirmed the feasibility of a hotel in downtown Norwood. Joseph W. Shea, Sr., known affectionately by all as Pappy Shea, had just resigned from the city council after a lifetime of political service; he agreed to become Norwood's first and, as it turned out, only urban-renewal director. Mr. Shea turned Norwood around. The old gentleman was to become the driving force that pushed the program through local obstacles and the sometimes ridiculous jungle of federal urban-renewal bureaucracy.

Mr. Shea and I agreed that it was opportune to take advantage of the ground swell and interest in a hotel facility, and he engineered a major public-information campaign, which coincided with a municipal election and bond issue. An overwhelming endorsement was secured for urban renewal of downtown Norwood, which, in time, would create a new focal point and rallying center for the city. Based on the approved GNRP, the city council requested permission from HHFA to tackle the entire sixty-five-acre area as a single urban-renewal project. This position reflected our suspicion of all federal programs, which, all good intentions notwithstanding, all too often are discontinued or drastically changed in midstream, leaving the local participants holding the bag. HHFA agreed to manage the renewal effort in three projects, as portrayed by figure 8-2. The city council was assured repeatedly by field representatives and the regional director in Chicago that the approval of the GNRP should be guarantee enough that HHFA fully intended to see the program through to its ultimate conclusion.

Pappy Shea, being a pragmatist, wasted no time with theory. He moved swiftly into the first project, which, of course, would produce the much-needed hotel and restaurant. Project Ohio R-71 was a resounding success. Mr. Frisch of Frisch's Big Boy, a native of Norwood, took great personal pride in building an attractive 151-room medium-highrise building. Located on relatively high elevation, it can be seen clearly for some distance, and access by way of the Norwood lateral is convenient. The Norwood Quality Courts Hotel is one of the few hotels in the region that enjoys nearly 100 percent occupancy the week around. It is now in its second decade, and its elegant, spacious restaurant was recently further enlarged, having become a major gathering place for all kinds of public and private groups and individuals, not only in Norwood but from the entire metropolitan area.

Encouraged by this success, Norwood almost routinely endorsed the second project, Ohio R-83, the southernmost element of the CBD. This was the acid test of the theory that, in most situations of CBD decay, it is preferable to remove the blight, clear the site, and build a modern retail facility, accompanied by such other uses, as offices and apartments, as can be accommodated under prevailing conditions. A large superblock was carved out, code-named Nor-Center Shopping Plaza. More than one hundred properties were involved; utilities and access streets had to be reconstructed, and complex negotiations for business relocation payments had to be carried out. Technical services were provided by several engineering firms and myself and by appraisers and attorneys. All did their assigned jobs very well, which was not surprising, because Pappy Shea not only remained the spiritual leader of the group but had emerged as a capable executive who could handle every situation. He could do it in a way that made people cooperate and caused those adversely affected by his decisions to walk away, perhaps not thrilled, but with the conviction that they had been dealt with fairly. Jack Cotton, partner of Howard, Needles, Tammen and

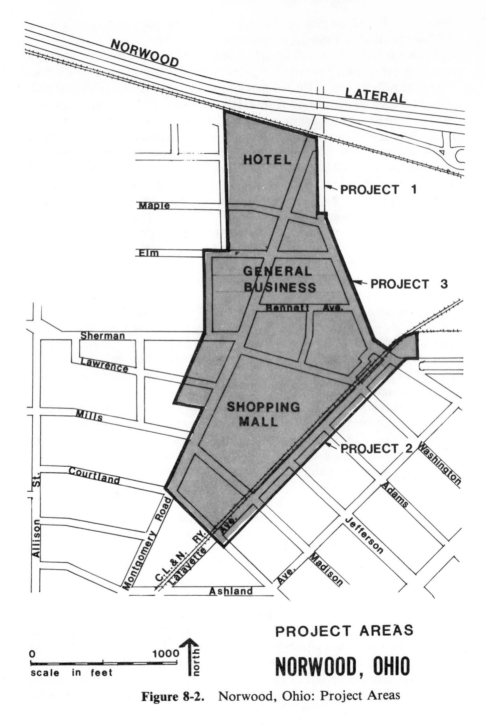

Figure 8-2.   Norwood, Ohio: Project Areas

Bergendoff, then engineer in charge of street and utility design for Nor-Center II, remarked that Pappy Shea was the "very soul" of the redevelopment program.[5] Joseph Shea, Sr., was a dedicated, highly principled man whose greatest reward was to be beloved by the people of Norwood. Nor-Center II was cleared in October 1965 and sold to an investment group headed by Carl and Robert Lindner, Cincinnati financiers. In accordance with the urban-renewal plans, a shopping mall was constructed, which enjoys a thriving business. Surrey Square has replaced an obsolete downtown and, with the Quality Courts Hotel, has given Norwood a new identity. All told, a public investment of some $8 million has produced a major addition to the local tax base in place of urban blight, as well as numerous jobs and inducements to others to upgrade their facilities. While the urban renewal program was under way, General Motors constructed a major parking garage adjacent to the area, and Mr. Steinberg replaced his old store with an attractive new one. Norwood kept its promise; I wish I could report that the government kept its commitment too.

Guess Who Copped Out?

The third project, widening of the remainder of Montgomery Road between Nor-Center I and Nor-Center II, became the victim of changed federal policy when commercial projects were suddenly out of favor. To this day, that linkage remains to be accomplished. However, the people of Norwood have not given up. A recent property acquisition in that small section and the authorization of a new commercial building carefully observed the setback lines, established under the renewal plans years ago, so that the widened Montgomery Road, when and if accomplished, will have no difficulty fitting into its predetermined slot. That is planning; that is the right spirit.[6]

Council Bluffs, Iowa, Follows the Norwood Model

Similarities

Like Norwood, Council Bluffs, Iowa, is part of a larger metropolitan community. The Omaha-Council Bluffs area consists of two distinct elements: the Nebraska part and the Iowa part. Most urban development over the years has occurred in Nebraska, and Omaha's physical characteristics are typical of the river town: a lopsided development away from the river with a central industrial and business district that lacks the fourth side of the trade area. In the Omaha region, Council Bluffs, on the opposite side of the Missouri, held its own for many years and was more than a mere satellite. It was a trade center in its own right and the focal point of an extensive agricultural region to the east.

Retail business prospered until the advent of the regional shopping center began to undermine the once-solid position of downtown Council Bluffs. Merchants, property owners, and financial institutions realized in the late 1960s that the central business district was rapidly approaching collapse, while Omaha seemed to have adjusted very well to changing conditions. A planning team was called in, under my direction, which proceeded systematically to lay before the city council the issues and perils perceived by all who had taken the trouble to examine prevailing conditions in the area. There was much talk about possible refurbishing of buildings, provision of more free off-street parking, and other amenities to halt the rapidly progressing decline. Based on my experience in Norwood, I advised the city administration that any piecemeal measure would merely be a waste of the taxpayer's money, would raise false hopes, and might contribute to even more accelerated deterioration and loss of business, which, of course, always equates with loss of tax revenue.

Action

The community was very fortunate to have enterprising leadership in Pete Pakey, city manager, and Dale Ball, vice-president of the First National Bank of Council Bluffs, which had considerable financial interests in the area. Both gentlemen accepted the notion that only drastic measures would have a chance to turn matters around. If Council Bluffs was to retain any kind of strength in the retail business of the metropolitan region, it would have to come up with a first-rate retail center. Under prevailing circumstances, this would only be possible through clearance of an adequate downtown site for a shopping mall, as was done in Norwood with much success.

The city council, with some reluctance, eventually approved the urban-renewal approach to the problem and authorized the initiation of an areawide planning program in the form of a general neighborhood-renewal program and a current clearance project of a ten-block area (Iowa R-29).[7] This ten-block pilot project was planned to be one of five projects. It would provide approximately twenty acres of land for a compact shopping mall and related facilities. In addition to the clearance effort, traffic circulation would be substantially improved through relocation of several streets and corresponding intersectional modifications, as portrayed in figure 8-3. In some areas, where appropriate, rehabilitation programs were initiated to accommodate business enterprises that probably would not locate in the new shopping mall.

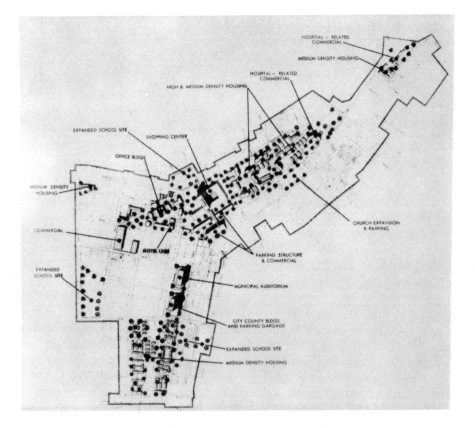

Figure 8-3.   Council Bluffs, Iowa: Downtown Renewal Plan

Because of a change in federal policies, the initial project was to become the only clearance project in the Council Bluffs central business district. Nevertheless, the ten-block site was cleared, and the reconditioned site was sold to the Midland Corporation, a locally organized development company. Midland Mall was built, containing a retail mall and office space, altogether approximately 350,000 square feet of enclosed space, plus off-street parking for 1,250 cars. The parking facility was provided by the city. Principal stores in the mall are Sears, Roebuck and Company and Brandeis and Philips department stores. These companies, together with some fifty other enterprises, are now the core of the new central business district of Council Bluffs. Since there can be no more federally financed urban renewal in the foreseeable future, and since there appears to be no other source of funds for similar operations, one could not expect acquisition of one's deteriorating property by others. This condition, and the apparent success of the mall that opened in 1976, induced several property owners to make substantial improvements on their own. A process had been triggered that allowed Council Bluffs to regain a lost position within the economic community of the Omaha-Council Bluffs metropolitan area.[8]

Notes

1. Cincinnati, Ohio, City Plan Commission, "Metropolitan Master Plan," 1948 (Prepared by Sherwood L. Reeder, director; Ladislas Segoe and Tracy Augur, general consultants; and De Leuw, Cather and Co.).

2. Norwood, Ohio, "Master Plan," 1960 (Prepared by L. Segoe and Associates; W.G. Roeseler, planner-in-charge).

3. Norwood, Ohio, "General Neighborhood Renewal Plan for the Central Business District," 1963, Ohio 57 GN (W.G. Roeseler, planner-in-charge). As a municipality with less than 50,000 population, Norwood qualified under Title I rules for a three-fourths federal capital grant to cover the net cost of every urban-renewal project. The balance had to be covered by local cash and noncash contributions. Cost was computed to include land acquisition; demolition of existing structures and site preparation; construction of required public facilities, such as streets and utilities; land-disposition costs; and planning, engineering, and administrative expenses. Proceeds from the sale of the land would be deducted from gross costs to arrive at net project costs. Relocation expenses were covered by separate grants not charged against the project. These projects were carried out under the Housing Act of 1949, as amended in 1954 and subsequently.

4. Ibid.

5. Project reports to the old Housing and Home Finance Agency, later the U.S. Department of Housing and Urban Development, for projects Ohio R-71 and Ohio R-83. Note, also, the 1969 update of the Norwood master plan by Howard, Needles, Tammen and Bergendoff (Douglas C. Smith, planner-in-charge).

6. "Norwood, Ohio—Central Business District Redevelopment, Third Phase," 1973 (Prepared by W.G. Roeseler, consulting city planner).

7. Council Bluffs, Iowa, "General Neighborhood Renewal Plan," 1967, Iowa R-21 GN (Prepared by Howard, Needles, Tammen and Bergendoff, Consulting Engineers, Kansas City, under the direction of W.G. Roeseler); Council Bluffs, Iowa, "Moving Ahead" (Popular brochure on the program, by Douglas C. Smith).

8. Council Bluffs, Iowa, "Regional and Urban Comprehensive Plan," 1969 (Prepared by Howard, Needles, Tammen and Bergendoff, Consulting Engineers, Kansas City, under the direction of Clare A. Russie).

Autonomous Cities

Winona and Rochester, Minnesota:
Cities of the Northern Plains

The urban plans for Winona in 1959[1] and for Rochester in 1960[2] are classics in the comprehensive-planning literature. Urban and regional planning, like other applied sciences, finds its literary expression not so much in works about the process as in the plan documents written for a specific situation. This is where the planner merges theory and practice into a useful tool and where effectiveness or failure quickly becomes evident. In other words, the impact of urban planning can be studied only by examining the plans directly in the actual context in which they were prepared and applied over some discernible period of time and under competent direction.

The Winona and Rochester plans are useful examples for several reasons. Both cities are well established and clearly structured from the point of view of physical form and layout; and both communities are homogeneous in the composition of their populations. The plan documents would easily satisfy the criteria of comprehensive planning as set forth by the planning purists but would also typify the plans of the much more aggressive Segoe planning organization, by addressing, if not solving, specific categorical problems that may well have caused the planning process to be initiated in the first place. As to form, both documents contain about a hundred letter-sized pages of explanatory text, which is well organized and accompanied by essential technical data in tabular or graphic form. Both documents are generously illustrated by some thirty designs, plans, maps, and photographs.

Data Base

In both instances, the foundation for planning is carefully laid by thorough demographic studies and microeconomic analysis. The full spectrum of social characteristics is traced over several decades, and causes of change are identified and explained where possible and significant for planning purposes. Data are not produced for their own sake merely because something might be interesting to know; they are researched for specific reasons relating directly to the planning process. To orient the reader and to

153

allow him to see the data base in perspective, to put the reader in a position to judge whether a statistical configuration may suggest positive or negative tendencies, and to establish applicable norms against which local conditions may be measured, the plan base studies compare communities of the same or slightly larger size with the state as a whole (Minnesota in this case); with all other urban communities in the state (Minnesota urban); with the respective counties (Winona and Olmsted); and with the United States. Initially, trends are projected then adjusted into forecasts on the basis of a variety of factors flowing from both subsequent demographic analysis and microeconomic studies.

One of these is a study of population composition, which offers insights into demand for specialized facilities, such as schools and recreation areas for various age groups. Characteristics of age, sex, ethnic origin, education, occupation, and family income and size are among the elements analyzed and forecasted. The cohort-survival method of population forecasting is used, augmented by studies of inmigration and outmigration, possibly prompted during the plan-forecast period by anticipated changes in economic factors that affect the communities. Economic analysis takes place concurrently with the population studies, and each must be calibrated or adjusted against the other. During the plan phases of the program, demographic findings are transformed into plan elements to serve the public as effectively as possible.

The demographic element concludes with a range of probable future population levels and some indication of most likely characteristics of composition. In the case of Winona, not much change was anticipated. The city was expected to remain at approximately 30,000, on a steady, even course. For the Mayo Clinic city, Rochester, however, substantial growth was anticipated over the next quarter-century, and the forecasts called for an increase from the existing 40,000 in 1960 to some 60,000 by 1980. Both prognostications turned out to be realistic.

Neither plan was satisfied with mere numerical forecasts. Based on a study of the existing distribution of population and the conditions under which residential and nonresidential development had taken place, an attempt was made to anticipate probable future population and activities distribution. In one instance, this meant merely minor adjustments; in the other, it meant accommodating new growth. More than any other phase of comprehensive planning, these population-distribution scenarios illustrate the intricate interactive nature of the process, the consistent holistic, analytical methodology that penetrates all procedures, from the data base through the physical design into fiscal or regulatory efforts for implementation and administration.

Demographic and microeconomic analyses rely on technical and fundamental interpretation of data and trends. In many ways, they are really one and the same operation, looking at the client from different points of view. Purely technical, statistical relationship will provide a quick, initial overview of the situation, while the more penetrating analysis of fundamentals will eventually provide greater insight into the workings and, consequently, probable future behavior of the local economy in the context of regional and national trends. Our two sample plans developed this information on the basis of sector analyses for the two economies that included intensive dialogues with management and labor at the local and regional level. Winona emerged as a diversified industrial and trade center in a strong agricultural region, well served by all modes of transportation. Rochester, of course, is, first of all, the world-renowned medical center, focused on the Mayo Clinic and its supporting facilities. However, it is also an agricultural-trade center, and, at the time of plan preparation, it had just entered the era of sophisticated electronics manufacturing, with the location of a giant IBM plant designed by Eero Saarinen.

Following these studies, both plans take a long, hard look at the physical characteristics of the community. Land use is painstakingly surveyed in the field and mapped at a scale of 1 inch for 200 feet, with base maps taken from a recent aerial-mapping program. Some thirty categories of land use are distinguished and portrayed in color, by hand. An atlas is produced, which is to serve as a major reference work in the zoning-enforcement office. This activity is also an invaluable tool for the plan designer, for nothing provides such an intimate view of the community as land-use field observation and subsequent recording. Augmenting the land-use data, utilities, public services in general, and street conditions are also mapped or noted. Service capability is reviewed with the respective agencies, and urban-service scenarios are developed for assumed varying levels of population from which, ultimately, a key element of the land-use plan emerges.

Traffic flow, including specific traffic problems, is surveyed and documented, together with a comprehensive field survey of parking requirements in the central business district. These surveys allow for pleasant and interesting interactions with the community, for they can be successfully executed only with much community support. News media, civic organizations, and high-school or college classes became fine participants in the survey process to gain a better insight into the objectives of planning. Understanding the process and its purposes goes a long way toward acceptance, and that, in turn, makes a convincing salesperson. The community must be a part of the effort, or nothing will happen. Finally, urban-development suitability is further analyzed by studies of soils and subsoils, topography, water- and air-pollution matters, and other environmental issues. In Winona and Rochester, water courses and hillsides received particular attention. The majestic Mississippi River and the bluffs at Winona stand in sharp contrast to the flat, barely rolling landscape of the northern prairie at Rochester.

Creative Planning

The plan elements of the comprehensive plans feature, first and foremost, circulation, which required much attention in both cities. Accordingly, the thoroughfare plans are meticulously executed. A well-defined street-classification system is established, appropriately illustrating engineering street cross sections for each type of street and thoroughfare. Every primary and secondary artery for which changes, extensions, or new sections are recommended is reviewed in the text in sufficient detail to allow the engineer to pick up where the planners left off, fully understanding the intent of the proposal. Occasionally, alternatives are offered, with comments on pros and cons for each. With an eye on reserving certain private property for future public use where reasonable, suggested setback lines are set forth on the thoroughfare-plan map. Desirable ultimate roadway width is also given, with the suggestion that it may be achieved in stages. Negotiating agreement during the initial planning stages on future street right-of-way width can save the taxpayer substantial funds in the future, because much of that right-of-way can be acquired gradually through the subdivision process without undue hardship to the developer. In fact, a firm commitment to future streets—their classification and width—offers numerous advantages to the subdivider and is welcome by all competent land developers, as it removes uncertainty from land planning by private enterprise within the framework planning by municipal and county planning agencies. The street plan is rounded out by a series of sketches of more complex, specific intersectional situations. This technique is also applied to ingress-egress solutions for major traffic generators, such as shopping centers. Management of traffic, from curb cuts to signalization and directional control, is viewed as an integral part of the planning process. In this sense, both plans mold long-range elements and shorter-range objectives into useful tools for the municipal technical manager in planning, engineering, and fiscal affairs. Other plan elements—such as public buildings, public schools, and public-recreation facilities—are treated with the care and particularity warranted at the time. Both communities had vital interests in the future of their central business districts. In both situations, plans of considerable sophistication were presented. In Winona, these plans sparked substantial urban-renewal and rehabilitation programs. The culmination of each plan, however, was the land-use plan, which Ladislas Segoe called the one element of the planning process that "really was *the plan.*"

The land-use plans, figures 9-1 and 9-2, pull all the plan elements together and provide the ultimate test of effective integration and coordination. They are, first, maps that portray the study area at some point in time when all will have been accomplished that is envisaged by the plan—all public and private improvement. Since it is unlikely that all proposals will ever be carried out, or carried out as anticipated at the time of plan conception, one must take any land-use plan as a scenario of probable future achievement, not as an undisputable dictum. It is a holistic design and, to some extent, merely the sum total of concepts and quantities of services and facilities that should eventually be provided if the standards of urbanization set forth in the planning process are to prevail. Since change is the very essence of life, the land-use plan in this sense may be looked upon primarily as a gauge of accomplishments and as a means that requires decision makers and the public to justify and document to themselves why they found it advisable to deviate from the plan. The plan itself, as Alfred Bettman would remind us time and again, is considered to further the public health, safety, morals, convenience, and general welfare, because those who designed it are presumed to have applied scientific principles representing the state of the art at the time the document was produced. It follows, then, that any amendment or modification must also meet these criteria, and a change of conditions must have occurred to justify the plan revision. Without such change of condition, any modification of plans would be clearly illogical.

In this context, the land-use plan is not merely a composite picture of the plan elements. Public policy and reasons for regulatory or fiscal measures are enunciated in it. To this end, both plans had previously divided the cities into residential neighborhoods and nonresidential planning areas. Each such planning entity would relate geographically to other units of surveying or measuring, such as traffic zones (or U.S. census tracts in the larger cities). The planning areas would serve, of course, as convenient units of reference and organization. More important, however, they would become the organizational nucleus of public participation, as every effort would be made to secure permanent representation of the public at large from these entities. Naturally, organizations have their ups and downs and will vary with circumstances. By and large, unless there is an immediate local crisis, people tend to lose interest. Consequently, the seasoned planning administrator will be careful not to overextend his welcome in this group and will call on the citizens only if and when it is truly warranted and their time is not wasted with trivia.

The planning-area analysis pioneered by Segoe in the early Cincinnati, Ohio, and Madison, Wisconsin, plan offers opportunities to outline, in the plan document, reasons for recommendations relating to population density or nonresidential intensity of land use in relation to the capacity of the urban-service infrastructure: height and bulk limitations of structures for

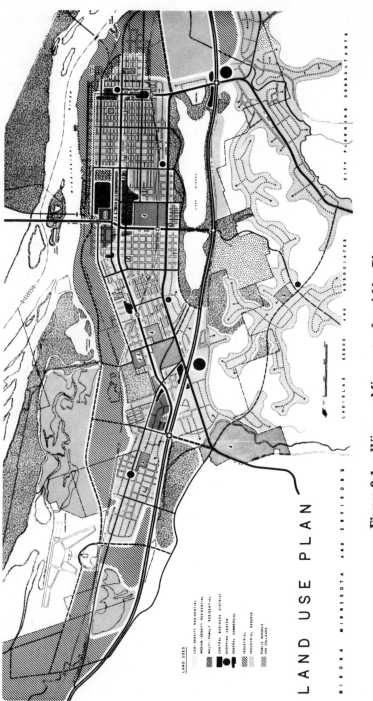

Figure 9-1.   Winona, Minnesota: Land-Use Plan

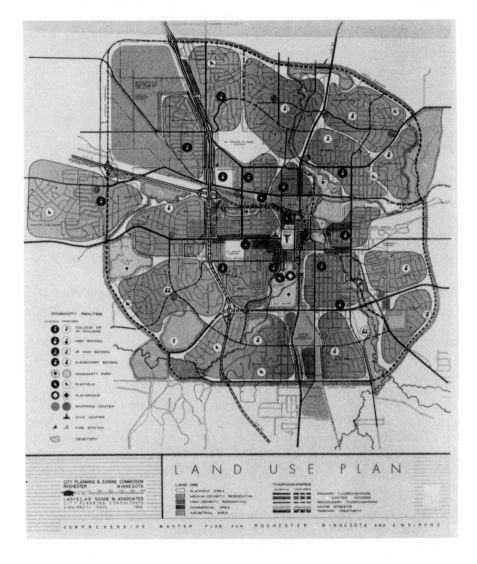

Figure 9-2. Rochester, Minnesota: Land-Use Plan

light and air access, fire safety, or purely aesthetic objectives of view and exposure; development hazards, such as landslides or flooding; or any other locally significant ecological consideration. If these issues are not settled, at least a sound basis for further study and deliberation is established. When issues can be settled and find their way in some form into regulatory measures, especially zoning ordiances, a thorough discussion of all pertinent

factors in the land-use plan will offer a formidable defense in case of litigation under any of the police-power applications of plan implementation.
Conversely, failure to provide scientific justification and evidence has
caused many a lawsuit to be lost for lack of adequate planning foundation.

The land-use plan is also where issues of special community concern,
which may well have been the underlying cause of the political actions that
led to the current planning program, may be reviewed. In Winona, in addition to circulation problems, matters of hospital and general medical-care-
delivery systems were of interest, as were riverfront development and control, railroad grade separations, and downtown renewal. In Rochester, the
main problem was circulation, of course, but equally pressing were
problems of managing and coordinating growth; annexation policies,
medical-center development, downtown reclamation, public-works programming for capital improvements, and tax issues. Both communities were
keenly interested in effective zoning and subdivision administration and in
strengthening in-house capabilities for planning.

Winona adopted its plans and regulations swiftly under the expert
leadership of Mayor Lloyd E. Peiffer, city council president William P.
Theurer, planning commission chairman E.J. Sievers, and city engineer
James J. Kleinschmidt—effectively supported by the council and the plan
commission. The city worked in unison; the public at large was in concert
with their business leadership, and that leadership was the political force,
because public service was both an honor and a responsibility. The results
are significant. In Rochester, it took a few years longer to secure plan and
regulation adoption. However, ably managed by planning director Tom O.
Moore and with new people on boards and commissions, in time, all proper
steps were taken. Professionals serving on the planning commission—John
Brengman and Don Grue, for example—did their best to achieve success.
Both plan documents have been kept current. Says Mr. Moore in a recent
survey:

> Under the Plan, many streets and utility systems were developed, too
> numerous to list; seven new schools, four new parks, and one new fire sta-
> tion were built; and parking facilities constructed. The Zoning and Sub-
> division Ordinances were adopted. The Plan pulled things together and
> gave the community direction. It allowed private interests to gear their
> activities in harmony with the city and provided a basis for all operating
> departments of the city to follow an integrated program.[3]

However, with respect to downtown, Mr. Moore comments that the
plan was "too visionary" for the people at the time. Had they taken the
plan's warning seriously, they might have prevented the ultimate loss of
their key position in retailing in the area. One cannot blame the merchants
of that period, for, so long as there is income, there is reluctance to change.

The economist and planner is often cast in a frustrating role; he can see the problem, and prescribe a good solution, but he cannot step in and provide the capital needed to carry out his prescriptions. It is really not his role, and he cannot prove that his analysis is absolutely fail-safe. Therein lies the fundamental difference of planner-analyst functioning in the public sector or in private industry. In the private environment, the planner becomes a responsible manager at times, when he changes roles and function. Nevertheless, the Rochester planning program initiated over twenty years ago, according to Tom Moore—who has been an active participant from the beginning—was successful and has served a very useful purpose.

In Winona, Adolph Bremer of the *Winona Daily News* reported in a recent telephone interview that the 1959 comprehensive plan was the unquestioned catalyst that pulled the town together behind attainable objectives. It led to numerous achievements, including the construction of a truck route along the Mississippi River, flood-control works by the U.S. Army Corps of Engineers; downtown refurbishing; riverfront and park developments; hospital improvements; and the evolution of an effective community development program staffed by competent personnel. Much of the credit for this success story goes to Adolph Bremer and the *Winona Daily News*. Mr. Bremer, a sensitive, capable reporter with a keen interest in public affairs, was the best friend a young planner could have found twenty years ago. It was with much pride that I personally prepared the documentation called for in nominating the *Winona Daily News* for the National Journalism Award of the American Society of Planning Officials (ASPO) in 1960. I was humbled, indeed, when the *Winona Daily News* asked me to accept the coveted award for them from ASPO executive director Dennis O'Harrow at the National Planning Conference in Miami Beach that same year. Five other newspapers received the recognition at that time, including the *Chicago Sun Times,* the *Milwaukee Journal,* the *New York Times,* the *Monterey Peninsula Herald,* and the *Minneapolis Star*—distinguished company, indeed. The award reads: "To the *Winona Daily News* (Minnesota), for excellence in continued interpretation of planning, and creating public opinion favorable for adoption of specific planning programs."[4]

Zanesville, Ohio: Echoes of Appalachia

In the 1950s, Zanesville, Ohio, though not entirely depressed, nevertheless gave the impression of being a bit "down at the heels." Zanesville's once-prosperous tile and pottery industry had fallen on hard times. A number of manufacturers had gone out of business, and conditions generally left much to be desired. Actually, Zanesville by that time had managed to diversify considerably, and economic downtrends had been arrested. However, in the eyes of the public, much remained to be done, particularly in city government. Located at the confluence of the Muskingum and Licking Rivers, some fifty miles east of Columbus, Zanesville had received national attention on several occasions in the past. It is the only city in North America with a Y-shaped concrete bridge (constructed in 1902), which connects the east bank of the Muskingum with both sides of the Licking River on the west bank. Following the devastating flood of 1913, which severely affected several Ohio Towns, Zanesville benefited from massive federal aid in the form of flood works constructed by the U.S. Army Corps of Engineers in the Muskingum Valley, including some fourteen reservoirs. The last of the major flood works, the Dillon Dam and Reservoir on the Licking River, was not completed until 1960. During the period following World War II, public works had fallen into disrepair, and the overall impression of the city was less than favorable. However, civic interests were rekindled, perhaps in response to a wide variety of government-sponsored programs and activities that promised solutions for conditions that otherwise might have been written off as hopeless. Moreover, in central Ohio, communities watched with keen interest the plans for Interstate 70 advanced by the Ohio Department of Highways, which would bring employment and cash to many places along the way, especially to those eastern Ohio communities that were not doing well at that time. The immediate result of the newly developing public interest was the installation of the council-manager form of municipal government, replacing the antiquated commission form, which was blamed, perhaps rightfully, for much of the inefficiency and decay.

The new administration initiated a comprehensive urban-planning program. Such people as Paul Mobes, Marvin Rutherford, and others provided the required political leadership to assure reasonable public support and involvement in the new planning activities. City managers Richard Custer and Samuel Grey and planner Theodore G. Steinbach provided outstanding managerial and technical direction, and, within a rather short period of time, the Zanesville city government was transformed into a businesslike operation.

In the planning area, Segoe and Associates of Cincinnati was engaged to prepare, under the effective direction of Charles W. Matthews, a comprehensive plan, zoning regulations, a subdivision ordinance, and a capital-improvements program.[5] These instruments were prepared in 1960-1962 and adopted in 1964. Each year, the plan is adjusted as required, and the capital-improvements program is carried forward for the next budget period. Housing maintenance and fire-prevention codes were added to the list of regulatory measures, together with an architectural-design code for certain areas and selected improvements. The plan was sufficiently broad to serve as the basis for a number of federal-assistance programs that were then available to communities with a somewhat depressed economy.

The Economic Development Administration, in particular, under its accelerated public-works program, made several capital grants to the city, which produced a safety center and major additions to the much-neglected sewerage and water systems of the community. One immediate and initially not anticipated result of the improved sanitary facilities was the location of a two-year college of the Ohio system in Zanesville.

Interstate 70 was constructed through the northern section of the city, and U.S. 20 was relocated by the Ohio Department of Highways, in accordance with the comprehensive plan. Numerous other street improvements were made—some with local funds, some jointly with state allocations. Several parks were acquired and developed.

The community regained pride in itself but remained frustrated by the fact that substantial urban blight continued to persist, particularly in the central area of town. It was at that juncture that the city council authorized an exploratory study of urban renewal in the form of a community-renewal program (CRP). That was the mechanism of the period to move from the broad master-plan concepts closer to specific redevelopment programs without actually initiating a project.

From a planning-systems point of view, the concept of community-renewal programs advanced by the U.S. Department of Housing and Urban Development had its merits. It provided the community with an equivalent to the transportation studies sponsored by the U.S. Department of Transportation—a mechanism to deal more directly with specific issues of development than can be achieved under the typical comprehensive plan. Of course, by necessity, the CRP could never attain the kind of impact that a transportation study would have, because many of the CRP's issues were with privately owned property, where entirely different standards and considerations of legitimate public interest prevail. However, in skillful hands, the CRP could serve a good purpose, as it did in Zanesville.

A series of four studies was produced by consultants that outlined opportunities with respect to social, economic, and environmental-physical resources of the community, as potentially augmented by then-existing federal-assistance programs, and the urban-design concepts that might be given consideration in that process.[6] Much of the city was subjected to critical analysis, leading repeatedly to the conclusion that lower-income housing and jobs were the most important elements of further economic recovery. The order of magnitude of redevelopment needs was truly overwhelming. By federal standards, perhaps as much as one-third of the community would in some way be eligible for slum clearance.

In order to establish priorities within the framework of anticipated market conditions in central Ohio, many avenues were explored.

To provide some relief for those most adversely affected by economic decline, Mr. Steinbach, with the never-tiring support of Harley Flack, an

outstanding black community leader, initiated several significant social programs, including the Older American Program for a wide range of activities; the Community Action Program for the public at large; day-care
centers; a health program; neighborhood play-lot programs. As Mr.
Steinbach points out, although the comprehensive plan was excellent with
respect to physical features and facilities, it lacked the short-term view so
essential in social-services planning. That gap was filled by the CRP.[7]
However, the physical-planning aspects were by no means neglected. Of the
several redevelopment opportunities that enjoyed support, I urged the
council to select, as its first attempt in this controversial field, a project that
was immediately named Project Job Opportunity (see figure 9-3).

Located adjacent to the downtown area, in the Underwood neighborhood, the ninety-acre tract abutted Interstate 70, one of the country's most
important and busiest highways, practically at the outskirts of Ohio's state

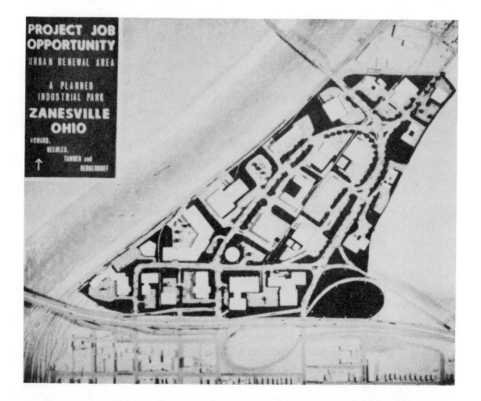

Figure 9-3. Project "Job Opportunity," Zanesville, Ohio

capital. Relocation seemed manageable for Zanesville, although some 500 families—all low-income—would have to be housed in standard dwellings under city and federal regulations, and about fifty business establishments would be displaced.

City government wasted no time in authorizing the planners to initiate a total slum-clearance project there, to be known as Ohio R-97. This was no simple task. In order to accomplish the relocation of the families, the city's housing authority began construction of nearly 300 dwelling units under HUD's Section 221-d-3 and 236 housing programs. In retrospect, this seems reasonable. Unfortunately, HUD's bureaucracy made the entire program nearly a nightmare, involving everybody from the local congressman to a deputy undersecretary, as well as the Chicago regional office. The inability of the federal agency to make swift and binding commitments unquestionably was the ultimate downfall of the entire urban-redevelopment program under Title I of the several housing and urban development acts. The popular Community Block Grant Program was, indeed, a material improvement over past practices.

Eventually, however, the job was accomplished. In a recent survey, John Ray, community development director of Zanesville since 1976, reported that Project Job Opportunity was a successful project.[8] He stated that all but two parcels have been sold and that a substantial amount of construction has been accomplished by private enterprise, including a Pepsi-Cola bottling plant, a pipeline-supply contracting establishment, office buildings, and other related establishments. He also mentioned that the Ohio Department of Highways completed its part in the project—the reconstruction of Underwood Street, including construction of a new bridge across the Muskingum River. Moreover, unsightly and unhealthy slums have been removed. The former occupants of that area are now housed in standard dwellings at rental rates they can afford. New employment opportunities have been created by the enterprises that have moved to town and located in the project area. The area has been equipped with a modern urban infrastructure in streets and utilities and enjoys sensible, protective zoning restrictions that should maximize investment and effectively prevent the recurrence of blight in the future. The public is proud of the project, says Mr. Ray, in assessing the effectiveness of urban renewal there. However, the city council would be reluctant to work again with any federal agency under conditions similar to those of the old categorical urban-renewal program under Title I of the housing act, directed, in fact, by administrators who were hundreds of miles away from the public they attempted to serve. It is to the credit of the planning profession that many individuals managed to achieve good results under these often-frustrating circumstances.

The last major accomplishment under Zanesville's urban-planning effort of the last twenty-five years was the acquisition and development of five parks under an open-space program. Plans for this project were drawn up in 1968 by Charles W. Matthews, of Cincinnati. These plans established eligibility for the city for grants under the federal open-space program.

Although I have been critical of the administration of various federal programs, Zanesville nevertheless demonstrates one inescapable fact of American urban affairs: not all communities have the financial resources to retain or regain economic vitality, though they may very well have the capacity to sustain it once established. There is a legitimate role for the federal government as an equalizer, but is must perform its function without direct involvement in program execution, as it now attempts with revenue sharing and block grants.

Notes

1. City of Winona, Minnesota, "Master Plan of Winona, Minnesota," 1959 (Prepared by Ladislas Segoe and Associates, under the direction of W.G. Roeseler, together with zoning and subdivision regulations).

2. City of Rochester, Minnesota, "Master Plan for Rochester, Minnesota," 1960 (Prepared by Ladislas Segoe and Associates, under the direction of W.G. Roeseler, together with zoning and subdivision regulations).

3. "Survey of Effectiveness of Comprehensive Planning," (Unpublished research documents, 1976-1981, Texas A&M University, Department of Urban and Regional Planning, College Station, Texas).

4. American Society of Planning Officials, press release, 23 May 1960, Chicago.

5. City of Zanesville, Ohio, "Comprehensive Plan," 1960 (Prepared by Ladislas Segoe and Associates; directed by Charles W. Matthews, principal associate).

6. Zanesville, Ohio, "Community Renewal Program," 1966, Vols. 1-4: 1. Physical Inventory; 2. Social Resources; 3. Economic Potential; 4. Plans and Programs (Prepared by Howard, Needles, Tammen and Bergendoff, Kansas City, under the direction of W.G. Roeseler, assisted by Douglas C. Smith).

7. "Survey of Effectiveness of Comprehensive Plans," (Unpublished research records, 1976-1981, Texas A&M University, Department of Urban and Regional Planning).

8. Telephone interview with John Ray, 5 March 1981.

10 From Suburb to Community

Our discussion of the medium-sized community would be incomplete without some observations regarding one of the key phenomena of the post World War II period—the American suburb. It is here to stay and to perform a major function in housing metropolitan populations of all walks of life and ethnic backgrounds. Initially considered a mere bedroom town for upper-middle-income and upper-income workers of the central city, suburbs have undergone sociological and economic changes during their relatively short existence that indicate that they are now well on their way to becoming permanent elements in today's urban form.

Economically fully integrated with the metropolitan area, especially its central city, the suburb found immediate acceptance by the public, as evidenced by the sacrifices American families and unrelated individuals are willing to make for their suburban houses, apartments, or condominiums, their clubs and schools, and other amenities that are deeply established in American life. As Richard Kellenberg, noted midwestern land planner, points out, there can be no better evidence of suburban stability than the history of property values that suburbs produced initially and have maintained through the fluctuations of the economic cycle, high interest rates, and other adversities of real-estate investment.

In Overland Park, Kansas, development did not begin in earnest until its incorporation in 1960, with a population of about 25,000. Today, the city accommodates nearly 90,000 people and enjoys a well-balanced land-use pattern and corresponding tax base. The city manager employed in 1963, Don Pipes, is still chief administrative officer, and the quality of the city council has been beyond question in all these years. They are dedicated men and women, with a primary interest in civic affairs not conventional politics. In 1963, Mr. Kellenberg produced a general plan for the area, but he points out that that was not the thrust of his professional efforts. Actually, even before the incorporation, he served the township administration and was instrumental in securing rights-of-way of sufficient width along the old U.S. survey-section lines, which had served rural road development for a century.

Although there was some rigidity in that method, it worked because, during the critical years, it gave the planner a base of negotiation with the rural people who could accept that reasoning. Many a good plan is lost because it is beyond the delivery capacity of existing authorities. Moreover, one must keep in mind that even the most enlightened public and its representatives, as a body politic, absorb only a limited amount of highly technical options in any given situation. In situations such as this, the day-by-day decisions of city manager, planner, and engineer are more important than formal plans and can be equally or more beneficial. In Mr. Kellenberg's practice, the major street plan and the informal layout of undeveloped sections on the basis of well-established methodology—as, for example, the neighborhood principle of design, with its protected residential-access streets, its central school locations, its peripheral service establishments along traffic-carrying perimeter streets—the negotiations with developers and city council, and the ultimate resolution of issue after issue became the foundation of his distinguished service in guiding suburban growth. An equitable and consistent course of action does much to assure success.[1]

Although Overland Park relies primarily on traditional regulatory measures and periodic capital improvements to achieve its objectives, other cities in the suburbs have experimented with more modern practices in land management. Roy Potter, formerly planning director of Fremont, reports that desired development objectives in that California community in the San Francisco region were achieved through extensive use of the planned-unit-development technique. Review of these development units was based on a comprehensive-guide plan, designed by consulting city planner Sydney H. Williams and later augmented by park plans conceived by landscape architect Donald B. Austin. Under Mr. Potter's direction, the planning program brought about the merger of five small villages with some 25,000 people into a city that currently claims more than 120,000 residents. A General Motors plant and other nonresidential investments balanced the land-use pattern of the area, and the latest in transportation technology, the Bay Area Rapid Transit System, selected Fremont as the terminal station of its East Bay line into Oakland and San Francisco.[2]

Upper Arlington, Ohio, a pleasant suburb of Columbus, was laid out on the model of Kansas City's Country Club area. In 1962, manager and city council employed consultants primarily (1) to review and rewrite the city's zoning and subdivision regulations; and (2) to lay out remaining undeveloped sections as well as some possible modifications of the existing street system. Concurrently with this program, in neighboring Westerville, the assignment was to mold together, through appropriate design, several older and newer subdivisions that had been joined into a municipal corporation and to integrate this development with major metropolitan highway programs, which were then in the planning stage. Planning at that scale required a very sensitive approach, with extensive contacts with public officials and private interests in order to assure workable solutions to current and longer-range issues. The demarcation between current and long-range planning and programming was elusive in view of the rapid changes of that period. Events that, at best, had been anticipated to occur some day would suddenly confront the surprised city council, and action would have to be taken instantly.

There were major problems—such as the location of a thoroughfare or a school—but there were just as many concerns with minutiae of planning: whether sidewalks should be separated from the curb by a park strip, and, if so, whether there should be trees in that parkstrip; whether residential streets should be wide enough to allow for curb parking at least on one side of the roadway; whether neighborhood playgrounds should be provided at city expense or at subdivider's expense; whether single-family homes should contain minimum living space; whether people should be allowed to park recreational vehicles in their yards and, if so, where; what signs should be permitted; whether churches and clubs should be required to provide off-street parking; whether there should be noise control; what kind of land use was wanted in the community; and so on. Minutiae are not to be confused with trivia and petty quarrels. Minutiae in this context may make the difference between a mediocre environment and a superior, high-quality habitat. Conversely, minutiae can just as easily become unwarranted and burdensome. Once again, we are at a point where planning, the science, becomes planning and composition, the art.[3]

These experiences were repeated from coast to coast between about 1955 and 1970. Reports from Arlington, Virginia, and Arlington, Texas; Mission Hills, Kansas, and the Pacific Palisades in Los Angeles; Southern California's San Fernando Valley and Green Hills, Ohio; Silver Spring, Maryland, and Park Forest, Illinois; Clayton, Missouri, and Wauwatosa, Wisconsin—all convey the same pattern. Urban planning is equated with sound judgment and such compliance with required formality as time and circumstances would permit. In the course of this experience, many superb neighborhoods emerged, as did numerous communities of modest housing. It is significant, however, that, by and large, our suburbs are equipped with adequate infrastructures of essential urban facilities and services, are laid out to reasonable standards of land planning, and enjoy, for the most part, good management. Given today's technology and financial constraints, our suburbs compare well with post World War II urbanization around the world.

Notes

1. Overland Park, Kansas, "General Plan," 1963 (Prepared by Richard H. Kellenberg); and interview with the author on 21 March 1981.

2. "Survey of Effectiveness of Comprehensive Plans," 1976-81 (Unpublished research records, Texas A&M University, Department of Urban and Regional Planning).

3. City of Upper Arlington, Ohio, "Comprehensive Master Plan," 1962 (Prepared by Ladislas Segoe and Associates, Cincinnati; W.G. Roeseler, planner-in charge); City of Westerville, Ohio, "Comprehensive Master Plan," 1962 (Prepared by Ladislas Segoe and Associates, Cincinnati; W.G. Roeseler, planner-in-charge).

Part IV:
The Central- Area Issue

Technological obsolescence is a hallmark of the age of industrialization. No sooner has a significant function managed to find a mode of operation and physical form than a new technology renders it ineffective and replaces the old by something different, which catches the imagination of the consumer. The private automobile and the physical urban patterns it produced dethroned the American central business district from its powerful position and caused it either to vanish altogether or to assume a new role and function.

With few exceptions, American cities are products of trade and commerce, and the physical form of our cities represents that tradition. The sections that housed commercial and industrial activities formed the central elements of the city, surrounded by residential areas, at first within walking distance, later within the service radius of public transport. The retail and banking functions typically constituted the focal points of that pattern, both physically and with respect to economic power. The cathedral and the castle of the medieval European city was replaced in America by department stores at the "100 percent" corner of downtown and by the skyscrapers housing the local banks and the offices of the functionaries of the power structure.

The boom years before the Great Depression, Henry Ford's successful mass production of trucks and cars, swiftly copied by automakers around the world, and the gradual outmigration of people into the newly created subdivisions of the suburbs prompted the establishment of secondary business districts in the large cities. In Kansas City, J.C. Nichols took the boldest step by developing the County Club Plaza business center, which was to become the prototype for shopping-center development many years later. These trends were significant, as they heralded a new era of urbanization in the United States—the era of decentralization. The depression years, the war, and postwar adjustment delayed the decentralization movement by about twenty years. However, when it eventually came into its own, the movement struck with such enormous power that it produced entirely new urban forms and patterns, without much resistance. On the contrary, the public embraced the new life-styles, and the central-area interest groups were simply swept away in the new direction.

For the last thirty years, America's metropolitan areas have changed from highly centralized entities to decentralized, nucleated areas. The retail function was the first to move into the suburban communities and to set the pattern of this decentralization. It is regrettable that retail business did not take the form of the Nichols Country Club Plaza, with its charming architecture and altogether human scale, its pleasing intimacy, and its relaxed, though elegant, atmosphere. Instead, with frightening uniformity, retail business followed the awkward, if not clumsy, pattern carved out by Victor Gruen with the Northland Center in Detroit—a gigantic warehouse of marketing surrounded by an ocean of parking spaces. Although Mr. Gruen later produced several substantially more interesting shopping centers, the basic principle has survived to this day and is still imitated from coast to coast. There are, however, remarkable exceptions.

Office-based commerce and industry followed in due course, creating integrated developments in parklike settings, frequently adjacent to the retail centers. In time, these new concentrations of business became focal points, not only aesthetically but also for community functions, political activities, and general social interaction. Downtown, which for generations had performed this basic function, was relegated to a second-rate position in the urban spectrum. As would be all too obvious, downtown space became a "drag on the market," deteriorated, and invited occupancies that produced social liabilities.

Although, years ago, the central business districts were major revenue producers for municipal and county government, they now became deficit areas, where service demand exceeded tax revenue or was rapidly moving in that direction. Municipal administrators were pressed by remaining downtown interests to do something about it, and, as is so frequently the case these days, these hard-pressed officials, by and large, looked to Washington for help: send more money, and we promise to solve the problem. Congressional delegations were also besieged by requests from local constituents. In time, urban-renewal legislation was produced that enabled localities to embark on grandiose reclamation efforts. Forced reclamation rarely produces anything but boondoggles, as, for example, Philadelphia's so-called—and at one time much heralded—renaissance.

I find it intriguing that planners so often tend to cling to obsolescence in order to preserve the status quo. A friend of mine used to say that so many planners are masters of the obvious—after the fact. I would hope that this is not true, and that it is more appropriate to say that planners at their best are, indeed, masters of the obvious, but before the fact, which requires little more than technical skill and some ingenuity. With respect to the central-area issue, planners have been far less effective than they were in most other areas of urban development. Causes of that failure are complex, as they relate as much to the intangible, emotional, and power-political as to the physical and generally tangible spheres of life.

Planning agencies and commissions throughout the land are still brooding over central-area decline, and they listen, too readily, to available architectural total solutions to the downtown dilemma. Unfortunately, that is precisely the concern they should not have. It is a legitimate concern of planners to address depressed conditions anywhere in their jurisdiction. It is inappropriate, however, to overstate and overemphasize any one area or sector, especially if it occurs at the expense of others. Experience shows that the appropriateness of solutions to central-area utilization or reutilization is very much a function of size and scale.

Moreover, it matters greatly whether the central area under consideration pertains to a large metropolitan region, to a satellite community within a metropolitan area, or to an autonomous city. In the last category, relative size may again be significant. The issue, incidentally, is not particularly American. European cities, too, have wrestled with the problem, especially those communities that were devastated by the bombing raids of World War II. The extensive apartment areas that typically surrounded business sections of the European cities were wiped out, and questions of rebuilding or changing the traditional patterns arose. It is here that American planners often make a cardinal mistake. They see and rightfully admire the Europeans for their work in rebuilding and, at the same time, modernizing the old cities. The large European metropolitan area had been more decentralized than its American cousin, especially on the continent. Berlin, for example, had distinct focal points of retail business and other commercial activities for over a century, and the area most closely resembling an American central business district was at best a first-among-equals concentration, composed of several segments: retail, banking, education, diplomatic representation, and some general government, but by no means all of these.

In the smaller metropolitan areas, where retail and office activities more closely resembled those in America, the daily travel pattern for work, shopping, and other business purposes is primarily accomplished by public transport, not by individual car; 75 to 80 percent of all work trips are transit trips. This travel characteristic produces a daytime population of pedestrians and largely eliminates the need for parking facilities to the extent that American cities require them. Consequently, it is logical for the German or Dutch planner to convert secondary streets, not needed for direct property access, to pedestrian preserves, and to encounter overwhelming public support for such action. Since the central-street rights-of-way of the older European cities are typically narrow, such adaptation is all the more feasible, as walking distances between building lines are short, often shorter than those within the malls of American regional shopping centers. These physical features create an atmosphere of intimacy mindful of the ancient Greek agora or the North African and Mideastern bazaar. Why is it difficult, if not entirely inappropriate, to transfer that technology from Europe to North America?

First, the European public is accustomed to the universal availability of excellent public transit, operating at high levels of service. Despite the popularity of the private automobile, transit is expected to be provided and is heavily used, especially for work trips but also for shopping and other purposes. Transit comes in various forms, including the traditional streetcar or light-rail system, the bus, the electric trolley with the capacity to operate without overhead wires in outlying areas, the subway, paratransit, and the ultramodern rapid transit. These systems require heavy public subsidies because of the high level of service expected: twenty-four-hour operation at considerably greater frequency than is available even in New York or Chicago. The public is prepared to underwrite these costs through taxation and to spend a proportionately greater amount on transit than on highway construction and operation. Generally, however, the tax burden for transportation is comparable there to that carried by the American taxpayer. It is just applied differently in response to public demand.

The second consideration is the scarcity of land in Europe, especially in Western Europe's industrial countries. It is simply not possible to accommodate the automobile and its support space to the same degree there as is feasible here. Consequently, land-development and density controls in the form of national policy and local regulation are taken very seriously, for without these measures there would be total chaos. The European public is keenly aware of the issues and very astute politically in its efforts to maintain a reasonable balance. Careful land management, customary heavy use of public transit, and a deeply rooted appreciation for an aesthetically appealing urban environment are the underlying elements of Europe's central-area policies. Although technology is transferable, policy, to the extent that it reflects fundamentally different attitudes of the general public, is not. The American planner has to rely on his own imagination to resolve the central-area issue.

During the nineteenth century, the planner's problem in this regard was simple: banking and retail, together with other commercial functions, belong in the central area simply because they must be accessible to one another as well as to the general public. The central area is at or near the port, later the railroad station, and taxis and public transit move people to their ultimate destinations. Prior to the transit era, congestion problems arose because it was often difficult to accommodate the large numbers of horses and buggies that brought people to town. Since the cities were small by today's standards, these problems were hardly more than temporary inconveniences. Today, the planner looks at the typical downtown area and discovers that much of it is a pathetic wasteland of deterioration, social decay, and ugliness. The once-solid residential areas of the downtown fringe are long gone and have become home for large numbers of people carving out a living near the very bottom of the economic system, often harrassed by gangs of frustrated youngsters and other deprived groups. At best, the planner is confronted with physical decay; at worst, with that and the full gamut of social disarray.

Public planning calls for a high degree of realism. It is my contention that the planner can do nothing of any consequence to resolve the nation's social problems. That is squarely the responsibility of the U.S. Congress, the president, and the agencies specifically charged with that responsibility at the federal and state level. The buck should not be passed to the planner. And the planner should not allow himself to be maneuvered into the position of a social reformer—as some advocates did in the 1960s. That is not his function, and, indeed, he is ill prepared to attempt what the most powerful elements of our country have not been able to resolve. That problem is one that can rightfully be returned to Washington. Social reform and urban planning are not synonymous, although we readily accept the fact that many issues in the planning process lead directly to underlying social causes and, in order to be resolved, call for fundamental changes. However, these changes concern society as a whole and can be brought about only through the channels provided by the political and judicial processes, so that the correction of a given wrong does not come about by creating two new problems for someone else. It is appropriate for us to point to these needs; it is inappropriate to attempt a do-it-yourself solution, for the self-appointed crusader swiftly loses his professional effectiveness.

If, after due consideration, it becomes apparent that the local central-area issue does, indeed, go beyond local capability and responsibility, let those who are responsible take action. If, however, that is not the case, and there is an opportunity to act within the means of local general-purpose government, one must identify the fundamental requirements and objectives that are not now attained because of the conditions of the area, as the Norwood and Council Bluffs case studies reported earlier have amply demonstrated. By and large, obsolescence will be the overriding cause. In our times, we have already identified one major cause of central-area obsolescence: the private automobile and its universal acceptance in all of America, except New York and, to some extent, Chicago. The other cause—perhaps soon to be recognized as the even more significant cause of this era—is the revolution in communication. Actually, from the very beginning, the telephone removed the justification for physical proximity. It was just as convenient to call as it was to go and see and confer; in time, it became convincingly more convenient. Today, it is a perfectly acceptable substitute for most personal contacts. Since the technology has long been available to add the visual element to the voice and the computer and its infinite capacity for communication to both, the time has come for substantial reduction in travel to be accepted business practice, especially in view of the ever-increasing complications and rising costs of transportation.[1]

In the United States, after the turn of the century, the skyscraper became an effective answer to space economies in New York and other giant cities. New York became a leader in design and operation of that symbol of modern America, including an often-overlooked major element—the safety of such buildings, by no means to be taken for granted. New York's safety record of skyscraper construction and operation became a standard for the world. Unfortunately, there was a time after World War II when New York discovered that construction had become more and more expensive under its standards. In view of the strong safety record of the past, New York—and with it the rest of the world—was persuaded to lower standards and to encourage more construction, not to levels recklessly below previous practice but to levels that experts considered reasonable in view of the record. The lower standards produced more buildings, including the vulgar glass box, which typically resembles a vertical ice-cube tray rather than a building for human activity or housing.

Yet, even this new cut-rate construction has become prohibitive for many because of ever-rising labor and capital costs. (Sometimes one hears the argument that planning and zoning regulations cause these price spirals. If anything, they reduce development costs. They certainly do not cause interest rates to rise or wages to be negotiated beyond productivity.)

If one takes these various technological changes into consideration, it becomes apparent that artificial support of obsolescence surely must be counterproductive. One cannot merely recreate a condition of the past and superficially retrofit a central area by adding on various features to make it more acceptable to present-day taste and practice. Principles that led to highly compact land utilization decades ago are often no longer valid. Transportation-mode changes are so contingent on conditions outside the central area, and so very slow, that they offer no solution. This becomes all the more clear when public attitudes are taken into consideration, as well as the life-styles that have evolved in this country, life-styles that offer to most people more positive aspects than negative ones and, as such, call for change.

In time, all urban land finds its level of maximum productivity, depending on numerous influences. We have looked into some of the more obvious and overriding impacts. There are, of course, many others within the spectrum of microeconomics in a given situation. Areas that have outlived their usefulness and have become technologically obsolete will eventually be rediscovered for some purpose. For example, old river ports in many cities have become impressive civic centers for local government and trade fairs; stockyards have been converted into sports arenas and gathering places for commercial and recreational livestock shows; phased-out military installations have been reclaimed for industrial development; quarries have become attractive zoos and general parks. The list is endless. There is no reason to assume that the central areas of yesteryear, which no longer perform a useful service, will forever remain in this state. On the contrary, total neglect and decay may very well be the most direct way to the cure of the ailment, which is so frequently aggravated by absentee ownership and unrealistic expectations.

Considering the well-known fact that the real-estate market is a very imperfect market and rarely produces the compatibility that is conducive to maximizing land productivity, it is appropriate for the planner to assist in bringing about a framework within which reclamation of obsolescence will occur more rapidly than it would without such a framework, provided that the objectives of such efforts are in scale with the remainder of the urban entity and are not brought about at the expense of those not directly concerned. Local government may facilitate, but the initiative has to come from those who have direct financial interests in the matter.

In all these efforts, several warnings must be kept in mind. Perhaps most important in this context should be the realization that the replacement of a spot of blight by a new activity within an extensive blighted area will not induce similar action by others. On the contrary, spot clearance, by and large, will only further manifest decay, because the remaining property will be kept in its deplorable state in anticipation of a purchase offer for additional redevelopment—an event that is rarely realized. If an effort is to be made toward redevelopment, it must be massive. It must be undertaken only if there is sufficient capital to absorb the risk, not a marginal operation. If redevelopment is for public reuse, the issue of risk does not arise; if it is for private venture, it does.

Physical relationships of area or regional character are most crucial. In retail planning, travel time becomes a most significant element. Most shopping trips, even in the largest cities, do not exceed twenty to thirty minutes of travel time. If that time span is increased substantially—by 50 percent, for example—the density of population required to support a given retail-center destination would have to nearly double, theoretically, to maintain the original level of expenditures. The outmigration of the last three decades, the evolution of decentralized urban areas, and the corresponding redistribution of population are simply facts of American life that must be carefully considered in attempting major reclamation programs. These forces have reshaped the urban form entirely. What was historically an integrated single-focus entity has become a multicentered configuration of overlapping systems. New centers have sprung up, constituting an array of urban nodes, frequently connected by intensely developed so-called corridors along the urban highways. New generations have grown up in this environment, no longer identifying with the city but rather with the neighborhood of their youth and its principal features. It is appropriate to view the urban settlement as an amorphous mass, in the sense that it has no finite form, but, nevertheless, as being rather well organized with respect to land use, infrastructures, service, and administration at the immediate local level.

Another key problem is disturbing residential areas, however modest or deplorable. Aside from legal obligations, careful relocation programs are essential if substantial numbers of people and business operations are involved.[2] Actually, in the majority of central-area reclamations, the relocation issue is marginal, as the structures involved are primarily vacant commercial and industrial buildings. The residential problems arise almost entirely in the fringe areas of central or industrial districts and call for different solutions. In general, we have done well with respect to physical reclamation, but we have yet to solve the ever-increasing complexity of human plight and despair, particularly in the major metropolitan regions of the Eastern Seaboard, where the very scale of human deprivation is overwhelming. Indeed, it constitutes an issue of its own. Elsewhere in the large cities of North America, there is hope, despite often adverse circumstances. Examples of encouraging experiences can be found everywhere, and the three cases I am about to describe will give some insight into requisites that are conducive to positive action.

Notes

1. W.G. Roeseler, "Transportation Planning and Urban Renewal" (Paper presented at American Society of Civil Engineers annual meeting, Baton Rouge, Louisiana, 1966); D.W. Jones, Jr., "Must We Travel: The Potential of Communications as a Substitute for Urban Travel" (Urban Mass Transportation Administration, NTIS, 1973).

2. The Uniform Relocation Assistance and Real Property Acquisition Policies Act of 1970, as amended, provides for specific procedures in property acquisition and payment of compensation for relocation expenses. All projects that entirely, or in part, include financial assistance in the form of loans and grants by the federal government must comply with these regulations. Several states have enacted similar laws pertaining to state-funded programs.

11 Fundamental Alternatives

Owner-Investor Solution: New Town-in-Town

In urban action, it is impossible to overestimate the power and the advantages that flow from legal ownership and central management of land and improvements. Nowhere does this fundamental truth become more readily apparent than in large-scale development and redevelopment.[1]

Once more I shall discuss Kansas City, for it was there that the theory of center-city recovery through complete replacement of a blighted and topographically difficult area was put to a critical test to an extent and scope rarely attempted in the modern city here and abroad. The project is known as Crown Center. It is an undertaking solely of the Hallmark Corporation, the widely known manufacturer of greeting cards and other fascinating products. Hallmark's major production plant for many years represented the firm's base and headquarters. It is located near Union Station in the general downtown area, some ten blocks south of the central business district of Kansas City. By 1950, the plant was in need of major modernization, lest it follow the beginning exodus to the suburbs.

Joyce C. Hall, founder and president of the corporation, who was dedicated to the city that had brought him success and fortune, chose to remain in the established location of the plant and initiated a comprehensive refurbishing program, which was completed in 1956. However, it became apparent that the improvements of the Hallmark property would have very little positive impact on the surrounding blighted area. Matters were further complicated by topographic conditions that were adverse to normal urban construction. Immediately to the west of the plant was a pronounced hill, composed entirely of solid limestone and characterized by rather steep slopes. For years, Signboard Hill was considered undevelopable by the city planners.

Nevertheless, the area in general had amenities that, if properly integrated into an area plan, could become an anchor point of new development. These landmarks included Union Station, the World War I Liberty Memorial on another prominent knoll, Penn Valley Park and historic Union Cemetery, and, several blocks to the east, the Medical Center of the University of Missouri. Joyce C. Hall, and, since 1966, his son, Donald J. Hall decided correctly that any attempt at staying or reversing blight in that sector of the central area of Kansas City could succeed only with massive infusion of capital, with corresponding equally massive construction. Piecemeal renewal federal style, without clearly defined authority and responsibility, would not accomplish the desired purpose.

Local government, however, would have a role to play in this planning and programming effort. Under the provisions of the Missouri Redevelopment Corporations Act, the power of eminent domain for land acquisition could be used, and real-property taxes on new improvements could be waived entirely for the first ten years of the life of the structures and reduced to 50 percent for another fifteen years thereafter, based on an assessed valuation of the construction year. In a recent conversation, Donald Hall asserted that incentives of this type are absolutely necessary to achieve the economic objectives of central-city revitalization. He shares my views that these incentives take nothing away from the taxpayer, because blighted property, if allowed to persist, merely perpetuates poor tax-revenue production and certainly provides no employment.

Crown Center was conceived by the Halls as a means to convert blight into productivity. The risk was considerable, and the experiment is far from complete, let alone conclusive. However, the achievements to date are impressive and deserve recognition. The program was initiated in the early 1960s with the establishment of the Crown Center Redevelopment Corporation. Following procedures prescribed by Kansas City's redevelopment ordinance, the corporation produced, in less than twelve years, a remarkable statement in concrete and steel of the capacity of private industry to make contributions of great substance to the urban-development process. It is all the more remarkable that these contributions invariably are superb examples of meticulous planning. Figure 11-1 gives an indication of the magnitude of the project.

Financed entirely by private capital, Crown Center is being developed on eighty-five acres surrounding the international headquarters of the Hallmark greeting-card firm. By the mid 1980s, the development will be an investment of $500 million and will have added fifty new buildings to the city's skyline, offering quality living, working, shopping, and guest accommodations in a prestigious and parklike setting. Construction began in 1968. As of this writing, completed portions of the project include five interconnected seven-story office buildings containing 660,000 square feet; the dramatic Crown Center Hotel, with 730 guest rooms and famous indoor tropical garden; the Hyatt Regency Kansas City, with 750 guest rooms and the city's largest ballroom; a multilevel retail complex, with 85 specialty stores and boutiques spread over 400,000 square feet on three floors; eight restaurants; a full-service bank; a sophisticated meeting center, with advanced audiovisual capabilities; a children's art workshop; a ten-acre cen-

Figure 11-1. Crown Center, Kansas City, Missouri

tral square; a secondary office complex of 600,000 square feet; a 245-unit apartment and condominium community; and structured parking for nearly 5,000 cars. The entire site of twenty-five square blocks is surrounded by public parkland, the largest being Penn Valley Park, a 220-acre expanse of rolling hills, mentioned earlier.

The office environment at Crown Center offers a convenient location and exceptional amenities. Stairstepped to meet the sloping contour of the land, the first-phase five-building office complex overlooks the open court and landscaped terraces of the ten-acre Crown Center Square. Close at hand are all the services needed to conduct the most sophisticated business endeavors, including facilities and equipment for special meetings and the normal amenities for smooth-running day-to-day operations. The five interconnected office buildings were designed by New York architect Edward Larrabee Barnes, who, in association with Marshall and Brown of Kansas City, designed Crown Center's master plan and serves as coordinating architect for the entire development. In 1975, the project's developers began a new construction program that would approximately double the original amount of planned office space in Crown Center some three years ahead of schedule.

In this departure from the original plans, a combination of outside interests constructed a twenty-eight story office tower of 600,000 square feet and a four-story satellite building for the Mutual Benefit Life Insurance Company of New Jersey and IBM. The building, designed by Fujikawa, Conterato, Lohan and Associates of Chicago, was completed in mid 1977 at a cost of $35 million.

Convention activities are focused in the 730-room Crown Center Hotel and the 750-room Hyatt Regency Kansas City. Crown Center Hotel, one of the most dramatic and commanding structures in the entire development, is actually two distinct but connected buildings—a multilevel lobby wing set into a rocky hillside at street level and an L-shaped guest tower rising fifteen stories atop the hill. Designed by Chicago architect Harry Weese, the structure has attracted much attention because of its interesting features. For example, a stunning backdrop to the lobby interior is provided by a hillside garden carved from the hill's natural limestone, highlighted by tropical landscaping and a sixty-foot-high waterfall. Guest rooms on two sides of the hotel overlook a hilltop park surrounding a circular, recessed swimming pool. High-speed outside elevators afford passengers a panoramic view of the city.

In the fall of the 1977, Crown Center announced its plans to build a second hotel within the development, a 750-room Hyatt Regency. The $50 million Hyatt, completed in the summer of 1980, is located on the eastern edge of the development, just north of the first-phase office complex. The Hyatt features a forty-story guest tower, with revolving cocktail lounge on the penthouse level and the city's largest ballroom. It was designed by the Kansas City, Missouri, firm of PBNDML Architects, Planners, Inc. Supplementing Crown Center's hotel-based meeting facilities is The Multimedia Forum and Producers Video Center, which are located above the development's retail complex. Planned primarily for business meetings and sales-training sessions, The Forum is equipped with audiovisual equipment, allowing for multiscreen slide and film presentations, audio and video recording, and live television broadcasting. Its 400-seat Presentation Hall also is used for various artistic performances.

Crown Center's trilevel retail area covers 400,000 square feet and is occupied by eighty-five shops and boutiques, a modern-day farmers' market, and three distinctive restaurants. A highly unusual area of the retail complex is West Village, a multilevel collection of cubic boutiques that form the basis of a unique shopping town for contemporary items. It was designed by Francois Dallegret of Canada.

Much of the public entertainment at Crown Center takes place on the square, where trees, fountains, and grassy terraces make an ideal setting for art fairs, craft shows, ethnic festivals, and outdoor concerts, ranging from symphony to rock. "Shiva," a major stabile by the late Alexander Calder, is permanently displayed on the square, as is "Wagon III," a large forged-iron piece by the late David Smith. In the winter months, the Ice Terrace at one corner of the square is open for public skating and ice shows. For children, the highlight of Crown Center is Kaleidoscope, a creative-art workshop for five- to twelve-year-olds.

In the last months of 1976, Crown Center opened its first residential community, rounding out the classic superblock, multiple-use design. Known as Crown Center West, the six-acre urban neighborhood includes 110 garden apartments, 135 high-rise luxury condominiums, a clubhouse, tennis courts, swimming pool, and gardens.

The condominiums, ranging in size from one- to four-bedroom units, are housed in a thirty-story tower immediately to the south of the Crown Center Shops. An adjacent seven-story building contains 110 rental apartments. The condominiums and apartments were designed by The Architects Collaborative of Cambridge, Massachusetts, under the direction of Norman Fletcher, and are provided with a 450-space parking garage.

Although Crown Center's residential units are designed for upper-income groups, future plans call for a variety of moderate- to middle-income units on the eastern and southern boundaries of the project. More than 2,000 residential units are planned for the eighty-five acre development, which has allocated 50 percent of its land for residential use.

When Crown Center is completed in the late 1980s, the total community is expected to generate a daytime population of 75,000, including some 8,000 permanent residents. It will have more than two million square feet of office space, over 2,000 residential units, two retail complexes, two hotels, numerous cultural and entertainment facilities, and structured parking for more than 7,000 cars. Concept and implementation attest to the principle that compatibility of land uses—industrial, retail commercial, offices, entertainment, hotels, arts and crafts, and restaurants in one complex structure group—is more a matter of design and performance than of use type.

Moreover, it is noted that Hallmark has also become active in reclamation and modernization of buildings in the adjacent Longfellow neighborhood. Modern apartments have been provided in several 1920s-vintage buildings. The corporation is also experimenting with various loan programs for low-income and elderly residents, which intend to solve human as well as physical urban problems. The decision to move boldly into a blighted area and to take advantage of the power of eminent domain and the tax-abatement procedures under Missouri law allowed the owner-developer to retain complete control over his business decisions and to make his moves when, in his best judgment, the time was ripe. Any attempt to deprive the developer, no matter how well intended, invariably invites failure. The role of government in this context is to simplify, facilitate, and assure that no injustice is done. In other words, government performs its traditional duty: to intervene only when absolutely necessary and to apply only means that are neither arbitrary nor unduly oppressive.

Diverse Interests: Association Power

In many central areas, opportunities for massive privately financed actions are not present. The circumstances that led to a $500 million new town-in-town in Kansas City were unique, as perhaps evidenced by the fact that no other comparable attempt has yet been made elsewhere.

Conversely, the kind of direct local governmental intervention reported earlier in Norwood, Ohio, and Council Bluffs, Iowa, is only feasible under the following conditions: (1) that the problem is not overly complex from a managerial point of view and is relatively small in scale, physically and in regards to the local economy; and (2) that some higher level of government, state or federal, is prepared to furnish the funding for the public share of the venture. We have seen the limitations and hazards even if these conditions prevail. Decisions are often delayed to the point of placing the project in jeopardy, and there is the ever-present threat that politics could change program terms and conditions at higher levels of government. Yet the problems of decay persist.

What, then, might be done in such a case when neither of the foregoing circumstances exists? Through trial and error and, in part, through transfer

of concepts from Europe by European architects, a number of cities, ranging from medium-size communities to large metropolitan areas, have attempted to reverse downward trends in central areas by a combination of interactive measures of commercial and trade associations, local government,
and civic and professional groups, who made it their business to address
downtown problems. The motivation for these efforts is typically a mix of
business interests, tax-revenue concerns, and, not to be underestimated,
nostalgia. Many of these efforts have failed to materialize, but enough have
succeeded to warrant recognition in this context, if for no other reason than
the extraordinary intellectual efforts of the numerous groups and individuals who participated in the venture. Perhaps no other planning activity has generated as much voluntary participation by citizens in all walks of
life than have the attempts to refurbish downtown areas and to provide
amenities otherwise found in suburban shopping centers.

Historically, I believe the first such attempt was implemented in Miami
Beach in 1959 with the conversion of Lincoln Road to a pedestrian mall.
The street conversion was coupled with substantial construction of off-
street parking facilities immediately behind both commercial street front-
ages. It gave the Miami Beach central business district a new lease on life;
however, it could not stem the tide. The solid consumers moved away, leaving the city to low-income elderly persons. Another early attempt of conversion, which is still reasonably viable, was the mall in downtown
Kalamazoo, Michigan. As the threat of major community and regional
shopping center invasions continued, more and more interest in similar
measures was generated. Paradoxically, by then, the key retailers and banks
had established themselves in suburbia as well, and the movement lost much
of its initial impetus. It is not surprising that, in the 1960s, the notion
evolved that the old central business districts should be viewed in a new light—
as one of several commercial centers in town, perhaps with an emphasis on
nonretail functions. Correspondingly, the key department stores began to
experiment with an adjustment of marketing practice, aiming now no
longer at the affluent but more and more at the residents of the central-area
fringe, primarily lower- and lower-middle-income families and unrelated individuals. The preponderance of these customers would occasionally be at
cross purposes when high-priced apartments and condominiums were introduced in the downtown areas to offset the downward trends. However,
these people were not significantly strong in numbers to have much impact,
except in the new-town concept of the self-contained Crown Center.

Most public-planning agencies eagerly joined forces with the central-
area groups and made provisions within the framework of their comprehensive and categorical plans to accommodate specific downtown programs,
which, in most instances, were financed by the downtown interests.

City after city produced its downtown program in the form of public investments in state and federal office buildings, city halls, courthouses, convention halls, and gigantic sports facilities, accompanied by a wide variety of privately financed developments, most in the form of office buildings. These major investments throughout the country were invariably augmented by conversion of some downtown streets into pedestrian preserves or malls, landscaped and otherwise modified to create an atmosphere of tranquility in contrast to the traditional hustle and bustle of downtowns. These malls and other features varied greatly in quality and included such features as skywalks in Minneapolis and Cincinnati or a few flower beds and a newspaper kiosk in Middletown. All represented countless committee-hours of activity and the creative imagination of a gifted architect. Despite impressions to the contrary, many of these programs had some input from economists; too many of them unfortunately looked at their clients through rose-colored glasses. The experiences of San Diego, California, and Tulsa, Oklahoma, may be considered representative of that era.

San Diegans, Inc.

For some ten years, the downtown merchants of San Diego debated the issues of their declining area. They attempted to secure publicly financed off-street parking, and they tried urban renewal and other solutions. Urban renewal ran into strong opposition, initially under the leadership of a person with substantial suburban interests. All told, very little was accomplished until John E. Hirten, an experienced planner and manager, was retained by San Diegans, Inc., as executive vice president. The corporation was impressed with the success of San Francisco's redevelopment program and hoped to duplicate it to some extent in San Diego. Mr. Hirten moved swiftly into a redevelopment program—one that would rely significantly on California's Community Redevelopment Law. That law offers the use of eminent domain for land acquisition in accordance with an acceptable plan, together with a tax-increment financing process. The property is evaluated for tax purposes, the developer obligates himself to make payments in lieu of taxes to the city or its designated renewal authority, and that entity, in turn, may issue revenue bonds for project financing. This method is widely used throughout California.

The first success came with the city of San Diego's adoption of a fifteen-block area in the heart of downtown—known as Horton Plaza—immediately followed by a decision by a major savings and loan association to construct a major building in the area. A special entity was established to carry out urban redevelopment on the tax-increment basis. This nonprofit redevelopment corporation has since been instrumental in inducing a substantial number of projects, commercial and multifamily residential. Attention was paid to the waterfront, which constitutes a major feature of central San Diego. The San Diego Civic Center became a major catalyst of the renewal effort, together with the C Street pedestrian preserve in the form of a modified mall.

The following self-assessment of San Diegans, Inc.—provided by its executive vice-president, Ray Potter—is typical of the role and function that ad hoc associations of diverse downtown business interests have assumed throughout the country in their efforts to strengthen, if not regain, central-area survival—with mixed results, to be sure.

> Downtown San Diego . . . is being revitalized through a number of projects which have been completed or are now just being implemented. San Diegans, Inc., a group of business and civic leaders, has played a leading role in the revitalization. Founded in 1959, San Diegans, Inc. has remained united in the belief that the vitality, strength and attractiveness of the Centre City was and would continue to be the most important contributing factor to the health, growth and prosperity of San Diego.
>
> The purpose of San Diegans, Inc. is to bring about the full revitalization of the Centre Area. San Diegans, Inc. and its ninety member firms has worked in close cooperation with local government, civic organizations and private investors/developers in the building of a broad base of support for Centre City revitalization and has, through its broad and diverse membership, provided the private sector with the leadership needed to make things happen.[2]

The internal ups and downs of the organization, the common problem of holding people together without direct central managerial control, the need to be part of a broader effort, and other concerns are in evidence between the lines of this policy statement. To the credit of San Diegans, Inc., are not merely the group's achievements in inducing investment and new construction in its project areas but its longevity, which surely is a fine reflection of leadership. The organization takes pride in its participation in the general urban-planning process of San Diego and defines its place in this context as one driving force among many. No one will question that this very attitude by a major merchants' group in a major American city today is the direct result of our finest tradition in urban planning, as practiced from coast to coast by many outstanding individuals. No doubt, the position carved out by San Diegans, Inc., may give us a clue to its effectiveness. The following is a statement from their 1980 report to the public, which describes the matter from their own viewpoint:

> San Diegans, Inc.'s efforts are primarily focussed on the Centre City area which includes approximately 1,200 blocks. . . . Members have played a key role in the implementation of the Community Concourse which includes the Civic Theater, Exhibit Hall, Convention Auditorium, City Administration Building, Operations Building, and parking areas. They raised $1,600,000 to assist in the financing of the Concourse.

A number of studies relating to the downtown area were sponsored by San Diegans, Inc. to assist the city in decision making. Among these studies prepared by nationally known research organizations were, in 1960, an economic analysis of Centre City; in 1961, a governmental feasibility study; in 1964, a market analysis of the South Broadway area, and a housing market analysis of Centre City; and in 1969, a feasibility study of the Horton Plaza Redevelopment Project.[3]

Further, the report goes on to say that San Diegans, Inc.,

. . . has assisted in the successful effort to adopt the City's General Plan; has served as a prototype for other community planning organizations; initiated redevelopment planning for Horton Plaza expansion. . . . Also recommended that a major retail center be built in the area; organized Centre City Way beautification and financing by private property owners and tenants; initiated transportation proposals for Centre City; recommended joint action by City, County and Port District for the preparation of the City Centre Plan to update the 1975 City Centre Plan; recommended the formation of a non-profit development corporation to be responsible for all redevelopment efforts in the Centre City area . . . suggested the building of a major convention center within the Centre City and supported the use of tax increment (bonds) and transient occupancy tax as a means of financing the project, supported the expansion of City College from 3.5 acres to 35 acres; recommended the initiation and adoption of the Marina and Columbia area redevelopment plans . . . in 1976 (for housing); and developed the "Design for Action" program for the Centre City area, 1976.[4]

In San Diego, the often perplexing and complex interaction between commercial interests and government has produced significant results and deserves full recognition. However, even under the best of circumstances, it remains far more hazardous than the alternative of central management by reason of unified ownership. Mayor Pete Wilson and County Board of Supervisors chairman Roger Hedgecock have repeatedly acknowledged the contributions of San Diegans, Inc.

Tulcenter

Comparable in environmental quality and aesthetic attractiveness to San Diego, the Tulsa metropolitan area experienced spectacular growth during the last two decades. The urbanized area doubled in population from about 250,000 in 1960 to over 500,000 by 1980. Traditionally, Tulsa had taken great pride in the appearance of the city. Shortly after the turn of the century, the city banished oil wells from the incorporated municipal jurisdiction and made special arrangements for improved circulation, railroad grade separations, and other amenities. Tulsa was one of the first American cities to enact land-use restrictions and to initiate integrated city-county regional-planning administration under the competent professional direction of Irving Hand and Erling Helland.

Mr. Helland is a planning consultant in Tulsa. He has been prominently involved in numerous development efforts there, following his service as planning director there in 1953-1954. Mr. Hand was his predecessor in public office. In this position, he organized the Tulsa Metropolitan Area Planning Commission, the planning arm of both the city and county governments. The commission became operational in 1952. Under the direction of outstanding professionals—Glen Turner, Robert Wegner, Donald Osgood, and others—the Tulsa Metropolitan Area Planning Commission initiated a wide variety of programs that had substantial impact on the fast-growing metropolitan area. One of these, the Tulsa Community Renewal Program, in 1962-1963, earned a citation of excellence from the regional director of the U.S. Department of Housing and Urban Development, Leonard E. Church, on 7 November 1963. It was to become the basis of all urban redevelopment activities in the city.[5]

In 1960, the Tulsa Metropolitan Area Planning Commission adopted the first comprehensive plan for the area under the general guidance of Washington, D.C., planning consultant Harold Wise. This plan included the all-important major street and highway plan, which is generally recognized as the catalyst of Tulsa's planned development. Implementation of that plan element provided the city with the kind of urban freeway system that became a key factor in the arrangement and organization of urban space in the United States during the last twenty-five years. Not unlike the Kansas City and Dallas systems, an inner-dispersal loop is the focal element of Tulsa's urban-freeway design. Rex M. Ball, a prominent Oklahoma architect, calls the system "immensely successful," although he is critical of the city's inability to match the freeways with adequate parking facilities.[6]

Within this framework, in 1958-1959, some eighty downtown firms raised $100,000 for funding a specific redevelopment study for the central area. The Richard J. Neutra firm of Los Angeles was retained, and Mr. Neutra and his partner, Robert Alexander—assisted by Howard Miller and my colleague Robert S. Cornish—produced an imaginative plan for central Tulsa. Local leadership was provided by several individuals, most notably, Murray McCune, an architect and member of Tulsa's Urban Renewal Authority. Mr. McCune was particularly interested in restoration of architecturally significant buildings and their effective integration with new development. Mr. Neutra coined the term *Tulcenter,* which became the focal area of major activities of the downtown group. Tulcenter was actually part of a broader plan for central Tulsa, which incorporated other programs well under way at the time. The most important and striking accomplishments of these was the ambitious fifteen-block Civic Center. It provided a new city hall and courthouse; a county administration building; the city-county

TULCENTER

Figure 11-2.   Tulcenter, Tulsa, Oklahoma

public library; a federal building; a state office building; and the assembly center—a remarkable civic achievement.

Through the efforts of Downtown Tulsa Unlimited, a private association, in close cooperation with the city government, two elements of the Neutra plan for Tulcenter have been accomplished: the implementation of a superblock concept at First Place (First National Bank) and at Williams Center (Bank of Oklahoma); and the Tulcenter Mall, between Third and Fourth Streets. Although the pleasing effect of these improvements adds much to the general appearance of downtown Tulsa (see figure 11-2), informed people agree that these efforts have not been able to reverse the retail slump in the central business district. Perhaps they have helped to arrest the trend, as evidenced by decisions of key stores to maintain retail outlets downtown that at one time had been slated for closing. Perhaps, in time, if and when residential development returns in sufficient strength to downtown, the efforts by committees and associations of interested parties without central ownership and management will yield greater tangible results. It should be noted that Tulsa received the All-America Cities award in 1973, partly due to its central area and general planning efforts.

Notes

1. Crown Center data furnished by Steve Doyal, Crown Center Redevelopment Corporation, Kansas City, Missouri.

2. "San Diegans, Inc., 1980" (San Diegans, Inc., public report, San Diego, California).

3. Ibid.

4. Ibid.

5. W.G. Roeseler, "Tulsa, Oklahoma, CRP Recommends Long-range Renewal for Metropolitan Area," *Journal of Housing,* 15 October 1964.

6. Rex M. Ball, "Award Winning Design of City Scale," *Property Journal* (Tulsa, Oklahoma), Winter 1978.

12 An Affair of Two Nations: The United States and Mexico

Not all central-area issues are prompted by commercial considerations and the desire to cope with urban decline and obsolescence, blight and poverty. Political, cultural, and historical objectives may also lead to significant action in the central area of cities, provided there is sufficient interest to initiate plans and programs for restoration or modification of the existing pattern. The painstaking restoration of Pennsylvania Avenue in Washington, D.C., initiated by President Harry S Truman and continued under Presidents Kennedy and Johnson—with much guidance by planner Harland Bartholomew of St. Louis, assisted by able architects—is one well-known example. Others include the world-famous Vieux Carré of New Orleans, the historic elements of St. Augustine, Florida, and so on.

There are, however, other less-noted situations, which, nevertheless, have had rather substantial impact on specific local communities. Imaginative solutions have occasionally emerged in response to issues that arose historically many years ago and were simply brushed aside until growth and development pressures and the demands of modern economies required reconsideration and attention. One such situation brought about a major international effort of collaboration and resulted in the Chamizal International Border Improvement Project in the heart of the El Paso-Ciudad Juarez metropolitan area on the Texas-Chihuahua border, the only truly international metropolitan region along the long border between the United States and Mexico, where people think of themselves as residents of a single urban economic, if not social, entity.

Generally known as the Chamizal Settlement, the program involved realignment of the international border, whereby 630 acres of land were transferred from the United States to Mexico and 193 acres from Mexico to the United States. This correction was necessitated by a shift in the course of the Rio Grande River over a century ago, caused by avulsion. Several treaties between the two countries failed to resolve required adjustments effectively until negotiations were reopened by Presidents John F. Kennedy and Adolfo Lopez Mateos and concluded by President Lyndon B. Johnson in 1963. The settlement brought about the border relocation and the river rechanneling. Private property, both commercial and residential, and public facilities were directly affected.

Edwin J.W. Hamlyn, a professional planner in El Paso, reports that the Chamizal Settlement might have amounted to little more than a legal, bu-

reaucratic measure disposing of an old political issue, as such of little interest to the public, except for those directly involved. Several disputes over
trivial matters ensued between the participating agencies on the Mexican
and American sides, notably, the Immigration and Naturalization Service's
preoccupation with a border detention center, issues of compensation of
private interests, and so forth. However, the city of El Paso was not
prepared to let an opportunity of such significance pass without maximizing
direct return to the citizens of both nations.[1]

All negotiations on behalf of the city were delegated to the late
Jonathan Cunningham, planning director. Jon Cunningham was a native of
the region who returned home from the Pacific Northwest in 1958 at the in-
vitation of Major Raymond Telles, the city's first Mexican-American chief
administrative officer. Single-handedly, Mr. Cunningham built an effective
planning department and pioneered in this far-western outpost numerous
methods and techniques of development. He was particularly concerned
with the preservation of natural features and became a champion of the
Wilderness Park development there. These efforts helped him establish
good rapport with the U.S. Department of Interior, which was a major
force on the federal side in the Chamizal matter. Mr. Cunningham was to
manage his assignment well, indeed.

It is well known in El Paso, as confirmed by Mr. Hamlyn, that Jon
Cunningham—with the full support of mayor and city council—was most
effective in advancing the city's position with many agencies involved in the
settlement. Unfortunately, Mr. Cunningham was not given to much formality, and he left neither plan documents, reports, nor even notes of his
successful work in this context. Perhaps that was the secret of his success—to plan and make decisions "by the seat of his pants," as the saying
goes. He certainly possessed the competence to achieve his stated goals in
this manner.

The international problem to be coped with became an opportunity to
be seized upon and to be taken as far as possible under the circumstances in
attaining other tangible results along the way. The Chamizal Settlement
brought about several major improvements that had been in the planning
stage in some form or other for years but otherwise had little, if any, chance
to be taken seriously. The accomplishments include a highway paralleling
the border, relieving traffic congestion in a bottleneck formed between the
mountain and the river; partial relocation of an irrigation canal, which
previously passed through a densely populated neighborhood; construction
of a senior high school on part of the land transferred from Mexico to the
United States, replacing a substandard facility; and establishment of a national monument park, also on part of this transferred land, com-
memorating the peaceful settlement and creating, at the same time, much-
needed open space as well as an attractive setting for the juxtaposition of

the two nations. On the Mexican side, the Juarez Convention Center and the Juarez Museum, with substantial private investment, represent fitting complements to the American effort. Although the municipalities in the case did not play as critical a role as, for example, the U.S. International Boundary and Water Commission, El Paso's input on facilities of secondary impact and planner Cunningham's negotiating skills produced lasting results for the benefit of the central-area functions of both El Paso and Ciudad Juarez.[2]

Notes

1. Report to the author from Edwin J.W. Hamlyn, February 1981.

2. U.S. Department of Interior, "The Chamizal International Border Improvement Project," 1963.

Index

About the Author

W.G. Roeseler has been a practicing urban planner since 1949, following postdoctoral studies at the University of Wisconsin in Madison. He received his professional education at Philipps State University of Hesse at Marburg, West Germany, where he received the Ph.D. in 1948. As a public official and a private consultant, Dr. Roeseler has directed major urban and regional planning projects throughout the United States and abroad. He has published numerous articles in technical periodicals and is the author of more than 150 major plan documents and of the introductory text, *General Policies and Principles for Prototype Zoning Ordinances and Related Measures* (1976). He is professor of urban and regional planning at Texas A&M University and head of his department. Dr. Roeseler is a member of the Institute of Transportation Engineers and of the American Institute of Certified Planners.